Managing the Development of Software-Intensive Systems

WILEY SERIES ON
QUANTITATIVE SOFTWARE ENGINEERING

Larry Bernstein, *Series Editor*

The Quantitative Software Engineering Series focuses on the convergence of systems engineering and software engineering with emphasis on quantitative engineering trade-off analysis. Each title brings the principles and theory of programming in-the-large and industrial strength software into focus.

This practical series helps software developers, software engineers, systems engineers, and graduate students understand and benefit from this convergence through the unique weaving of software engineering case histories, quantitative analysis, and technology into the project effort. You will find that each publication reinforces the series goal of assisting the reader with producing useful, well-engineered software systems.

Published titles:

Trustworthy Systems through Quantitative Software Engineering
Lawrence Bernstein and C. M. Yuhas

Software Measurement and Estimation: A Practical Approach
Linda M. Laird and M. Carol Brennan

Web Application Design and Implementation: Apache 2, PHP5, MySQL, JavaScript, and Linux/UNIX
Steven A. Gabarro

Trustworthy Systems for Quantitative Software Engineering
Larry Bernstein and C. M. Yuhas

Software Measurement and Estimation: A Practical Approach
Linda M. Laird and M. Carol Brennan

World Wide Web Application Engineering and Implementation
Steven A. Gabarro

Managing the Development of Software-Intensive Systems
James McDonald

Trustworthy Compilers
Vladimir O. Safonov

Managing the Development of Software-Intensive Systems

James McDonald

WILEY

A John Wiley & Sons, Inc., Publication

Published by John Wiley & Sons, Inc., Hoboken, New Jersey.
Published simultaneously in Canada.

For general information on our other products and services or for technical support, please contact our
Customer Care Department within the United States at (800) 762-2974, outside the United States at
(317) 572-3993 or fax (317) 572-4002.

Wiley also publishes its books in a variety of electronic formats. Some content that appears in print
may not be available in electronic formats. For more information about Wiley products, visit our web
site at www.wiley.com.

Library of Congress Cataloging-in-Publication Data:

McDonald, James, 1941–
    Managing the development of software intensive systems / James McDonald.
      p. cm.
    Includes bibliographical references and index.
    ISBN 978-0-470-53762-6 (cloth)
  1. Computer software–Development–Management. 2. Project management. I. Title.
    QA76.76.D47M3945 2010
    005.1–dc22

                                  2009035851

Printed in the United States of America.

Contents

Supplemental materials available at ftp://ftp.wiley.com/public/sci_tech_med/software_intensive

Preface

This book is titled *Managing the Development of Software-Intensive Systems*. It probably could have been called simply "Software Project Management" because it covers virtually all aspects of traditional project management as it is applied to software. However, I chose the alternative title because I wanted it to be broader and, in some ways, deeper than the "Software Project Management" title would imply. Software projects come in a wide variety of shapes and sizes. They range from pure software projects, which operate wholly within a commercial computer/operating system environment, to those that operate in a commercial computer/operating system environment and interface with a wide variety of external computers and software applications for the purposes of monitoring and controlling those computers and applications, to those that are embedded and that operate as permanently or semipermanently installed software, usually on custom-designed hardware. In this book, we will be discussing the application of project management techniques to the development of software, and sometimes hardware, in all of these environments.

Project management has come to be well known and well specified by the Project Management Body of Knowledge (PMBOK) (*Guide to the Project Management Body of Knowledge* (Upper Darby, PA: Project Management Institute, 2000)). Individuals can study the materials specified in the PMBOK, take a test administered by the Project Management Institute (PMI) and work as a project manager for a specified period of time, and then be certified by the PMI as a project management professional (PMP). Certification as a PMP provides some assurance that the certified individual is very familiar with the knowledge areas specified in the PMBOK and has had some experience in applying that knowledge to real projects. However, certification provides no assurance that an individual is capable of managing software-intensive development projects, particularly those that require the simultaneous development of hardware. That is what this book is all about.

I personally learned many of the things contained in the PMBOK during a workshop that I attended many years ago when the software development community was beginning to realize that projects might benefit from the application of project management techniques to software projects. Shortly after that time, I had an opportunity to become the manager of a department in Bell Laboratories, which was responsible for developing application software that was being or would be used in all of the Bell Operating Companies. That assignment was eye-opening for me. I found that knowledge of project management techniques and the direct application of those techniques to the development of software was far from straightforward. I struggled for about 5 years to implement a modest software project management process in an organization that had primary responsibility for one project that required the efforts of about 30 people and for a second larger project in which about

70 people were involved. A third exploratory development project employing four people was later added to this mix.

At about that time, AT&T divested itself of the regional Bell Operating Companies, and I was able to move to a different part of the organization where I became responsible for a department that developed somewhat smaller systems. Those projects typically involved project teams of 5–25 people with seven or eight projects taking place in the organization at any one time. None of the teams in that organization had ever used anything resembling project management for the management of their development work. These projects were smaller, but they had an added complication in that almost all of them required the simultaneous development of software as well as the development of customized electronic hardware. This presented me with a second set of learning experiences.

In that environment, it became clear that instituting the use of project management tools and techniques was much easier than it had been on very large software projects. But the added complications that resulted from the need to get employees with very different technical capabilities (circuit and physical design in addition to software development) to work together and to use similar management techniques made the management of each project more difficult. The additional risks involved with hardware development, which included the possibility of long delays if a fault was inserted into the hardware design, also made the overall management of these projects at least as difficult as the management of very large software projects. After 8 or 9 years of managing this organization, I became quite successful at integrating the software and hardware developers into teams that used similar techniques for managing their projects. In fact, by 1994, we obtained ISO (International Standards Organization) 9000 certification for the combined hardware and software development process, including the project management of those projects.

Fortunately for me, I was then asked to develop a project management workshop for all AT&T employees who were involved in both software and hardware development. During preparation for that workshop, many of the ideas contained in this book were formulated.

One of the things that I learned during the experiences described above was that there was a need for a strong relationship between the project management processes and the underlying technical and business processes that are used to develop software or hardware, or both, and the difficulty of integrating the management processes with the technical processes used for product development. That integration will be the focus of this book. Instead of discussing project management abstractly as a set of management processes and techniques, we will try to integrate that discussion with a discussion of the underlying technical processes, which present both opportunities and challenges for the managers of software-intensive development projects and organizations.

During the next 3.5 years, I had the privilege of delivering the workshop with a small team of other employees. During that time, the workshop was offered about every third week in a variety of locations in the United States and in Europe where most of the AT&T and Lucent Technologies product and system development teams were based. About 1800 employees participated in the workshop.

In 1999, I retired from Lucent Technologies and joined Monmouth University's Software Engineering Department where I have been teaching software project management and a variety of other software engineering topics for the past 10 years. Each year, I have taught at least one software project management course and sometimes two. The bulk of the students in my graduate level software project management courses at Monmouth University have been employees of the U.S. Army's Software Engineering Center at Fort Monmouth, NJ. From my interactions with those students, I believe that I have acquired yet a third perspective on the management of software development, this time in a government organization for which most of the software development work was done by external contract organizations. That situation presents yet another set of difficulties and complications that we will discuss in Chapter 11.

Throughout this book, we will discuss the standard project management processes of planning, organizing, monitoring, and controlling. We will emphasize the relationship of those processes to the underlying technical process that software-based product developers use to specify, design, develop, and deploy software and hardware. Specifically, we will describe how managers can exploit those relationships to develop high-quality products in predictable ways.

In Chapter 1, we introduce the management of software development and describe a model that emphasizes the relationship between project management and the underlying technical processes. Chapter 2 is dedicated to explaining and providing examples of the most important project management process: planning. Chapter 3 provides a wide variety of material related to one of the most difficult parts of the planning process, that is, estimating the time, effort, and cost that will be required to develop software and any hardware that may be required. Chapter 4 is about verification and validation, with particular emphasis on inspections and testing.

Chapters 5–7 introduce the other important project management processes of organizing, monitoring, and controlling and the relationship of those processes to the underlying technical software development processes. Chapter 8 introduces risk management and describes two techniques that managers might use to help manage the risks that are inherent in all software-based product development work. Chapter 9 discusses a variety of audit, review, and assessment techniques. Chapters 10–12 discuss what we will call multi-projects, development outsourcing, and the management of globally disbursed development work. Finally, Chapter 13 introduces the topic of retrospectives, which, while it is neither a pure project management process nor an underlying technical process, provides a way for development managers to look back at their successes and failures as a way to help improve their capabilities in the future.

Each chapter is accompanied by a case study based on an actual situation with which the author is familiar. Readers of the text can benefit from reading the text in each chapter, then using the case study at the end of the chapter as the basis for a group or classroom discussion. In addition, Case Study 2 at the end of Chapter 2 provides the basis of an extended facilitated case study that can be used throughout the remainder of the book to give participants some practice in the most important of the project management processes: planning.

The text can be used as reading material in support of a one-semester course on software project management. In the author's experience, coverage of the entire text as well as the case studies could easily extend to a two-semester course. I have occasionally used selected chapters, for example, Chapters 1 through 7 and the Central Control Position System (CCPS) planning project in Chapter 2 for a one-semester course, allowing for facilitated group project work during alternate class sessions. I have also used the material from the entire text in the form of lecture materials and several of the case studies for a 4.5-day workshop.

I wish the readers of this book well and I hope you find the content helpful.

Supplemental materials available at ftp://ftp.wiley.com/public/sci_tech_med/ software_intensive

JAMES MCDONALD
West Long Branch, NJ
June 2009

Acknowledgments

I would like to thank Glenn Secor, who jointly taught a software project management workshop with the author while both were employed by Bell Laboratories and Lucent Technologies. Glenn was the primary developer of the CCPS project planning exercise, which appears throughout this text. He continually developed its content while serving as a facilitator for many student groups that successfully completed the exercise. I would also like to thank Larry Bernstein, who suggested many times that I should write a book that contained all of the materials included in the workshop. I have had numerous discussions about project management with my professional colleagues and students during the past several years. Those discussions have contributed immensely to the materials contained in this book. Among those who have spent countless hours with me in recent years have been employees of the U.S. Army's Software Engineering Center, Tata Consultancy Services, Ltd., and Telcordia Technologies, Inc.

I would like to thank my wife, Gail, my son, Michael, and my daughter, Amy, and their families, who have been supportive throughout the development and operation of the workshop and this text. They were very patient during the long weeks that I spent teaching the workshop throughout the world. Finally, I would like to thank the faculty and administration of Monmouth University for giving me the opportunity to teach software project management courses in the Software Engineering Department at that institution and for giving me the opportunity to work on writing this book during the 2008–2009 academic year.

Acknowledgments

About the Author

James McDonald, PhD, is Associate Professor of Software Engineering at Monmouth University in West Long Branch, NJ. He has bachelor's and master's degrees in electrical engineering from New Jersey Institute of Technology and Massachusetts Institute of Technology, respectively, and a PhD from New York University. Dr. McDonald has an extensive industrial and academic background in electrical, computer, and software engineering. Prior to joining the Monmouth University faculty, he worked at AT&T, Bell Laboratories, Telcordia Technologies, Inc., and Lucent Technologies. During his last 10 years at Bell Laboratories and Lucent Technologies, he managed a department that was responsible for the development of microprocessor and digital signal processor-based hardware and software and taught several week-long project management workshops. He served as chair of Monmouth University's Department of Software and Electrical Engineering from 1999 until 2008. He has returned several times to some of the former AT&T companies to teach a project management workshop during the past 10 years.

Dr. McDonald is very active in the software engineering community, teaching at Monmouth University, regularly publishing in technical journals and in conference proceedings, and evaluating academic software, electrical, and computer engineering programs as an evaluator for the Accreditation Board for Engineering and Technology (ABET). He is a senior life member of the Institute of Electrical and Electronics Engineers (IEEE) and the IEEE Computer Society and a member of both the Association for Computing Machinery and the American Society for Engineering Education. He has been a recipient of the North Atlantic Treaty Organization (NATO) Systems Science Prize.

Chapter 1

Overview and Introduction

This is a book about managing the development of software-based applications and products. When we say "the development of software-based products," we mean the activities involved in deciding what the product needs to do, commonly called requirements engineering, designing the product at both high levels, sometimes called architecture, and low levels, called detailed design, coding the software, sometimes integrating the software with custom-designed hardware, testing the product, deploying it to users, and maintaining its evolution. So, we include the management of all phases of the development life cycle in our understanding of the phrase "development of software-based products." We also include all types and kinds of software. This covers the range from software that drives static web pages, interactive web pages, and scientific applications to large data management systems based on commercial database management systems to applications that monitor and control real-world distributed systems such as air flight control systems or telecommunication switches and transmission systems that are geographically disbursed. These software applications typically run in service on commercial computers. We also include embedded and real-time software that typically interacts intimately with electrical and mechanical devices and systems and that is frequently loaded permanently (or at least semipermanently) into the hardware devices or systems that it controls. When we develop the latter type of software, we will also need to be concerned about integrating both new software and the newly developed hardware on which and with which it operates.

With the inclusion of this broad array of software types and all phases of the life cycle, it quickly becomes obvious that the same rigidly defined management methods and techniques cannot be used to manage all software development work. In addition, some software applications will involve only a small number of people working together to do the work, sometimes only two or three people. Other projects will require hundreds, or occasionally thousands, of people to do the job. In the industrial environment of Bell Laboratories where I worked for several years, there were typically a few hundred software development projects under way at any one time. The number of people involved in each ranged from four or five up to approximately 1500 on the very largest undertaking. The average number of people involved

Managing the Development of Software-Intensive Systems, by James McDonald
Copyright © 2010 John Wiley & Sons, Inc.

on each project was about 20. So, as with the kinds of work and types of software being developed, the sizes of the teams doing the work also vary tremendously.

This extremely large variation among possible environments in which development managers could be working implies that any method that we will be discussing will need to be appropriately tailored to the environment in which it will be used. Tailoring is difficult and it is almost impossible to be prescriptive about which techniques should be applied under which conditions. However, by the time the readers finish with all of the materials in this book, they will have developed enough understanding and skill so that they will feel confident in their ability to tailor their use of the methods and techniques discussed to their particular environment.

I have found that one of the primary determinants of which techniques are appropriate is the size of the project, measured in terms of the product's size and functionality and the maximum number of people who will need to be employed to develop the product. For example, it should be quite obvious that a development team of four or five people does not require the same quantity or quality of management as would a team of several hundred people. It is likely that some readers of this book will be involved with small projects, involving only a handful of people. Others might be involved in projects that require a few tens of people to accomplish their objectives. A few may be lucky (or, perhaps, unlucky) enough to work with teams of a hundred or more people.

So, how should each reader review the content of this book? I would suggest that you start by temporarily backing away from the environment in which you are currently involved. Try to imagine that you are working with a team of 20 other developers on a project that will require that maximum number of people to accomplish the work. Also assume, for now, that you are starting at the very beginning of a brand new undertaking and that you will have an opportunity to influence not only what will be developed but also how that work will be done and, most importantly for this book, how it will be managed. Most of the examples discussed in this book will be drawn from projects like the one described here. For those projects, we will describe all of the things that need to be done to make them successful. For larger projects, it is safe to assume that all of the things that we discuss will need to be done (along, perhaps, with a few additional things) with great care and diligence. For smaller projects involving a few up to about 20 people, the methods and techniques that we will discuss will need to be selectively scaled back, with some not requiring as much care or thoroughness as we will imply and some that may need none at all. However, while reading, please try to concentrate on the project involving 20 people described above. Toward the end of the book, we will provide some guidelines for "backing off" from some of the more burdensome activities.

Throughout this book, you will read about the four major project management processes of planning, organizing, monitoring, and controlling and how those processes can be applied effectively by software project managers. We will also talk about two underlying processes that the manager needs to use to facilitate the process management processes. They are communicating and negotiating. These process are used somewhat sequentially as shown in Fig. 1.1 with significant amounts of feedback from the processes toward the right in the figure to the processes on the left.

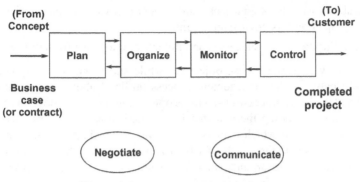

Figure 1.1 Project management processes.

Most product or system development undertakings will start with a concept and, perhaps, a business case or a contract that has been negotiated with a customer or with the management of the parent organization. The person responsible for managing the work needs to plan what will be done, organize the team that will do the work, monitor how the work is progressing, and, when necessary, take control to modify how the work is being done or by whom it is being done. These processes are intended to take the job from concept to delivery of a completed product to the customer. The two supporting activities labeled "communicate" and "negotiate" in Fig. 1.1 are used by the manager in support of the four major project management processes.

In this book, we will try to achieve several objectives. They are to develop

- a broad understanding of how project management can be applied to software development projects;
- an understanding of the estimation methods that are available and the pros and cons of each;
- the ability to properly apply project management methods to the requirements, architecture, design, testing, and delivery of software products;
- an understanding of common organizational structures, team building, and conflict resolution;
- the ability to monitor and to report on the status of software development work;
- the ability to use audits, reviews, and assessments effectively;
- the ability to minimize risk;
- methods for working with partners and vendors;
- the ability to manage projects in complicated but typical, multi-project, and multiple organization environments;
- an understanding of the complications and the costs involved in outsourcing portions of development projects;

- an ability to tailor the project management processes to appropriately match the project and its environment; and
- the ability to review successes and failures and to learn from our experiences.

We will try to achieve these objectives while simultaneously emphasizing the relationship between the management process outlined above and the underlying technical and business processes used by people doing the actual development work.

In addition to reading the text that is provided in each chapter, there are two significant activities in which readers might want to participate. These are, first, a series of short case studies, each of which is associated with the materials in the chapters where they appear, and, second, a major longer case study (Case Study 2 at the end of Chapter 2) in which readers can go through all of the steps involved in developing a project plan for a real project. Both the case studies and the project are best done by groups of four to eight participants, so they are best suited for use in classes and workshops in which all participants are going through the text together and working on the case studies and the project in groups. However, the case studies may also be of use to an individual reader who would like to get some real-world experience in thinking about how the content of the text might be related to situations faced by managers of software-based development work.

In the remainder of this chapter, we will address our first objective. That is "developing a broad understanding of how project management can be applied to software and software/hardware development projects." We will do this by discussing a model that will provide a context for the remainder of the book, some definitions of terms, characteristics of software projects, managers' roles, software life cycles, processes in the life cycle, and process management.

1.1 OUR MODEL

Throughout this book, we will assume that development of a new product or expansion of the capabilities of an older product follows the model shown in Fig. 1.2. In this model, we assume that product or system development work requires the successful completion of the business and technical tasks shown in the lower portion of the figure. They include the work required to develop requirements and to design and implement the necessary software and hardware, and the associated business processes such as development of a business case, a proposal, or a contract. This is work done by people using whatever business and technical processes the organization has decided to use to accomplish its work. Sitting above these business and technical processes is a box that contains the project management processes. These are also tasks that are done by people using a variety of management methods, some of which include the planning, organizing, monitoring, and controlling processes that make up a major portion of the material discussed in this book. These processes are also executed by people who can make use of a wide variety of management methods.

We will assume that most development work starts with a customer who is making use of a presently available product or system. That customer, whether they

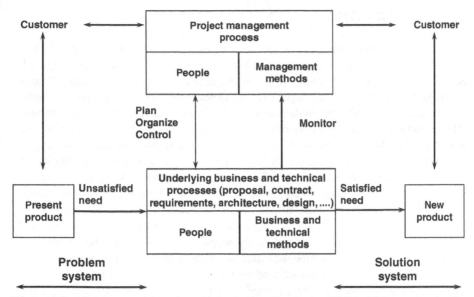

Figure 1.2 Model assumed throughout this book (from Crawford and Fallah 1985, reproduced with permission of IEEE © 1985 IEEE).

are inside or outside the organization in which the work will be done, is assumed to have a problem or an unmet need to which we will refer as the problem system. The customer interacts with some of the people who execute both the management and the underlying technical processes shown in the upper and lower paths shown in Fig. 1.2. The people in those blocks then execute their processes, sometimes over a short period of time, such as a few weeks or months, or over a longer period of time, sometimes extending to as much as several months or even several years. At the end of the overall development process, the development team delivers a new product or system to the customer that satisfies their needs. We will call that product the solution system.

Two important parts of this model are the lines connecting the project management process box with the underlying business and technical processes box. The reader should note that the line labeled "plan," "organize," and "control" is two headed, indicating that information flows both ways along this link. Those processes require that information flows both from the project management process to the underlying business and technical processes and that information flows from the underlying processes to the project management process. The one-headed arrow labeled "monitor" indicates that for monitoring, the primary flow of information is from the underlying business and technical processes to the project management process.

This model is a very simplified description of what usually takes place in practice. When we start talking about development models in more detail, we will discuss the waterfall model, the spiral model, and the agile model that bring out more of the gory details of real development processes.

1.2 DEFINITIONS

Most books like this one have titles like "Software Project Management." They contain many terms drawn from the traditional project management body of knowledge which had its early roots in the management of the development of large complex systems for the U.S. Department of Defense and for commercial and public works construction projects. In this book, we will make use of many standard project management terms. So, let us get started by defining a few of them. The first one we will define is the word "project." A project is an activity performed by people, sometimes with assistance from a variety of tools, like backhoes, cement trucks, or, in our case, computers, compilers, software development environments, test equipment, and so on. Most projects are faced with a variety of constraints like the availability of funds, the availability of people, or the need to have the new product or system available by a specified date. A project can be described by a set of tasks and processes where tasks are activities done by people and processes are the connections between those tasks that describe the order in which the tasks must be accomplished. Some of the tasks are typically dependent on the completion of other tasks, while some are completely independent of other tasks. In the case of software development, a task might be something like coding and compiling a program. Another task might be testing the program to determine if it works properly and, if not, what is wrong with it. Obviously, the testing task cannot begin until there is some code that has been written and compiled, so there is a process relating the testing task to the coding and compiling task. Projects need to be planned, organized, monitored, and controlled, and we will spend at least a chapter discussing both the meaning of those terms and how the manager can optimally manage those processes.

All of these tasks and processes are similar to other activities in which humans engage. However, there are two characteristics that make projects different from those other activities: (1) a project is a temporary endeavor, meaning that it has definite starting and ending points; and (2) a project creates a unique product or service. After a project ends, the world will be different than before the project was started.

These characteristics distinguish projects from repetitive or cyclic operations. Cyclic operations are processes that are repeated over and over again, as, for example, in a factory that produces pencils, refrigerators, automobiles, or even airplanes. Those cyclic processes lend themselves relatively easily to quantification and to statistical process control, making them susceptible to the use of a variety of metrics that can be used by the manager who is responsible for them. Software-based development work, while we continually try to make it a repetitive process, is not cyclic. It has intrinsic characteristics that make it very difficult to apply quantitative techniques to its management in the same ways that these techniques are used to help manage cyclic processes. We will talk about a few commonly used software metrics, but we will find that using more than a very few basic measurement methods is extremely difficult and unreliable.

Let us think about building a skyscraper. The underground portions of each skyscraper are somewhat unique, with their layout and structure being dependent upon things like the ultimate height of the building, the soil and geologic conditions where it is being built, and the creativity and discipline of the architects and structural engineers who designed the building. The first and second floors usually contain some unique facilities like escalators, spaces for retail establishments, and elevator lobbies. However, after the third floor, all of the floors are quite similar, with the fourth floor being just like the third floor, the fifth floor being just like the fourth floor, and so on. Once construction reaches the third floor, the manager who is supervising construction can tell the work crew, "The fourth floor needs to be just like the third floor, the fifth like the fourth and just keep going until I say 'Stop.'" Then the roof is usually unique. So, while the construction of the overall skyscraper does, indeed, produce something unique, the rising of floor upon floor is more like a repetitive or cyclic process.

The development of software and its corresponding hardware is different from our skyscraper project in that, unless we are very creative, or sometimes very rigid, in the application of our development processes, there is usually minimal repetition from one part of the project to the next. Another characteristic of software-based development projects that makes them difficult is the fact that it is extremely difficult to look at a piece of software and to know the status of the work involved in developing it. We will discuss that issue in more depth when we talk about the monitoring process in Chapter 6.

The manager who is responsible for supervising development work is usually charged with meeting or exceeding the expectations of customers and other project stakeholders and with negotiating those expectations so that the work can be done within agreed upon budget, time, and personnel constraints. The manager is usually faced with the difficult task of balancing competing demands among customer needs and wants (usually called requirements and sometimes scope), the project schedule (time), the cost of the work, customers with competing requirements when a product is being developed for use by multiple customers, and quality of the design. Finally, the manager is sometimes faced with identified requirements as well as with unidentified requirements. Unidentified requirements are created when customers or stakeholders have made assumptions about what the product will do or how it will do it but have not communicated those assumptions to the development team.

In the preceding paragraph, we have mentioned "stakeholders." Stakeholders are the set of everyone who has an interest in the work of the development team. They include customers such as those who will ultimately be hands-on users of the product, a manufacturing organization that might need to load the software onto a commercial or custom-designed hardware configuration, sales and marketing people who will sell the product if it is being developed for sale to multiple customers, the higher management of the organization that is developing the software, and finally, and perhaps most important, members of the team that is doing the design and development work.

Throughout this book, we will be talking about both project managers as well as software organization managers. Sometimes these will be different people and sometimes they will be the same people. We will make that distinction more clearly when we discuss the organizing process in Chapter 5.

Let us first talk about what development project managers typically do on a day-to-day basis. Project managers have to understand the environment in which they and their teams are working. This includes the problem system that we discussed earlier and the stakeholders for the work that is being done, including customers, supporters, and detractors. They need to understand the business rationale for the work that is being done. And they need to understand the goals and rules that will be applied to the work. By the goals and rules, we mean explicit rules (such as the need for profit in an industrial environment or the need to meet the budget as closely as possible in a government environment), constraints (such as schedule and scope and the relationships between those constraints), and what information can and cannot be shared with customers. It is normal for some of these rules to be explicit and well known, but sometimes, the rules may be implicit and never openly discussed.

The project manager must take the lead in planning the work that will be done. We will discuss planning extensively in Chapter 2. However, it can be briefly described as identifying every task that must be done, clearly defining those tasks, allocating resources to tasks, scheduling the tasks, and assigning responsibility for completion of tasks for the overall project.

He or she needs to negotiate a commitment including the budget, the schedule, the features that will be delivered, and the people who will do the work. This is the most clearly defining role of a project manager. We frequently hear that a project manager has been assigned to a project for which the budget, the schedule, the scope, and the team membership have been predetermined and the project manager does not have the freedom or the ability to negotiate any of those constraints. If that is the situation, then the person we are discussing cannot be called the project manager. They can only serve the role of a clerk, monitoring the status of the project and reporting its status. Real project managers must have the ability to negotiate the budget, the schedule, the scope and team membership, and the freedom to negotiate changes in at least one, and possibly more, of those constraints when the need arises. If the project manager does not have this ability, they are not the project manager and they can be assured that they will not be successful in their job. If you ever find yourself in that position, you have two options. You can try to locate a member of the management team who, with your assistance, has the ability to negotiate these constraints and to pair up with that person to create the project management team. Together you could be called the "real project manager." Your second choice, if you cannot accomplish the first, is to leave the position and to look for another job. So, when we talk about a project manager in this book, we are referring to someone in the organization who has that ability to negotiate, someone who knows enough about the technical aspects of the work being done to understand it, and someone who also knows enough about project management to execute the more routine responsibilities of a project manager.

A project manager needs to organize the work including staffing the project and considering the skills, knowledge and abilities of the people who will be, or are, on the team, and the structure of the organization in which the work is being done. They need to clearly define and manage the definition of interfaces, both technical interfaces, which will be implemented in the product being developed, and interpersonal interfaces through which intra-project communications will take place. And, finally, they need to make responsibilities clear.

They need to execute the plan by monitoring the status of the work, identifying and addressing issues as early as possible. This means tracking staffing, cost, progress of the work, and performance of the product being developed to identify discrepancies between the plan and the project status. Then, when discrepancies are identified, he or she must take control to resolve the underlying issues promptly.

They need to complete the project on time with appropriate quality, within budget and with features that satisfy the customers.

Throughout all of this work, the project manager needs to communicate goals, plans, project status, and changes to all of the stakeholders. We have been talking about things that the project manager does. You might be thinking what is the difference between what a project manager does on a day-to-day basis and the four major project management processes that we discussed earlier. The project manager is a person, an individual (or sometimes an individual acting with the assistance of others) who is responsible for executing the project management processes including planning, organizing, monitoring, and controlling. Ideally, the individual project manager would be a visionary who can formulate where the project is headed and can communicate that vision to stakeholders; a rebel who is willing, when necessary, to say "no" when one or more of the stakeholders is pressuring them to do something that is inappropriate or undoable; a planner who is able to get members of the team engaged in doing the difficult planning work that some team members invariably will resist; a team builder who can get team members and important stakeholders to work together creatively and efficiently; a leader who can help the team members stay motivated while heading as directly as possible toward the team goals; a communicator who can write to and talk with stakeholders on the team, in the organization, and outside the organization in which the work is being done; and a psychologist who sometimes needs to try to understand the reasons for behaviors of team members, bosses, and customers who may not appear to behave rationally.

That ideal project manager is often hard to find, but that is what we will be working toward throughout the remainder of this book.

1.3 LIFE CYCLE MODELS AND THE DEVELOPMENT PROCESSES

Almost any book or paper on general project management will start with, or at least assume, that a project timeline looks like the one shown in Fig. 1.3. The project starts with the development of an idea that states in very broad terms what will be done and what will be achieved. This takes place during the concept phase of the project. Then someone takes a first cut to determine whether the project is feasible. A team starts to define the product by developing requirements. The product is developed. Then it is deployed and goes into operation.

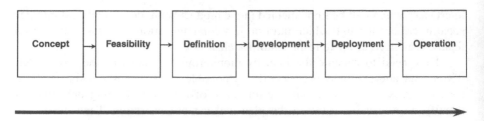

Time

Figure 1.3   Project phases and the project life cycle.

The major outputs of each of the phases shown in Fig. 1.3 are the following:

- Concept phase
  1. A statement of the opportunity
  2. An estimate of the resources to complete the feasibility phase of the project
- Feasibility phase
  1. A preliminary business case or a proposal
  2. Formation of a project team
  3. A draft of an architecture document
  4. A preliminary project plan
- Definition phase
  1. Baselined requirements
  2. A baselined architecture
  3. A baselined project plan
  4. An approved final business case or a signed contract
- Development phase
  1. Hardware designs captured, software coded, and both baselined.
  2. Unit, integration, system, and beta testing completed
  3. Customer documentation and training materials completed
  4. Information for reproduction transmitted to production facility
- Deployment phase
  1. Customer plans for use completed
  2. Production and customer support in place
- Operation phase
  1. Product generally available
  2. Product in use by customers
  3. Development team may be adding features and capabilities
  4. Project closed out

Of course, anyone who is familiar with the development of software-based products or applications knows that software is never developed using the exact phases and sequential life cycle shown in Fig. 1.3. The first attempt to specify a development process that was more realistic for the development of software was the waterfall process shown in Fig. 1.4. That process was described by Winston Royce in 1970

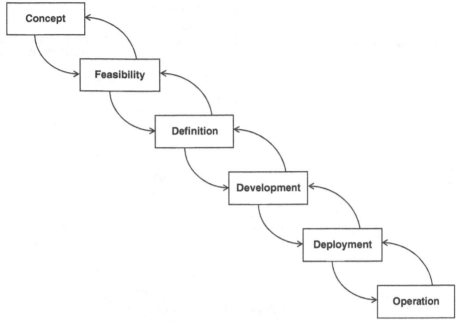

Figure 1.4 The waterfall model.

(Royce 1970). It is based on the traditional phased product development process of Fig. 1.3 but recognizes that it made more sense to iterate between adjacent phases to allow for some feedback from later phases to impact completion of earlier phases. It also allowed work on the succeeding phase to begin, to the degree possible, before the immediately prior phase is completely finished, thus shortening the interval from start to finish as compared to the linear depiction of Fig. 1.3.

Several years later, an alternative process, known as the spiral model, was introduced by Barry Boehm (1988). It is illustrated in Fig. 1.5.

The intent of the spiral model was to address some of the weaknesses of the waterfall model. It allows for the use of a waterfall model in that it calls for determination of objectives, specification and evaluation of alternatives, design and development of the product, and planning of future work. In this model, the distance from the origin is a measure of cumulative cost to date and the angular dimension represents progress in completing each cycle of the spiral. Notably, the spiral model explicitly specifies repetitive risk analysis steps and the use of prototypes, simulations, and modeling to help reduce risk. It also calls for frequent cycling during the early phases of the project to provide increased confidence that the concept, the requirements, the development plan, the prototypes, and the design are appropriate.

The third major contribution to the characterization of software development models was the development of the agile software development process. This method is based upon the content of a document that was developed and signed by a group of software consultants in 2001 (Beck et al. 2001). That document is called the Agile Software Development Manifesto. It includes four broad statements upon which the

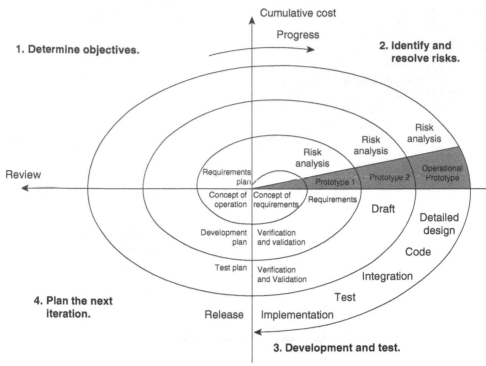

Figure 1.5   The spiral model (from Boehm 1988, reproduced with permission from IEEE © 1988 IEEE).

agile method is based. They are the following: (1) We value individuals and interactions over process and tools. (2) We value working software over comprehensive documentation. (3) We value customer collaboration over contract negotiation. (4) We value responding to change over following a plan.

   In some software development circles, the availability of the manifesto and the agile model has given members of development teams license to throw away what they call heavyweight software development methods and to do their development work using whatever alternative methods suit their fancy. However, some advocates of the method have made a valiant attempt to bring its ideas to software development teams in a way that is both understandable and responsible. Probably the most commonly used software model is called Agile with SCRUM (Schwaber 2004). Figure 1.6 is one representation of how this model works.

   Using this method, software development team members manage themselves and are responsible for figuring out how to turn a product backlog (list of capabilities desired by the customer) into increments of functionality in very short periods of time, typically of weeks or even days of duration. This is an incremental and iterative process. The loops in the figure are intended to show both the short iterations as well as the daily inspections of the work of the previous day that are done by members of the project team. The agile model can work for relatively small teams,

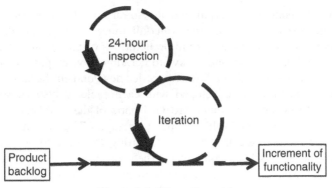

Figure 1.6   The agile model.

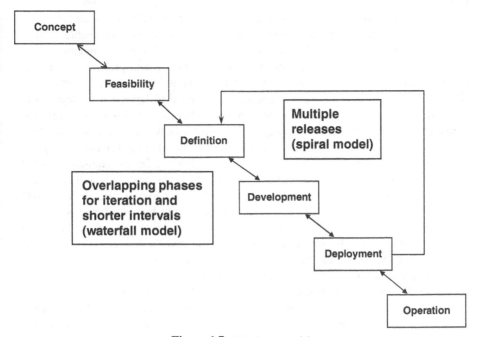

Figure 1.7   The better model.

and some of its advocates have attempted to scale it up for use on larger projects, but it has not been proven to be particularly useful for the kinds of projects that we will be discussing in this book. It is included here primarily for completeness.

To simplify our discussion, we will use a software development model that includes many of the characteristics of the waterfall model and the spiral model, and, perhaps, a bit of the agile model. It is shown in Fig. 1.7.

We will call it the "better model." It is better for several reasons. It is simpler than the spiral and agile models shown in Figs. 1.5 and 1.6 and contains characteristics of both the waterfall and the spiral models. It provides a shorter interval to the first delivery than the waterfall model of Fig. 1.4. It allows for significant customer feedback and multiple iterations of the spiral and recognizes the possibility of both forward and backward iteration between phases and between repetitions of the spiral. It also allows for easier development because only some of the product's features are developed with each cycle. It also allows for both prototyping and risk analysis, which are vital parts of the spiral model, although those characteristics are not explicitly shown in Fig. 1.7. Using this model does introduce some risks. There is the risk of starting the succeeding phase before the preceding phase has been completed. There are risks that later iterations of the spiral might require significant changes to the architecture. Customers might not want a partially completed product. It requires early formation of a cross-functional team so that people who are involved in later phases are ready to begin shortly after the work starts. Therefore, project managers need to be sure they have the agreement of both their customer and their management when they use this model. All phases need to be managed, and frequent visible outputs are required to facilitate project monitoring and control when necessary.

So far, we have been discussing development models and processes at a relatively high level. None of these models tell an individual team member what he or she should do. In order to resolve that issue, we need to have a somewhat more detailed process to tell individual team members what to do and when to do it. The actual process that will be used on a specific project can be defined in several alternative places. It can be in the heads of team members, which is usually not a great alternative. It can be defined in a project plan, which is a better alternative, but if the organization takes on new projects, with new plans, regularly creating new processes for each project can consume significant effort and cost. The process might be defined in organization-wide documents, which might be good for overall business processes, but which tend to be too rigid for low-level product development work. It could be included in locally developed and managed process documents if they are available and could be used by everyone in the organization, or they can be contained in a quality manual, which is required if the organization intends to seek ISO (International Standards Organization) 9000 certification for its development operations or if it plans to seek a Capability Maturity Model Integration (CMMI®) assessment. While any of these alternatives can be useful, I have found that developing a quality manual and seeking ISO 9000 certification to be quite effective. Getting such a certification is expensive, but many organizations have found it to be valuable, particularly if the products being developed are intended for sale in global commercial markets. We will talk more about ISO certification and CMMI assessments in Chapter 9 when we discuss audits and reviews.

1.4   PROCESS AND PROJECT MANAGEMENT

If a software process is to be defined, someone needs to prepare and document that definition. It could be done by an individual, by an individual with some assistance from other members of the development team or organization, or by a team charged with process management. Most observers would recommend that processes be managed by self-directed teams of people who are intimately familiar with the projects and the people in a product development organization. Self-directed teams can manage repeatable processes, and one of the purposes for developing a process specification is to drive software development in the direction of becoming a repeatable, or cyclic, process. The job of process management teams should be specification, management, and improvement of the process. They should not be charged with process enforcement. Their job is to define the process at an appropriate level that allows the process to be used repetitively by a group of people who may be working on one team or multiple development teams. It is sometimes desirable to provide the process management team with a management "coach" who can guide the team without acting as the supervisor of the team.

We have indicated earlier that software-based product development projects are not repeatable operations, so they cannot typically be self-managed. They can use the process that has been defined for the product they are working on or the organization they are working in, but someone must make the decision about whether the process can be used as is or whether it needs to be tailored for the current project. Software development projects frequently require prompt decision making and teams cannot usually make quick decisions. Therefore, while it is possible to have the process managed by a self-directed team, the project must be managed by an individual, sometimes with a staff, who has clear responsibility and authority for the project. That is the project manager.

So, while well-defined processes are necessary and helpful, they will not ensure successful projects. Both processes and projects must be planned, organized, monitored, and controlled.

1.5 SOME THINGS TO REMEMBER

The most important things we have discussed in this chapter are the following:

1. A product development *project* is a one-time, limited life endeavor that produces a unique output.

2. A *project manager* is responsible for producing the output on time, within budget, and meeting stakeholders' expectations.

3. A *project manager does* many things: plans, organizes, monitors, controls, leads, communicates, and motivates.

4. The *typical* project process (the "better" process) includes overlapped activities and multiple releases to achieve *speed*.

5. *Process management* is required to ensure good processes are in place and are working as planned.

6. A *development project* needs to be managed by an individual who has the ability to negotiate, scope, schedule, and budget.

CASE STUDY 1   *Implementing a Project Management System*

Purpose

1. Understand a situation faced by some newly trained development project managers.
2. Consider the criticality of several problems, including the lack of a project management process, competing for the manager's time and attention.
3. Practice planning the implementation of a project management system in a difficult environment.

Background

A few months after completing his study of this book, Stan Pasterchech was asked to take on his first job that involved software development. The move was not a promotion for Stan, but it gave him an opportunity to broaden his background, which had been in systems analysis and business planning. Stan was offered the opportunity to take on this new assignment because he had experience in two areas that the manager of the organization wanted to strengthen. They were in system requirements development and inventory management. Stan's previous assignment gave him the systems analysis background. His formal education had been in operations research and, in one of his early career assignments, he had become involved in several applications of inventory management theory to real-world problems.

When Stan arrived in his new assignment, he found himself managing an organization of 83 people. There were five supervisory groups in the organization, all of which reported to him. Three of the supervisory groups were responsible for software development. The fourth was responsible for customer support, and the fifth was a documentation and training group. Stan had been authorized to create and staff a sixth group that was to be responsible for requirements development. System test was the responsibility of a group in an organization managed by one of Stan's peers. His primary customers, who funded the work, were in other parts of his own corporation.

The people in Stan's new organization had spent several years developing and maintaining a large system based on a commercial database management application that tracked both physical inventory at a large number of geographically disbursed locations and the detailed financial records associated with the inventory investment. The system was in use at several locations throughout the world and was likely to require some enhancement and maintenance for several years into the future. However, the customers for the system were looking forward to a reduction in the needs for enhancements and a reduction in the cost and the need for staff on the project.

Fortunately for the staff, a new customer came along and asked if the organization could develop an inventory management system for a completely different application. The new application was not well defined, but there were several customer representatives who were looking forward to participating in the detailed definition of the new system.

The technology being used by the organization was very old. The existing application ran on IBM mainframes that were running the MVS operating system and the DB2 database management system. Most report-generating software and online transaction software were written in PL/I, and some of the online application softwares were even written in assembly language to assure adequate response time. Some of the older pieces of the inventory control software were written in FORTRAN. A few experiments had been carried out in which C++ had been used for report generation and online transactions. Formal detailed requirements were not usually written. A representative of the customers normally discussed their needs with one of the development group managers. One or more software developers would be assigned to the feature and would proceed to mock up a transaction or a report and then review it with the customer representative before it was implemented. There was no formal development methodology being used. There was no project management process and there was no inspection program in place.

Stan knew that the methods that had been used for development for more than 20 years could not be used for the new application. He wanted to avoid the use of PL/I, FORTRAN, and assembly language at all costs. When he suggested that they might consider moving completely to a modern high-level development language and a distributed architecture with graphical user interfaces, two of the software development managers explained that it would be very difficult to do that given the underlying architecture of the existing system, and that they would be risking unpredictable transaction response times. While getting to know some of the nonmanagement members of the organization in one-on-one meetings, he found that there was a small cadre of some very good software developers who wanted to implement a code inspection program but that they had not gotten support from their peers or their management. Stan also knew that unless he put his newly found project management knowledge into action, he would quickly forget what he learned and that the new undertaking would be a disaster. Finally, within a few months, his team would have to develop an estimate of the funding that would be required during the following year for both the old and the new applications and would have to negotiate with the funding organizations on the deliverables that they could expect.

Activity

Try to put yourself in Stan's position. Think, from his point of view, of the problems that he is facing. Develop and describe in writing your evaluation of the relative seriousness of the lack of a project management methodology versus his other problems. Finally, develop a written recommendation to Stan about how he should address the lack of a project management process by briefly describing the most important steps that he should take to get one implemented. In preparing this recommendation, you should consider the following: What can practically be done under these circumstances? Who might he go to for help? How can he start moving the organization in the right direction? In particular, prepare a prioritized list of the issues Stan was facing and a second list indicating what steps he could take to implement a project management process.

Output

If you are using this text in a class, at your next class meeting, you should be prepared to discuss your conclusions and recommendations. During that discussion, you should be prepared to answer the following questions:

1. What is the relative importance of project management compared to other issues that are normally faced by organizational managers?
2. Is it practical to impose project management process requirements on an organization like the one described above?
3. How are the activities associated with implementing a project management system the same as, or different from, the activities associated with the general management of an organization?
4. In order to have a practical project management system in an organization like the one described here, what part of the implementation needs to be done personally by the manager of the organization and what part can be delegated to the group managers or to the people in the managers' groups?

REFERENCES

BECK K. et al. (2001) *Manifesto for Agile Software Development*, February 2001. http://www.agilemanifesto.org (accessed October 31, 2008).

BOEHM B. (1988) A spiral model of software development. *IEEE Computer* **21** (5), 61–72.

CRAWFORD S. G. and M. H. FALLAH (1985) Software development audits—A general procedure. *Proceedings of the 8th International Conference on Software Engineering*, pp. 137–141, IEEE, Piscataway, NJ, August.

ROYCE W. W. (1970) Managing the development of large software systems. In *Proceedings of IEEE WESCOM*, IEEE Computer Society Presss, Los Alamitos, CA, August, 1970, pp 1–9.

SCHWABER K. (2004) *Agile Project Management with SCRUM*. Microsoft Press, Redmond, WA.

Chapter 2

Planning

In Chapter 1 we discussed the four major software project management processes. They were planning, organizing, monitoring, and controlling. Planning is the most important of these processes. For a typical development project, we need to plan how we are going to develop the requirements, how the architecture and the design will be specified, how the project will be implemented, how the product will be tested, how it will be distributed and installed, and how it will be maintained and enhanced. That planning process is the subject of this chapter.

Figure 2.1 shows the planning process at a high level. At that level, the process looks quite simple. Its inputs are a concept of what we are planning to implement and either a business case or a contract, which describes the development team's commitment to the business in which it is operating. The output from the planning process is a project plan.

2.1 INPUTS TO THE PLANNING PROCESS

If we are doing this work for a specific customer, the input will probably be a contract, or at least a draft version of a contract. Most readers probably know what we mean by a contract. In the simplest terms, a contract is an agreement between the provider and the buyer which says that the provider will deliver a product or a system on or before a specific date and the buyer will pay a specific price or will fund the development of the application. There are a variety of contract forms, some of which are most favorable to the buyer and others which are most favorable to the provider. We will not go into those details here, but the development team and the manager of the development work do need to know what is contained in the contract, if the team is operating in that environment.

On the other hand, readers might ask what is meant by a business case. A business case is usually used when the organization is proposing to develop a product on speculation; that is, there is no specific customer for the product, but the organization intends to market the product to one or more customers who have not yet been identified. Funding for the development work will be provided by the parent organization. The business case is a document that defines the business opportunity

Managing the Development of Software-Intensive Systems, by James McDonald
Copyright © 2010 John Wiley & Sons, Inc.

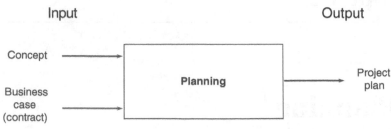

Figure 2.1   High-level view of the planning process.

that will be filled by the conceptual product and an initial estimate of the market for the product. It explains the marketing strategy for the product and provides an analysis of alternative products that are competing to fill that need. It should identify a few potential key customers who might provide early product evaluations. Finally, it should contain two types of financial analysis. The first is from the standpoint of the customer. That analysis looks at whether a typical customer can afford to pay the price that we would plan to charge for the product. The product analysis is from the point of view of the producing organization. The product financial analysis asks if our organization can make a profit on the product at the price we can charge in the market place after covering the estimated costs of developing, distributing, and maintaining the product.

We are not going to discuss how to develop a business case. However, it is important that the development team, and most importantly, the manager of that team, be familiar with its content so that it can be used as a basis for developing the project plan.

Whether we are working under a contract agreement or a business case, we will sometimes be told that the content of the business case or the contract is so confidential that we cannot gain access to it. Unfortunately, the contract or the business case almost always contains some description of the product we will be developing, dates on which deliveries are expected, and a specification of development resources that will be available, sometimes not explicitly specified, but frequently implied by the financial terms of the contract or by the assumptions in the business case.

If the manager of a product development team ever hears that they cannot get access to either of these documents, they should not accept that answer. The content of these documents is absolutely necessary for the development of a reasonable project plan. If we cannot see the contract or the business case, we will not be able to develop a project plan that is consistent with them. I have found that when I am unable to get a copy of the business case or contract, it is likely that it does not exist!

2.2   THE PLANNING PROCESS

Now let us discuss what takes place inside the planning process box of Fig. 2.1. The first thing we need to do is to assemble a core team. A core team is a set of people whom we expect to be working on a project from beginning to end and who can represent all of the functions required for the completion of the project. We will talk about functions in Chapter 5, The Organizing Process. For now, let us assume that for a typical software project, we might include someone from our marketing (or sales) organization or, if it is a product for internal use, a user or whomever is paying for the work, the person who will lead the requirements engineering effort, the project's chief architect, the leader of the people who will do the detailed design, coding, and integration, a person who will do or manage the testing, and someone who can represent those responsible for documentation, deployment, and customer support. A typical core team in an organization where most of those functions are done in different supervisory groups will have 7–10 members. That team needs to specify what will be done and how it will be done. They need to identify all of the tasks that need to be accomplished. They need to schedule those tasks and to assign them to individuals or groups of individuals. They, or the leader of the core team, need to develop cost estimates and to negotiate the budget and schedule for the deliveries that will result from doing the work.

In short, they will need to answer the following questions:

- What will be done?
- How will it be done?
- When will it be done?
- Who will do it?
- How much will it cost?

Answers to these questions make up the primary content of the project plan.

2.3 OUTPUT FROM THE PLANNING PROCESS— THE PROJECT PLAN

The content of a formal, written project plan can be outlined as shown in Table 2.1. It starts with three sections containing general information about the project in the Introduction, the Executive Summary, and the Architecture Summary. Then it gets into detail on 21 different topics, each of which has a section title that ends with the word "plan." That means that in each of those sections, answers should be provided for the questions "What are you going to do?" "How are you going to do it?" "Who is going to do it?" "When will it be done?" and "How much will it cost?" These are the sections with titles like "Feature and Deliverables Plan," "Management and Organization Plan," and "Documentation Plan." Finally, there are two sections titled "Master Schedule" and "Detailed Schedule." These sections do not address all of the questions required of a plan, but concentrate on answering questions about when things will be done. They will usually be referenced in other parts of the overall plan.

Now let us look at a project that the author worked on a few years ago. This was a project that involved the development of both hardware and software. It was being developed on speculation and was intended to be sold to businesses in the

Table 2.1 Content of a Project Plan

• Introduction	• Quality plan
• Executive summary	• Model plan
• Architecture summary	• Design transfer plan
• Feature and deliverables plan	• Configuration management plan
• Management and organization plan	• Qualification plan
• Master schedule	• Manufacturing plan
• Documentation plan	• Deployment and maintenance plan
• Hardware plan	• Risk plan
• Product definition plan	• Configuration management plan
• Software plan	• Training plan
• Budget and resources plan	• Facilities plan
• Risk management plan	• Tools plan
• Test plan	• Detailed schedule

Table 2.2 Prioritized Feature List

• F1—Test system interface	• F12—Enter/read site-dependent data
• F2—Local terminal interface	• F13—Read equipage
• F3—DACS interface	• F14—Software download
• F4—Maintenance position interface	• F15—Change pairs
• F5—DS1 access	• F16—Continuity check
• F6—Change DS1 access	• F17—Autoload site-dependent data
• F7—DS1 release	• F18—Scan performance
• F8—DS1 measure	• F19—Retrieve scan data
• F9—DS1 transmit	• F20—Enter/read scan site-dependent data
• F10—Set date	• F21—Insert errors
• F11—Set maintenance state	

telecommunications industry. The people working on this project were a group of people that had worked together for several years. They had developed two or three similar products in the past and they knew each other quite well. The core team was made up of eight people who were responsible for marketing, systems engineering (requirements), circuit design, physical design, software development, testing, manufacturing, and deployment/customer support.

We will walk through the steps that this team used to get the planning process started. The core team assembled in a hotel conference room for 3 days, away from their offices so that they would not be disturbed by telephone calls, e-mails, or their bosses. The team started this exercise by listing, *in priority order*, what they thought were the most important features that should be contained in the product. That list is shown in Table 2.2.

This list was prepared long before detailed requirements were developed, so the team was using its own collective knowledge and experience to produce this prioritized list of potential features. They planned to come back later to expand upon these one-liners and to elicit priorities from potential customers. It is not important to understand what each of the features on this list is. But it is important to notice that the team prioritized the features in an order based on their subjective opinions about the relative importance of each feature to their customers. It took the group about an hour and a half to brainstorm the content and to reach a consensus on the ordering of this list.

Because this team had previously developed several similar products, the next step, which was preparing a high-level list of tasks that they would need to accomplish, was quite easy for them. They spent about an hour coming up with the list of tasks, shown in Table 2.3, that they thought they would need to do to complete this project. These high-level tasks, at a minimum, needed to include things like requirements development, architecture, design, implementation, testing, manufacturing, distribution, installation, customer support, and maintenance plus other things that might be unique to the project at hand.

There are two characteristics about this list that are important. First, some of the tasks are relatively small in terms of the amount of work time that team members would have to put into them. Others are fairly large. For example, staffing the project is relatively small, probably requiring a small fraction of the time of a few people, perhaps over a few months. On the other hand, developing the software was a fairly large task, probably requiring four or five people working on it full-time, for a minimum of several months. Likewise, tasks associated with developing the hardware were of comparable size. A second thing that is important, for reasons that will become more obvious when we discuss monitoring in Chapter 6, is that for each task on our list, we need to know exactly how we will determine when the task has been completed.

To illustrate this, let us propose some possible endpoint definitions for tasks on our list of high-level tasks. For the first one, "Develop business case/proposal," we might use the completion of a review of the business case, which, for this project,

Table 2.3   High-Level Tasks

1. Develop business case/proposal
2. Develop project plan
3. Design system architecture
4. Develop requirements
5. Staff project
6. Develop new circuit packs
7. Develop new enclosure and wiring
8. Design software
9. Develop customer documentation and training
10. Manufacture hardware
11. Conduct internal testing
12. Develop sales materials
13. Conduct external testing
14. Provide continuing support for manufacturing, sales, and end-user operations

would mean that all members of the core team had reviewed the business case, provided their comments, and that appropriate comments had been incorporated into the business case. For the project plan, we might use "audit complete" as the end point. We will talk about project management audits (PMAs) in Chapter 9, but briefly, an audit is a detailed review of the project plan that the project manager might want to do when he or she thinks that the project plan is complete. For "Design system architecture," we could use "architecture review held." Architecture reviews is another topic we will discuss when we talk about audits and reviews later in Chapter 9. The most important property of the endpoint definitions that we choose should be that they need to be things that the project manager or any other stakeholder can easily see with a minimum of uncertainty about its status. The project manager does not want to get involved in asking members of the team what the status of a task is. He or she should be able to look at something for each task to determine in a very objective way what the status of a task is. The purpose of doing this is so that the project manager will never get an answer from a member of the team that says something like "the task is 80% complete." All that the project manager should be interested in are answers to questions like "Has work started on this task?" "Is the work in progress?" or "Is the work finished?" The reason for avoiding the percent complete questions and answers is they are frequently very inaccurate. This is not meant to imply that people doing the work will purposely lie (Glass et al. 2008), but software developers are usually very optimistic about their work. If you ask them the status question this week, you might get the 80% answer. Then, when you go back a week later and ask the same question, you might get an answer that says that the task is only 60% complete with an explanation indicating that there were some things that needed to be done that the person doing the task had forgotten when they gave their earlier answer.

When I teach this material to students, I usually ask them to propose good, visible end points for some of the tasks. Some of the answers that I get for item 4, writing requirements, are things like "when all of the writing has been finished," "when inspection of the requirements documents is finished," or "when the customer signs off on the requirements." Depending upon the circumstances, any of these could serve the purpose. However, to confirm that the writing has been finished, the manager monitoring the status of the project would need to read all of the requirements. That is not always feasible, particularly when for a large project the requirements might be several hundred, or even thousands of pages in length. The second one, "when requirements inspections have been completed," might be a practical one because the manager would need to review only what we will call "inspection reports" for each of the requirements inspection meetings to determine if the requirements have been completed. Getting the customer's signature on the requirements is an easy one for the manager to use and it is very visible, but it is not always possible to get the customer to read the requirements in enough detail to do that or, in some cases, to take the risk of signing when the customer knows that they might not be complete.

For staffing the project, I have heard answers ranging from "when the names of everyone who will work on the project are known" to "when everyone is sitting at their desk working on their tasks" to "when the project has been completed" because you never quite know when someone will leave the project, when they might get sick, or when they might leave for some other reason. In all of these cases, the staffing task needs to be restarted, so we usually never know when the staffing task is completed until the project has been completed.

The important point about all of this is that the project manager and the team need to reach agreements on what visible, observable end points will be used to determine when each task has been completed. We want to find definitions that can be confirmed with binary, that is, yes or no answers (Hurst 2000). We want to avoid answers like "The task is 80% complete."

Now that we have identified several high-level tasks, we need to decompose them into what we will call a work breakdown structure (WBS), consisting of smaller, lower-level tasks. We want to break them down in a way such that each low-level task represents the work that one person could do within a few weeks if they were working full-time on that task. We will use tasks at that level to do the detailed scheduling that will be necessary to answer some of the questions about when the work described in the project plan will be done.

Figure 2.2 shows a part of the WBS for the project that we have been discussing. It subdivides task 1, developing the business case, from our high-level list of tasks into several smaller tasks. In this case, the team decided that there were six smaller tasks that needed to be accomplished to develop the business case. They were describing the market needs, developing a quantitative market model, developing a market strategy, analyzing the competition, conducting a customer financial analysis, and doing a product financial analysis. If you remember, these were the things contained in a typical business case that we outlined earlier in this chapter.

The next thing they did was to make the assumption that one person would be working full-time on each task and asked themselves if one person could complete that task within a few weeks. They answered "yes" for tasks 1.1, 1.2, 1.3, 1.5, and 1.6, but they decided that the competitive analysis task, 1.4, would require multiple people to complete it, so they broke that task down to a lower level. The competitive analysis would require someone to send for literature on competitors' products (task

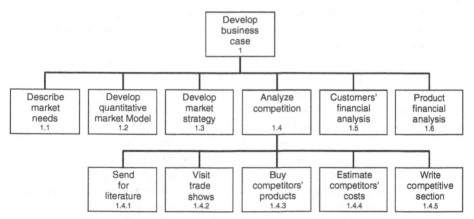

Figure 2.2 Part of the work breakdown structure.

1.4.1), one or more people to visit trade shows where those products were being displayed and demonstrated (task 1.4.2), someone to buy a sample of the competitors' products (task 1.4.3), someone to take them apart to estimate the competitors' costs (task 1.4.4), and, finally, someone to write the competitive section of the business case (task 1.4.5). When they got to this point, they asked the question again about whether one person, working full-time, could complete each task at the lowest level in the figure within a few weeks. They answered "yes" to that question, so this part of the WBS was finished.

The reader might be wondering about the meaning of the decimal numbers that we have created for each task in Fig. 2.2. These are simply expansions of the numbers associated with the parent tasks. They will be used as shorthand identifiers for tasks and subtasks as we move through the scheduling process. For example, 1 was the number of the first task on our high-level task list. The second digits, 1 through 6, are the tasks on the second level of the tree diagram in Fig. 2.2, and the third digits, 1 through 5, on the third level, are the numbers of the lowest-level tasks.

Next, the team went on to each of the other 13 high-level tasks and broke them down into lower-level tasks using the same rules that we used for task 1. When they finished this part of the exercise, they had developed 129 low-level tasks. Those tasks are shown in the list structured format of the WBS in Table 2.4. For each of the lowest-level tasks, they also had to specify a well-defined end point.

The next step in developing a schedule for this project involved estimation of the time that would be required to complete each task. For the tasks shown in Fig. 2.2, the people who would be doing the work happened to be members of the core team and they were in the room when these task durations were being estimated. So each person simply stated how long they thought it would take them to do each of their tasks if they were working on that task, uninterrupted, full-time. The person who would be describing the market needs said, "I think it will take me about 1 week of full-time work to do that." The person who was going to be responsible for developing the quantitative market model estimated that it would take about 6 weeks for that task, the person developing the market strategy said 3 weeks, and so on, for each of the 10 lowest-level tasks on this tree. The meeting scribe entered the team's estimates as shown in the lower-right corner of each task box in Fig. 2.3.

The rule of thumb that we usually use to determine when we should stop expanding the WBS is that every individual working on the project should have tasks assigned to them that can be completed within about 4 weeks of full-time work. And, in addition, the total number of tasks should not be greater than approximately 600. This achieves two things: (1) everyone on the project will be expected to confirm completion of a task at alternate project meetings (if project meetings are scheduled every 2 weeks, and (2) there are not so many tasks that the manager who is responsible for the project cannot comprehend the entire project. That allows for projects that require a maximum of approximately 50 staff years of effort, which are fairly large projects. Of course, there will occasionally be larger projects that need to be managed. In that case, we would break the project down into two or more projects that constitute a program and manage both the projects, as well as the program, which consists of both projects. We will talk briefly about program

Table 2.4 List Structured WBS

Task Number/Name	Task Number/Name
1. Develop business case/proposal	**6.2 Circuit pack 2**
1.1 Describe market needs	6.2.1 Design circuit pack 2
1.2 Develop quantitative market model	6.2.2 Inspect circuit pack 2 design
1.3 Develop market strategy	6.2.3 Physically layout circuit pack 2
1.4 Analyze competition	6.2.4 Procure parts for circuit pack 2
1.4.1 Send for literature	6.2.5 Build seven models of circuit pack 2
1.4.2 Visit trade shows	6.2.6 Debug circuit pack 2
1.4.3 Buy competitor's product	6.2.7 Transmit circuit pack 2 design to factory
1.4.4 Estimate competitor's costs	**6.3 Circuit pack 3**
1.4.5 Write competitive section	6.3.1 Design circuit pack 3
1.5 Customers' financial analysis	6.3.2 Inspect circuit pack 3 design
1.6 Product financial analysis	6.3.3 Physically layout circuit pack 3
1.7 Review business case/proposal	6.3.4 Procure parts for circuit pack 3
2 Develop project plan	6.3.4 Build 30 models of circuit pack 3
2.1 Plan initial planning meeting	6.3.5 Debug circuit pack 3
2.2 Hold initial planning meeting	6.3.6 Transmit circuit pack 3 design to factory
2.3 Write and print preliminary project plan	**7 Develop new enclosure and wiring**
2.4 Update project plan	7.1 Design enclosure, backplane, and wiring
2.5 Write and print final project plan	7.2 Physically layout backplane
2.6 Audit project plan	7.3 Inspect enclosure, backplane, and wiring
3 Design system architecture	design
3.1 Write initial draft of architecture document	7.4 Procure parts for enclosure and wiring models
3.2 Hold an architecture review	7.5 Build five models for testing
3.3 Revise architecture and republish	7.6 Integrate circuit pack 1 and circuit pack 2
document	into enclosure
4 Develop requirements	7.7 Debug enclosure + circuit pack 1 and circuit
4.1 Write/inspect general system requirements	pack 2
4.2 Write/inspect R1 feature requirements	7.8 Integrate circuit pack 3 into enclosure
4.3 Write/inspect R2 feature requirements	7.9 Debug enclosure + circuit pack 1 + circuit
4.4 Write/inspect R3 feature requirements	pack 2 + circuit pack 3
5 Staff project	7.10 Maintain five laboratory models
5.1 Assign planning team	7.11 Transmit enclosure and wiring design to factory
5.2 Assign additional team members	**8 Design software**
5.3 Assign replacement team members	**8.1 Develop common software**
6 Develop new circuit packs	8.1.1 Design common software and inspect
6.1 Circuit pack 1	8.1.2 Code/inspect unit test common software
6.1.1 Design circuit pack 1	8.1.3 Integrate common software with
6.1.2 Inspect circuit pack 1 design	hardware
6.1.3 Physically layout circuit pack 1	**8.2 Develop R1 software**
6.1.4 Procure parts for circuit pack 1	8.2.1 Design F1 software and inspect
6.1.5 Build seven models of circuit pack 1	8.2.2 Code/test/inspect F1 software
6.1.6 Debug circuit pack 1	8.2.3 Design F2 software and inspect
6.2.7 Transmit circuit pack 1 design to	8.2.4 Code/test/inspect F2 software
factory	8.2.4 Integrate R1 software into product

Table 2.4   Continued

Task Number/Name	Task Number/Name

8.3 Develop R2 software
- 8.3.1 Design F4 software and inspect
- 8.3.2 Code/test/inspect F4 software
- 8.3.3 Design F5 software and inspect
- 8.3.4 Code/test/inspect F5 software
- 8.3.5 Design F6 software and inspect
- 8.3.6 Code/test/inspect F6 software
- 8.3.7 Integrate R2 software into product

8.4 Develop R3 software
- 8.4.1 Design F3 software and inspect
- 8.4.2 Code/test/inspect F3 software
- 8.4.3 Design F7 software and inspect
- 8.4.4 Code/test/inspect F7 software
- 8.4.5 Design F8, F9, and F10 software and inspect
- 8.4.6 Code/test/inspect F8, F9, and F10 software
- 8.4.7 Design F11, F12, F13, and F14 software and inspect
- 8.4.8 Code/test/inspect F11, F12, F13, and F14 software
- 8.4.9 Design F15, F16, and F17 software and inspect
- 8.4.10 Code/test/inspect F15, F16, and F17 software
- 8.4.11 Design F17, F18, F19, F20, and F21 software and inspect
- 8.4.12 Code/test/inspect F17, F18, F19, F20, and F21 software
- 8.4.13 Integrate R3 software into product

9 Develop customer documentation and training
- 9.1 Documentation and Training for R1
- 9.2 Inspection of R1 documentation and training
- 9.3 Documentation and training for R21
- 9.4 Inspection of R2 documentation and training
- 9.5 Documentation and training for R3
- 9.6 Inspection of R3 documentation and training

10 Manufacture hardware (engineering portion only)
- 10.1 Procure parts
- 10.2 Set up manufacturing process
- 10.3 Set up quality control testing
- 10.4 Build first factory model

11 Conduct internal testing
- 11.1 Develop and inspect test plan
- 11.2 Develop R1 test scripts
- 11.3 Execute R1 tests
- 11.4 Transmit R1 software to factory
- 11.5 Develop R2 test scripts
- 11.6 Execute R2 tests and regression test R1
- 11.7 Transmit R2 software to factory
- 11.8 Develop R3 test scripts
- 11.9 Execute R3 tests and regression test R2
- 11.10 Transmit R3 software to factory
- 11.11 Design and execute stress tests

12 Develop sales materials

13 Conduct external testing
- 13.1 Negotiate three test sites with customers
- 13.2 Conduct three site surveys
- 13.3 Supply two test models for first two sites
- 13.4 Install R1 software and hardware at site 1
- 13.5 Train users at site 1
- 13.6 Jointly conduct R1 site 1 testing with customer
- 13.7 Install R2 software and test at site 1
- 13.8 Install circuit pack 3, R3 software, an test at site 1
- 13.9 Install R1 software and hardware at site
- 13.10 Train users at site 2
- 13.11 Jointly conduct R1 site 2 testing with customers
- 13.13 Install R2 software and test at site 2
- 13.14 Install circuit pack 3, R3 software and test at site 2
- 13.15 Supply one manufactured model for site 3
- 13.16 Install R1 software at site 3
- 13.17 Train users at site 3
- 13.18 Jointly conduct R1 site 3 testing with customers
- 13.19 Install R2 software and test at site 3
- 13.20 Install CP3, R3 software, and test at site

14 Provide continuing support

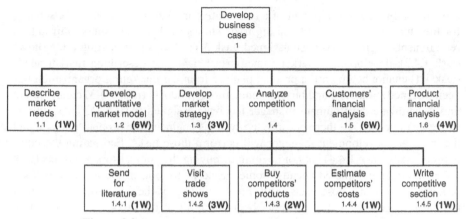

Figure 2.3 WBS with task duration estimates. W, weeks of effort.

management in Chapter 10. After completing the estimates shown in Fig. 2.3, the team went on to the areas of the WBS corresponding to each of the remaining 13 high-level tasks to estimate the task durations for each of their lowest-level tasks.

Now that we have identified all of our tasks and have estimated their durations, our next step will be to define precedence relationships among the tasks. Figure 2.4 shows the task dependencies that the core team defined among some of the tasks that resulted from breaking down high-level tasks 1 and 5. This chart says that the

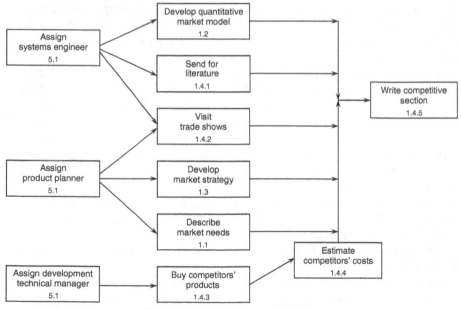

Figure 2.4 Precedence relationships.

tasks involving the development of a quantitative market model (task 1.2), sending for literature (task 1.4.1), and visiting trade shows (task 1.4.2) cannot start until a requirements engineer has been assigned (task 5.1). It says that visiting trade shows (task 1.4.2), developing a market strategy (task 1.3), and describing market needs (task 1.1) cannot begin until a product planner from the marketing organization has been assigned (task 5.1), and buying competitors' products (task 1.4.3) cannot begin until a hardware development manager has been assigned (task 5.1). These precedence relationships are there because the systems engineer, the product planner, and the hardware development manager will perform those tasks. Estimating the competitors' costs (task 1.4.4) cannot begin until buying the competitors' products (task 1.4.3) has been completed because someone needs to look inside the competitors' products to estimate those costs. And, finally, writing of the competitive section of the business case (task 1.4.5) cannot begin until all of the tasks shown preceding that task have been completed. We call the information in Fig. 2.4 a task precedence diagram. It describes the dependencies in time among the tasks included in the project. Of course, the complete task precedence diagram for this project is much larger than the portion shown in Fig. 2.4 because the complete diagram includes all of the 129 low-level tasks and task dependencies for the entire project.

Now that we have defined all of our tasks, estimated their durations, and specified their dependencies, we are ready to start putting this data into a scheduling tool like Microsoft Project™ or a similar tool. There are many different automated scheduling packages that can be used for this purpose, and we are not advocating Microsoft Project over any of the others. We are using it in our example because it is usually conveniently available in most academic and industrial settings.

Figure 2.5 shows some of the things that can be done with automated scheduling tools. Prior to printing the figure, we entered the number and description of each task. We then entered each task's duration and the precedence relationships that we had developed. The tool produced a network-based schedule, sometimes also called a Gantt chart, like the one shown in the figure. On the horizontal axis we have time shown along the top of the chart. The length of each horizontal bar is proportional to the task duration that we have estimated. The lines and arrows connecting the bars are based on the precedence relationships that we developed, and the solid horizontal bars show us what we call the critical path. The critical path, a portion of which is shown by the bars in Fig. 2.6, is the set of tasks that, when placed end to end according to our task precedence, determine the minimum time in which the project can be completed. If the entire project Gantt chart could be shown in Fig. 2.6, we would be able to see that the critical path for this project extends for 22 months. A file containing all of the tasks, the task precedence, and the critical path for this project is contained in the MS project file called "Figure 2.6.mpp" that can be downloaded from the FTP site for this book.

We have now specified what we are going to do in the form of a set of tasks. We have also specified how we are going to do the work (or, at least, the order in which tasks will be done) based on the precedence relationships among the tasks and the amount of time each task will take. The tool has helped us by suggesting when each task could be done and by placing the bars on the horizontal axis

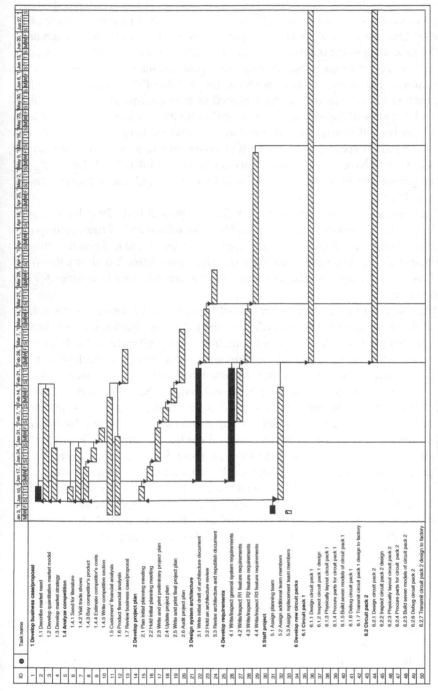

Figure 2.5 Use of automated scheduling tools.

31

corresponding to those times. It arranges the tasks so as to preserve the task precedence relationships and simultaneously to minimize the total time to complete all of the tasks. One thing that we have not yet specified is who will be doing each task.

The task assignment matrix, a portion of which is shown in Table 2.5, specifies who will be executing each task. Across the top of the matrix, we have listed the task numbers. Down the left side, we have the initials of the people who will be doing each task. In the matrix, we have placed an R in the row and column indicating which person will have primary responsibility for each task, an S where a second or third person will provide support for that task, and we have left a blank in cells where a person is expected to have no involvement in a task. So, a person with the initials DAG will have prime responsibility for tasks 1.2, 1.4.1, 1.4.2, 1.4.5, 1.5, and 1.6. The person with the initials JCK will assist with task 1.4.2 and will have primary responsibility for task 1.4.3.

The complete task assignment matrix for this project had 129 columns corresponding to the 129 low-level tasks that had been identified and 17 rows corresponding to the 17 different people who were expected to execute the tasks on this project. The same data can be entered into the scheduling tool. Table 2.6 shows the WBS as well as the task durations, the resources, and the precedence relationships for our sample project.

After we enter the resources, or responsible people, information into our scheduling tool, we can ask the tool to reschedule the project to avoid resource conflicts, that is, so that each person is doing only one thing at any given time. We want to do this because when we estimated the task durations, we assumed that each person was working full-time on one task at a time. In scheduling terms, this is called "resource leveling" and is a feature provided by most automated scheduling tools. Figure 2.6 shows the results of leveling for our sample project and also shows the initials of the people assigned to each task. Rescheduling stretches the overall time for completing the project because in our first version of the schedule, shown in Fig. 2.5, individual team members were allowed to work on more than one task at a time. In the Fig. 2.5 schedule, you can see that some of the tasks we have assigned to the person with initials DAG were scheduled to occur at the same time. DAG would probably never have been able to complete his work successfully on that schedule.

Now we have his work spread out. He starts his work on task 1.5 (customer financial analysis), then he moves to task 4.1 (Write and inspect general system

Table 2.5 Task Assignment Matrices

	1.1	1.2	1.3	1.4.1	1.4.2	1.4.3	1.4.4	1.4.5	1.5	1.6	4.3
DAG		R		R	R			R	R	R	
HPK											
JCK					S	R					
JKM	R		R		S						
JM							R				R
RWV											

R, responsible; S, support; blank, no involvement.

Table 2.6 Task Durations, Resource, and Precedence Relationships

Task Number/Name	Task Duration (Days)	Predecessor Task(s)	Resource Name(s)
1 Develop business case/proposal			
1.1 Describe market needs	5	5.1	JKM
1.2 Develop quantitative market model	30	5.1	DAG
1.3 Develop market strategy	15	5.1	JKM
1.4 Analyze competition			
1.4.1 Send for literature	5	5.1	JKM
1.4.2 Visit trade shows	15	5.1	JKM, DAG, DBH
1.4.3 Buy competitor's product	10	5.1	DBH
1.4.4 Estimate competitor's costs	5	1.4.3	DBH
1.4.5 Write competitive section	5	1.4.1, 1.4.2, 1.4.4	JKM
1.5 Customers' financial analysis	30		DAG
1.6 Product financial analysis	20		DAG
1.7 Review business case/ proposal	10	1.1, 1.2, 1.3, 1.4, 1.5, 1.7	HPK, JM, RWV
2 Develop project plan			
2.1 Plan initial planning meeting	5	5.1	JM
2.2 Hold initial planning meeting	5	2.1	JM
2.3 Write and print preliminary project plan	10	2.2	DBH
2.4 Update project plan	5	2.3	DBH
2.5 Write and print final project plan	5	2.4	DBH
2.6 Audit project plan	15	2.5	JM
3 Design system architecture			
3.1 Write initial draft of architecture document	30	1.1	JK, JCK
3.2 Hold an architecture review	15	3.1	JCK
3.3 Revise architecture and republish document	10	3.2	JCK
4 Develop requirements			
4.1 Write/inspect general system requirements	30	1.1	DAG
4.2 Write/inspect R1 feature requirements	15	2.3	DAG
4.3 Write/inspect R2 feature requirements	15	4.2	DAG
4.4 Write/inspect R3 feature requirements	40	4.3	DAG

Table 2.6   Continued

Task Number/Name	Task Duration (Days)	Predecessor Task(s)	Resource Name(s)
5 Staff project			
5.1 Assign planning team	3		HPK, JM, RWV
5.2 Assign additional team members	30	5.1	HPK, JM, RWV
5.3 Assign replacement team members	1		
6 Develop new circuit packs			
6.1 Circuit pack 1			
6.1.1 Design circuit pack 1	125	3.1, 4.1	CPD1
6.1.2 Inspect circuit pack 1 design	20	6.1.1	CPD1
6.1.3 Physically layout circuit pack 1	30	6.1.2	CPD1
6.1.4 Procure parts for circuit pack 1	90	6.1.2	CPD1
6.1.5 Build seven models of circuit pack 1	35	6.1.4	TECH1
6.1.6 Debug circuit pack 1	20	6.1.4	CPD1
6.2.7 Transmit circuit pack 1 design to factory	5	6.1.6	CPD1
6.2 Circuit Pack 2			
6.2.1 Design circuit pack 2	125	3.1, 4.1	CPD2
6.2.2 Inspect circuit pack 2 design	20	6.2.1	CPD2
6.2.3 Physically layout circuit pack 2	30	6.2.2	CPD2
6.2.4 Procure parts for circuit pack 2	90	6.2.2	CPD2
6.2.5 Build seven models of circuit pack 2	35	6.1.4	TECH2
6.2.6 Debug circuit pack 2	20	6.1.4	CPD2
6.2.7 Transmit circuit pack 2 design to factory	5	6.1.6	CPD2
6.3 Circuit pack 3			
6.3.1 Design circuit pack 3	125	3.1, 4.1	CPD1
6.3.2 Inspect circuit pack 3 design	20	6.3.1	CPD1
6.3.3 Physically layout circuit pack 3	30	6.3.2	CPD1
6.3.4 Procure parts for circuit pack 3	90	6.3.2	CPD1
6.3.4 Build 30 models of circuit pack 3	150	6.3.4	TECH1
6.3.5 Debug circuit pack 3	20	6.3.4	CPD1

Table 2.6 Continued

Task Number/Name	Task Duration (Days)	Predecessor Task(s)	Resource Name(s)
6.3.6 Transmit circuit pack 3 design to factory	5	6.3.6	CPD1
7 Develop new enclosure and wiring			
7.1 Design, enclosure, backplane, and wiring	125	3.1, 4.1	GP
7.2 Physically layout backplane	30	7.1	GP
7.3 Inspect enclosure, backplane, and wiring design	20	7.1	GP
7.4 Procure parts for enclosure and wiring models	90	7.2, 7.3	GP
7.5 Build five models for testing	25	7.4	TECH2
7.6 Integrate circuit pack 1 and circuit pack 2 into enclosure	10	6.1.4, 6.2.4, 7.4	GP, CPD1, CPD2
7.7 Debug enclosure + circuit pack 1 and circuit pack 2	10	7.6	GP, CPD1, CPD2
7.8 Integrate circuit pack 3 into enclosure	10	6.3.4, 7.6	CPD1
7.9 Debug enclosure + circuit pack 1 + circuit pack 2 + circuit pack 3	15	7.8	GP, CPD1
7.10 Maintain five laboratory models			
7.11 Transmit enclosure and wiring design to factory	5	7.9	GP
8 Design software			
8.1 Develop common software			
8.1.1 Design common software and inspect	20	4.1	JCK
8.1.2 Code/inspect unit test common software	20	8.1.1	JCK
8.1.3 Integrate common software with hardware	20	6.1.4, 6.2.4, 7.4, 8.1.2	CP1, JCK
8.2 Develop R1 software			
8.2.1 Design F1 software and inspect	20	4.2	SWD1
8.2.2 Code/test/inspect F1 software	20	8.2.1	SWD1
8.2.3 Design F2 software and inspect	20	4.2	SWD2
8.2.4 Code/test/inspect F2 software	20	8.2.3	SWD2
8.2.4 Integrate R1 software into product	20	8.1.3, 8.2.2, 8.2.3	JCK, SWD1, CPD2, SWD2, CPD1

Table 2.6   Continued

Task Number/Name	Task Duration (Days)	Predecessor Task(s)	Resource Name(s)
8.3 Develop R2 software			
8.3.1 Design F4 software and inspect	20	4.3	SWD1
8.3.2 Code/test/inspect F4 software	20	8.3.1	SWD1
8.3.3 Design F5 software and inspect	20	4.3	SWD2
8.3.4 Code/test/inspect F5 software	20	8.3.3	SWD2
8.3.5 Design F6 software and inspect	20	4.3	SWD3
8.3.6 Code/test/inspect F6 software	20	8.3.5	SWD3
8.3.7 Integrate R2 software into product	20	8.3.2, 8.3.4, 8.3.6	SWD1, SWD2, SWD3
8.4 Develop R3 software			
8.4.1 Design F3 software and inspect	20	4.4	SWD4
8.4.2 Code/test/inspect F3 software	20	8.4.1	SWD4
8.4.3 Design F7 software and inspect	20	4.4	SWD3
8.4.4 Code/test/inspect F7 software	20	8.4.3	SWD3
8.4.5 Design F8, F9, and F10 software and inspect	15	4.4	SWD1
8.4.6 Code/test/inspect F8, F9, and F10 software	15	8.4.5	SWD1
8.4.7 Design F11, F12, F13, and F14 software and inspect	10	4.4	SWD2
8.4.8 Code/test/inspect F11, F12, F13, and F14 software	10	8.4.7	SWD2
8.4.9 Design F15, F16, and F17 software and inspect	10	4.4	SWD5
8.4.10 Code/test/inspect F15, F16, and F17 software	10	8.4.9	SWD5
8.4.11 Design F17, F18, F19, F20, and F21 software and inspect	5	4.4	SWD6

Table 2.6   Continued

Task Number/Name	Task Duration (Days)	Predecessor Task(s)	Resource Name(s)
8.4.12 Code/test/inspect F17, F18, F19, F20, and F21 software	5	8.4.11	SWD6
8.4.13 Integrate R3 software into product	30	8.4.2, 8.4.4, 8.4.6, 8.4.8, 8.4.10, 8.4.12	SWD1, SWD2, SWD3, SWD4, SWD5, SWD6
9 Develop customer documentation and training			
9.1 Documentation and training for R1	30	4.2	SM
9.2 Inspection of R1 document and training	55	9.1	SM
9.3 Documentation and training for R21	30	4.3	SM
9.4 Inspection of R2 document and training	5	9.3	SM
9.5 Documentation and training for R3	30	4.4	SM
9.6 Inspection of R3 document and training	5	9.5	SM
10 Manufacture hardware (engineering portion only)			
10.1 Procure parts	90	6.1.7, 6.2.7, 6.3.6, 7.11	MFGENG1
10.2 Set up manufacturing process	30	6.1.7, 6.2.7, 6.3.6, 7.11	MFGENG2
10.3 Set up quality control testing	45	6.1.7, 6.2.7, 6.3.6, 7.12	MFGENG3
10.4 Build first factory model	30	10.1, 10.2, 10.3	
11 Conduct internal testing			
11.1 Develop and inspect test plan	25	4.1	HL
11.2 Develop R1 test scripts	15	4.2	HL
11.3 Execute R1 tests	15	8.2.4, 11.2, 6.1.5, 6.1.6, 6.2.5, 6.2.6	HL
11.4 Transmit R1 software to factory	5	11.3	HL
11.5 Develop R2 test scripts	25	4.3	RM
11.6 Execute R2 tests and regression test R1	15	8.3.7, 11.5	RM
11.7 Transmit R2 software to factory	5	11.6	RM

Table 2.6   Continued

Task Number/Name	Task Duration (Days)	Predecessor Task(s)	Resource Name(s)
11.8 Develop R3 test scripts	35	4.4	TEST3
11.9 Execute R3 tests and regression test R2	20	6.3.4, 8.4.13, 11.8	TEST3
11.10 Transmit R3 software to factory	5	11.9	TEST3
11.11 Design and execute stress tests	20	8.4.13	HL
12 Develop sales materials	30		
13 Conduct external testing			
13.1 Negotiate three test sites with customers	15		JKM, DAG
13.2 Conduct three site surveys	6	13.1	TEST3
13.3 Supply two test models for first two sites	10	7.5	TEST3
13.4 Install R1 software and hardware at site 1	2	11.4, 13.3	TEST3
13.5 Train users at site 1	5	13.4	SM, TEST3
13.6 Jointly conduct R1 site 1 testing with customer	5	13.5	TEST3
13.7 Install R2 software and test at site 1	2	11.7	TEST3
13.8 Install CP3, R3 software and test at site 1	2	6.3.6, 11.10	TEST3
13.9 Install R1 software and hardware at site 2	2	11.4, 13.3	RM
13.10 Train users at site 2	5	13.9	SM, RM
13.11 Jointly conduct R1 site 2 testing with customers	5	13.1	RM
13.13 Install R2 software and test at site 2	2	11.7	RM
13.14 Install CP3, R3 software and test at site 2	2	6.3.6, 11.10	RM
13.15 Supply one manufactured model for site 3	5	10.4	HL
13.16 Install R1 software at site 3	2	13.5	HL
13.17 Train users at site 3	6	13.6	SM, HL
13.18 Jointly conduct R1 site 3 testing with customers	6	13.7	HL
13.19 Install R2 software and test at site 3	2	11.7	HL
13.20 Install CP3, R3 software and test at site 3	2	6.3.6, 11.10	HL
14 Provide continuing support	1		

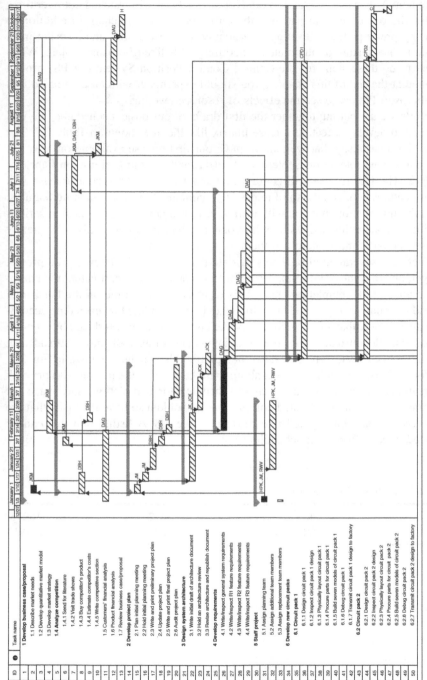

Figure 2.6 Gantt chart schedule with leveled resources.

requirements), then task 1.5, and so on. Not only is his work stretched out over time, but also the overall critical path for the entire project is stretched. In addition to producing pretty pictures, leveling is probably the most useful, and also the most difficult to use, feature of automated scheduling tools like Microsoft Project. When you get to do these steps for the Central Control Position System (CCPS) project presented at the end of this chapter, you should experiment with an automated tool like Microsoft Project to see the effects of resource leveling.

While we are putting together the first drafts of our project schedules, we will also need to develop a feature release matrix like the one shown in Table 2.7. The data in that matrix say that we plan to have our first release available on May 15, 2011, our second release on September 1, 2011, and our third release on February 10, 2012. The first release will contain features 1 and 2. The second release will contain features 4–6, and the third release will contain all of the remaining features. This is the information that you will need to have available during your first serious planning and budgeting discussion with your stakeholders because this is frequently the information of most interest to them.

There are several additional sets of data that will be of interest to the project manager, and to some or all of the stakeholders. The first is a chart called the cumulative planned task completion chart. This chart is a plot of time on the horizontal axis and the number of planned tasks that should be completed by each date according to the schedule that was developed above. This chart can be produced by copying the task completion dates from the automated scheduling tool into a spreadsheet application like Excel, sorting by date, then plotting the results as shown in Fig. 2.7.

You will also need a list of tasks along with the name of the person with primary responsibility for each, the date that is scheduled for completion, and space for recording its actual and estimated completion. It should also have the tasks that are on the critical path highlighted like those in Table 2.8. A listing like this can be produced directly from your scheduling tool.

Table 2.7   Feature Release Matrix

Features	Rel. 1 5/15/11	Rel. 2 9/1/11	Rel. 3 2/10/12
F1	X		
F2	X		
F3			X
F4		X	
F5		X	
F6		X	
F7			X
—			
—			
F(N-1)			X
FN			X

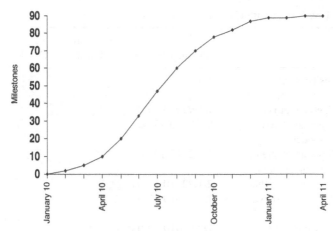

Figure 2.7 Planned completed task chart.

Another set of data that is likely to be helpful is a planned staffing profile chart like the one shown in Fig. 2.8. In that chart, we plot the staffing profile as a function of time. It can also be produced directly from the scheduling tool.

And, finally, we will use a planned cumulative cost chart like the one shown in Fig. 2.9. The purpose of the four charts in Figs. 2.7–2.9 and in Table 2.8 is so that we can use them as baselines for monitoring task completions, staffing, and costs as your project is executed.

At this point, we have most of the hard data that will serve as the basis for the project plan. It is primarily related to the schedule, resources, cost, and capabilities that we plan to deliver. Information related to these data will appear in several different sections of the plan. For example, the Gantt chart will become part of the master schedule and the detailed schedule. In each section of the plan, these data will need to be supplemented with appropriate text.

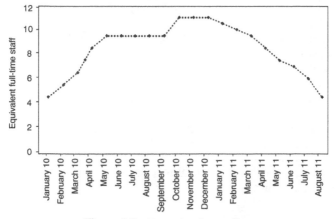

Figure 2.8 Planned project staffing.

Table 2.8   Task Listing with Completion Dates and Resources

Task Number/Name	Planned Finish	Estimated Finish	Actual Finish	Responsible Resource
1 Develop business case/ proposal				
1.1 Describe market needs*	1/15/2010 17:00			JKM
1.2 Develop quantitative market model	9/7/2010 17:00			DAG
1.3 Develop market strategy	3/5/2010 17:00			JKM
1.4 Analyze Competition				
1.4.1 Send for literature	2/12/2010 17:00			JKM
1.4.2 Visit trade shows	7/27/2010 17:00			JKM, DAG, DBH
1.4.3 Buy competitor's product	1/22/2010 17:00			DBH
1.4.4 Estimate competitor's costs	2/26/2010 17:00			DBH
1.4.5 Write competitive section	8/3/2010 17:00			JKM
1.5 Customers' financial analysis	2/16/2010 17:00			DAG
1.6 Product financial analysis	10/5/2010 17:00			DAG
1.7 Review business case/ proposal	10/19/2010 17:00			HPK, JM, RWV
2 Develop project plan				
2.1 Plan initial planning meeting	1/15/2010 17:00			JM
2.2 Hold initial planning meeting	1/22/2010 17:00			JM
2.3 Write and print preliminary project plan	2/5/2010 17:00			DBH
2.4 Update project plan	2/12/2010 17:00			DBH
2.5 Write and print final project plan	2/19/2010 17:00			DBH
2.6 Audit project plan	3/26/2010 17:00			JM
3 Design system architecture				
3.1 Write initial draft of architecture document	2/26/2010 17:00			JK, JCK
3.2 Hold an architecture review	3/19/2010 17:00			JCK
3.3 Revise architecture and republish document	4/2/2010 17:00			JCK
4 Develop requirements				
4.1 Write/inspect general system requirements*	3/30/2010 17:00			DAG

Table 2.8   Continued

Task Number/Name	Planned Finish	Estimated Finish	Actual Finish	Responsible Resource
4.2 Write/inspect R1 feature requirements	4/20/2010 17:00			DAG
4.3 Write/inspect R2 feature requirements	5/11/2010 17:00			DAG
4.4 Write/inspect R3 feature requirements	7/6/2010 17:00			DAG
5 Staff project				
5.1 Assign planning team*	1/8/2010 17:00			HPK, JM, RWV
5.2 Assign additional team members	3/5/2010 17:00			HPK, JM, RWV
5.3 Assign replacement team members	1/6/2010 17:00			HPK, JM, RWV
6 Develop new circuit packs				
6.1 Circuit Pack 1				
6.1.1 Design circuit pack 1*	9/21/2010 17:00			CPD1
6.1.2 Inspect circuit pack 1 design*	4/12/2011 17:00			CPD1
6.1.3 Physically layout circuit pack 1*	7/26/2012 17:00			CPD1
6.1.4 Procure parts for circuit pack 1	9/13/2011 17:00			CPD1
6.1.5 Build seven models of circuit pack 1	11/1/2011 17:00			TECH1
6.1.6 Debug circuit pack 1*	4/17/2012 17:00			CPD1
6.2.7 Transmit circuit pack 1 design to factory	5/22/2012 17:00			CPD1
6.2 Circuit pack 2				
6.2.1 Design circuit pack 2	9/21/2010 17:00			CPD2
6.2.2 Inspect circuit pack 2 design	10/19/2010 17:00			CPD2
6.2.3 Physically layout circuit pack 2	5/10/2011 17:00			CPD2
6.2.4 Procure parts for circuit pack 2	2/22/2011 17:00			CPD2
6.2.5 Build seven models of circuit pack 2	4/12/2011 17:00			TECH2
6.2.6 Debug circuit pack 2	3/22/2011 17:00			CPD2

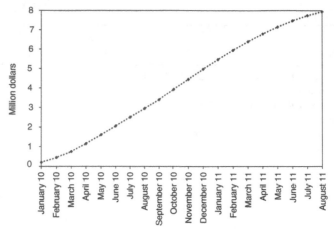

Figure 2.9 Planned cumulative cost.

2.4 PLANNING FOR REAL PROJECTS

The project that we have used to describe the beginnings of the planning process was an easy one. The core team members had previously completed several similar projects. They all knew each other well, and they knew what tasks needed to be completed to make the project successful. But, what do we do if that is not the case?

There is a method, called the "cards-on-the-wall" technique, that we use for a first-of-a-kind project. It is illustrated in Fig. 2.10. Using this method, the core team

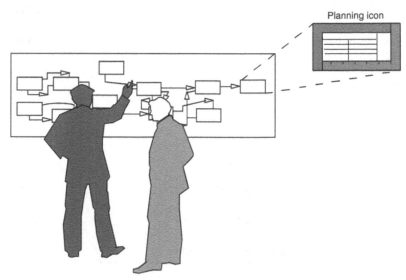

Figure 2.10 Cards-on-the-wall technique.

writes each task that needs to be executed on file cards or Post-it™ notes. Then they paste them on a whiteboard in an order approximating the order in which they think they will do the tasks. They connect the Post-its with lines drawn using erasable markers corresponding to the network precedences we discussed earlier. When they are satisfied that they have identified all of the tasks and their precedence relationships, they add time estimates for each task and an indicator of who will be doing each task. When all of this is done, they have the data that need to be entered into an automated scheduling tool.

This method works very well when the participants are just getting to know each other and when the team has never done a similar project before. I have seen it used on a massive project that involved a core team of about a hundred people and for which the planning chart went all the way around the four walls of a hotel ballroom. In that case, the planning technique worked very well, and the team was very satisfied that they had identified most of the tasks that would be required to complete the project and that they understood how those tasks would be networked.

2.5 SOME THINGS TO REMEMBER

The most important things that we have discussed in this chapter are the following:

1. Planning is the most important part of project management.
2. A project plan should be developed by a core team, which is a set of people who you expect to work on the project from beginning to end and who can represent all of the functions required for the completion of the project.
3. In addition to the scheduling that we have discussed in this chapter, we will need to add text in each section of the project plan to answer the following questions:
   What are you going to do?
   How are you going to do it?
   Who is going to do what?
   When will it be done?
   How much will it cost?

CASE STUDY 2   *Developing a Project Plan for the CCPS Project*

Purpose

This planning problem has three purposes:

1. To learn to plan and to write project plans
2. To learn about real project issues and how to plan and cope with them
3. To experience the PMA process

Background

You are a member of the Mini-Systems Development Shop (MSDS), an organization within a larger corporation. MSDS develops systems primarily for use within your company, but does a growing business outside. The second is important, and growth is encouraged.

Senior management wants to partner with AT Continental (referred to as ATCO in the remainder of this case), which plans to implement the CCPS.[1] Your management has worked hard to get MSDS the chance to bid on the development of CCPS.

You have been assigned to the core team for the CCPS project. You have been asked to develop a preliminary project plan[2] for CCPS. Based on that plan and your recommendation, MSDS will decide to bid, or not to bid, on CCPS.

Mark Money, who is the business manager for your part of MSDS, contacted you and a few of your peers on Monday, January 4, 2010 and asked for your assistance. He explained that on December 28, 2009, MSDS received a request for a proposal from ATCO and it was assigned to him. During the past week, he arranged for one of MSDS's hardware people, T. A. Edison, to talk with a company called BoardTech, with which he was familiar. He asked one of MSDS's systems engineers, F. L. Wright, to develop an initial architecture for the system being requested and R. T. Q. Writer, another of MSDS's systems engineers, to review and analyze the RFP from a business point of view. Mr. Edison's and Ms. Writer's responses are attached at the end of this case description. Then he secured agreement from your management and the managers of the other core team members to spend some time developing a project plan. He provided a broad overview of the problem, a description of the solution desired by the customer, the product that we would need to supply, the desired schedule, and a brief overview of the customer.

He described the problem as one in which ATCO was currently using a paper-driven method, which was slow and error prone, to drive their service operations. ATCO was planning to expand to at least 50 U.S. locations within the next few years. They believe that continued use of their paper-driven methods would be impractical because it created too many errors and delayed the acquisition of revenues. They are looking for a solution, which they call the CCPS, which would automate the entry, distribution, closure, and confirmation of service order data.

The environment in which CCPS would need to operate is shown in Fig. C2.1.

All data input and output would take place at the CCPS PC. The CCPS system would interact with four legacy systems called the billing, delivery, credit, and audit systems. More details of this environment are contained in the ATCO RFP, which appears near the end of this case description.

The architecture that Mr. Wright developed is shown in Fig. C2.2.

This architecture calls for the development or procurement of a special purpose PC board to allow the PC to communicate over a dial-up connection using an X.25 protocol with the audit and credit systems and 11 software modules as shown in the diagram, plus a simple database to temporarily hold active service orders. The customer will not permit any changes to the existing legacy system interfaces.

MSDS needs to "flesh out" the CCPS requirements, contract with ATCO and BoardTech, specify precisely what BoardTech will supply, design, code the internal CCPS software, integrate the new hardware and software, integrate the interfaces with ATCO's legacy systems, and perform system testing, site testing, and deployment to 50 locations.

---

[1] See the attached request for proposal (RFP) issued by ATCO.

[2] You need to develop only *costs*, not a price. If MSDS bids, the price will be determined separately.

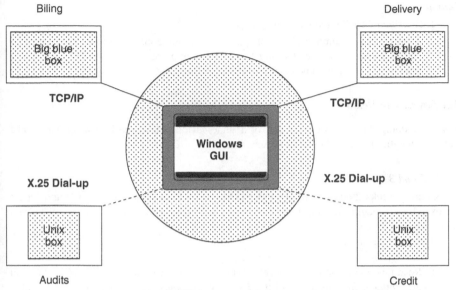

Figure C2.1 The CCPS environment.

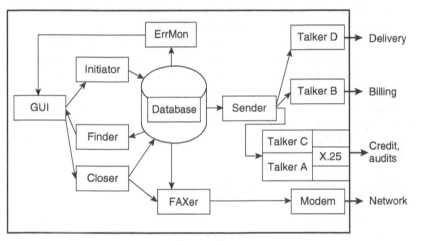

Figure C2.2 CCPS architecture.

Mark believes that ATCO wants the billing and delivery interfaces by 4Q2010 and could probably accept delivery of the credit and audit interfaces in 1Q2011.

Your job, and the job of the core team, will be to develop a project plan for this job; then, based on that plan, recommend whether MSDS should bid on the work.

Activity

Based on what we have discussed to this point and on the content of the remaining chapters of this book, you should develop *a written preliminary project plan and an oral summary of that plan.*

Output

1. *A written CCPS preliminary project plan.*[3]
2. *A presentation*, summarizing your plan and recommendation, to be given during a class session if you are studying from this book as part of a class. This simulates presenting your recommendation to management.

The Semester in Detail

If you are doing this case study as part of a semester-long class, the following paragraphs might be helpful in scheduling your time.

Weeks 2 and 3

Work during weeks 2 and 3 is to (1) understand your overall semester plan, (2) understand the exercise, (3) begin planning for the exercise, and (4) schedule your semester (what you will do during the semester).

The activities are as follows:

1. Read this document (during week 2), the *RFP*,[4] the *Analysis of the CCPS RFP*, and the *Preface, Introduction* and the *Executive Summary* sections of the project plan template.
2. *Identify features* that the CCPS product will offer, give them an identification number, and assign them a priority. Fill in columns 1–3 of the table in Section 4.2 of the template. (Start during week 2 and finish during week 3.)
3. *Assign the features to a release*, that is, complete the table in Section 4.2.[5] (week 3.)
4. *Start a list of project tasks.* Brainstorm *across the project life cycle. What do people do to create what output?* Strive for 50–60 tasks during week 3. Eventually, you should have well over 100 tasks.
5. *Select a project manager for the semester* (by the end of week 3).
6. *Develop a schedule for your semester*, assigning project plan sections to specific people (fill in the table in Section 1.2 of the project plan template and decide when each section is due (during week 3).

You should have the following at the end of the third week:

1. An understanding of the semester's work and the CCPS planning problem
2. Table in Section 4.2 of the plan completed
3. The start of a task list for the project.
4. A project manager
5. A schedule for the semester, with Table 2.1 in the plan completed.

---

[3] See the template for a project plan that can be downloaded from the FTP site for this book. It shows the sections for which you will provide the content, some partially completed sections, and the sections that you can skip.

[4] The attached RFP document is much less formal than a real RFP would be. It contains a minimum number of words and omits most of the legal wording that would be contained in a real RFP.

[5] *Advice:* Three columns for releases in the table of Section 4.2 does not mean that three releases should be used at this time.

Weeks 4, 5, and 6

During these weeks, you will (1) add to the task list, (2) create a "network diagram" using the cards on the wall technique, and (3) complete the network. You will also start sub-plans per your general schedule.

The activities are as follows:

1. Plan to meet as a group for 1–2 hours each week.
2. Select an estimating person/sub-team. The rest of the team is the planning sub-team (at the beginning of week 4).
3. The planning team is to use the "Post-its" to arrange tasks into a network chart on the wall.[6] During these sessions, you will rearrange the Post-its, add detail (duration and staffing), add tasks, and so on (week 4).
4. The estimating team is to review the architecture and make estimates of duration and staffing for the *design–code/capture–inspect–unit test*[7] task for each piece. They are also to *estimate duration and staffing for every other task in the network* (weeks 4 and 5).
5. Refine the chart for integration, system, and beta test ("soak" or first application) (week 5).
6. Start to collect/make policy statements for the Management and Organization section of the plan and begin a draft of that section of the plan (weeks 4 and 5).
7. Start writing selected sections of the plan per your schedule (week 5).
8. Review overall status of the semester's work, and make any adjustments required (before the end of session 5).
9. Review content of the plan, writing assignments, schedules, and so on, and get comfortable with the semester's schedule (before the end of week 6).

You should have the following at the end of week 6:

1. For the *architecture given*, tables (Sections 7.4.3, 8.3.3, 9.3.3, and 10.3.3 in the template) by deliverable, giving example estimates of staff and duration to develop the deliverable
2. A wall of Post-its showing precedence, positioned on a timeline. Each Post-it will have duration and staff estimates.
3. Some detail added to the wall as testing activities were refined.
4. The management policy in rough draft form
5. Several sections of plan started (per your schedule from week 3).

Weeks 7–11

Work during these weeks is intended (1) to ensure completion of work by class week 13 when the written project plan should be completed and (2) to wrap up some sections of your preliminary plan. You will continue or start most sections of the plan.

The activities are as follows:

1. Create the Risk Management section. Use "event analysis" *for at last one risk* (fill out the "Event Analysis Worksheet (s)" as applied to CCPS).

---

[6] See attached notes on use, especially item 5. In the Risk Management chapter of this book, a more sophisticated approach will be presented. It will use statistical methods to derive probabilistic schedules.

[7] For a preliminary plan on a small project, it is reasonable to lump these activities into one. As the estimate gets longer, refinement is needed.

2. Decide how to handle design transfer, deployment, maintenance, facilities, and tools, which we have not talked about in any detail, and will not.

3. Your resource expert should be looking at the overall schedule and resource implications of all the work so far, and beginning the Budget and Resources section of the plan.

4. Wrap up and review the Management and Organization section.

5. Enter all task, duration, relationship, and resource data into a scheduling tool such as Microsoft Project and produce a completed master schedule by the end of week 11.

6. Plan to write the Introduction and Executive Summary during week 9. They are summaries, so they are done last. They are also relatively short.

7. Plan to complete[8] everything by the end of week 12.

At the end of week 11, you should have (1) several sections of the plan completed and (2) all other sections being written.

Weeks 12 and 13

During weeks 12 and 13, you will (1) prepare a presentation outlining your plan, recommending what action to take and you will (2) get some experience having your project audited.

The activities are as follows:

1. Prepare for your session 14 presentation (about 20–25 minutes with PowerPoint slides). One person should give the whole presentation.

2. If you are studying this material in a class during week 13, other members of your class, taking on the functions of project auditors, will review your written plan and will interview members of your project team. Due to the criticality of this project, the audit has the highest priority. (Anyone on your team may be interviewed for up to 1 hour during this week.)

By the end of week 13, you will have completed the plan, prepared a presentation, and participated in an audit interview.

Week 14

During week 14, you will present a synopsis of your project plan during one of the class sessions. (See the last appendix for some notes.)

Appendices

Some Information about MSDS
"Cards-on-the-Wall" Instructions
Notes on Week 13 and 14 Activities

Attachments

Request for Proposal from AT Continental
System Engineer's notes concerning AT Continental and CCPS
Information regarding the circuit pack vendor of choice
Project plan template (can be downloaded from the FTP site for this book)

Appendix 1. Some Information about MSDS

MSDS is an organization of about 200 people, with annual revenue of $45 million. It is growing and has an aggressive management team that is seeking more growth. Of these

---

[8] *Completion* means the *original* copy of the plan has been printed and is available to others.

people, about 50 are located in Atlanta, 50 in San Jose, CA, and the remainder in Denver, CO. There is also a small headquarters location in Chicago, IL.

MSDS is an ISO (International Standards Organization) certified organization, with a good quality record, and has an ongoing quality improvement program. (For some performance numbers, see the Quality section of the prototype project plan.)

The staff is composed primarily of software people, with a few people who have some hardware design experience. It is rare, however, that they do hardware design, and typically, they serve as vendor managers. The software experience is varied, with UNIX, mainframe, server, and PC skills. The UNIX and mainframe applications are growing fewer, and PC and server applications are increasing. Over the years, MSDS has built a number of PC-based applications, but the interface has always been very simple and very structured. A number of software people have, however, studied such areas as Visual Basic and graphical user interface (GUI) development and have actually built prototype user interfaces for themselves. These people are anxious to use their skills.

Appendix 2. "Cards-on-the-Wall" Instructions
Below are instructions for using Post-its ("yellow stickies").[9] "Cards-on-the-wall" is an excellent way to start planning and can be carried to great detail.

1. Write a brief task name on the top of each Post-it.
2. Arrange the Post-its on a plastic sheet (or other *erasable* surface) so that related/ dependent tasks are close to one another.
3. Draw arrows *from* the *predecessor* tasks *to* the *successor* tasks.

Task/activity dependency

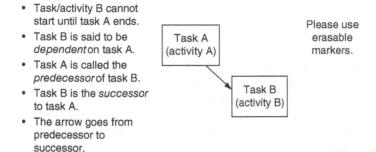

- Task/activity B cannot start until task A ends.
- Task B is said to be *dependent* on task A.
- Task A is called the *predecessor* of task B.
- Task B is the *successor* to task A.
- The arrow goes from predecessor to successor.

Task A (activity A)

Task B (activity B)

Please use erasable markers.

4. Add a duration and staffing estimate to each Post-it.
5. Once the arrangement of task stickies and dependencies (links) seems reasonable, and you have task duration estimates, you are ready to start project scheduling.[10]

---

[9] There are two simplifications in the process described here as compared to the approach used when we discuss risk modeling:
1. We use only start–finish dependencies.
2. We are not using "best, worst, most likely" estimates.

[10] The process up to here works with or without using software tools. Software will help with the details of scheduling. If you do not have a very complicated project, you may be as well off with cards and walls. If it is complex, or you want to do "what-if" exercises, or the graphics are important, consider software such as Microsoft Project.

- Guess an overall time requirement, and add some extra, just to get a reasonable scale.
- Draw a time scale on the bottom, in months, that will cover the whole schedule.
- Move the Post-its, starting from the left, so that each start date is at the right time. (A task's start date is the latest finish date of all predecessor tasks.)
- Draw links between tasks as appropriate.

6. You now have a "network" chart, with tasks located correctly in time.

Appendix 3. Notes on Week 13 and 14 Activities

The schedule discussed above combines two different management activities during weeks 13 and 14: a management review and a PMA.[11] These are complementary, but distinct.

Management Review

The planning teams present a synopsis of their plan. They should imagine that the audience is the higher management of their organization, and that those managers must make a decision afterward whether to fund/bid on the project. The input from the auditor may also be used in the decision. The goal of the planning team is *not to sell the project* but, rather, (1) to convince the higher management that they really understand the issues, based on their planning, and (2) to recommend a bid/no bid (fund/no fund) decision.

The planning teams should establish credibility for their recommendation by displaying the quality of their planning. Generally, a combination of material from the Executive Summary with some detail from the project plan works best. A suggested outline follows:

1. Problem statement—what business problem the customer has
2. Solution statement—how you propose to solve the problem
3. Architecture overview—what you are building
4. Organization—who is doing the job
5. Budget and resources—what it will take to do the job (include *both* a staffing profile *graph* and a cost profile *graph*)
6. Schedule—when it will happen (high-level Gantt chart)
7. Quality metrics and quality programs—how good the project/product must be and what will be done to make that happen
8. Risk analysis—what can go wrong and what the response should be
9. Recommendation—what the funder/sponsor should do (bid using your plan as a basis or decide not to bid)

There are a few key items that should be included:

1. Clear statement of risks and mitigation strategies
2. Clear statement of schedule, cost, and staff requirements
3. Clear recommendation for action, that is, bid/fund or not, typically on the last slide.

---

[11] Recall that a management review occurs at specified times and is to decide whether to continue or cancel the project. A PMA examines the project management process and methods, the extent to which they follow best practices, and suggests improvements. A PMA includes recommendations and is not necessarily consistent with some other concepts of audit (e.g., an ISO audit). The name is historical and widely used within the industry.

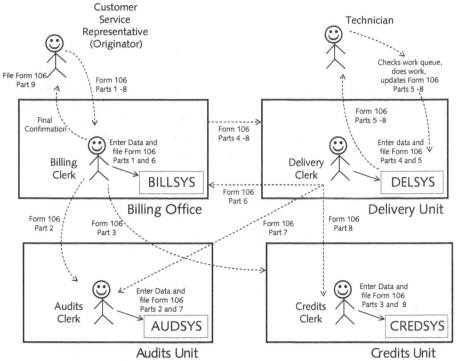

Figure C2.3   ATCO Work Flow Pre-CCPS.

Attachment 1. ATCO Request for Proposal Synopsis

The current work environment in ATCO is not mechanized. Information is transmitted using multipart forms. ATCO is expanding rapidly and desires to avoid certain inefficiencies associated with implementing new functions using current methods.

To avoid this, ATCO will create a "central control position" to coordinate information flow. The position will require a special workstation, the CCPS, which will automate most information transfer.

This document solicits proposals for delivery of CCPS as specified subsequently.

Problem System

Adding the new work functions *using current methods* would create an undesirable workflow described below and shown in Fig. C2.3

1. Receipt of paper request (ATCO Form 106) at billing unit, a *many-part* form
2. Manual entry of data into a system (BILLSYS) serving billing[12]
3. Forwarding of other parts of form from billing to audits, credit, and delivery units
4. Receipt of other parts of form at audits, credit, and delivery

---

[12] For brevity, call the system serving billing BILLSYS, the system saving credits CREDSYS, and the system serving delivery DELSYS.

5. Data entry at audits, credit, and delivery into the separate systems AUDSYS, CREDSYS, and DELSYS

6. Execution of work at delivery (Technician checks work queue on *DELSYS*, does work specified, and makes some entries on the form.)

7. Data entry to DELSYS (Technician updates system.)

8. Forwarding of remaining parts of original form to audits, billing, and credit (as notification of work completion)

9. Receipt of above parts of form at audits, billing, and credit

10. Data entry by audits, billing, and credit (into respective systems)

11. Final confirmation returned to originator from billing

Solution System

The approach ATCO has chosen is to create a work position called the "central control position," implemented by placing a PC in the billing unit. This PC will communicate with existing systems electronically. The envisioned CCPS environment is shown in Fig. C2.4

The intended workflow is discussed below and follows the figure.

1. Receipt of paper request at billing unit

2. Manual entry of data into BILLSYS, using PC as terminal

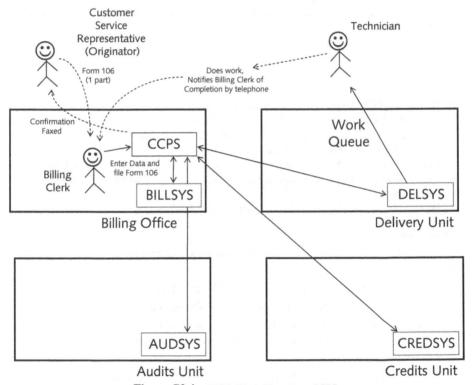

Figure C2.4 ATCO Work Flow Post-CCPS.

3. *Forwarding of data by PC to update systems AUDSYS, CREDSYS, and DELSYS* (previously updated manually)
4. Confirmation of update by PC with AUDSYS, CREDSYS, and DELSYS
5. Work done by technician (as before)
6. *Completion report from technician to billing via telephone*
7. Data entry by billing person, in real time, while on phone
8. *Forwarding of data by PC to update AUDSYS, CREDSYS, and DELSYS*
9. Confirmation of update by PC with AUDSYS, CREDSYS, and DELSYS
10. Preparation of final confirmation form by PC
11. Faxing of final confirmation form to originator

Other opportunities exist, for example, at billing. ATCO wishes to leave options open for these, but to take the first step described above.

Specifications

1. Hardware shall be, excepting special PC circuit packs, "off-the-shelf" industry products.
2. The product provided to ATCO shall be "turnkey" and shall include appropriate training and user manuals, as well as support through the deployment period.
3. A single workstation shall be "soaked" in the first site for 1 month, at the conclusion of which soak, if successful, the vendor shall be prepared to install the workstations at the rate of 10 per month.
4. The existing systems AUDSYS, BILLSYS, CREDSYS, and DELSYS are critical applications. No change will be made to accommodate CCPS.
5. A GUI running under Windows Vista is required on the PC.
6. The system shall "mimic" the existing ATCO Form 106, so that training will be minimal.
7. Existing terminal communications to the systems must be used, that is, IBM SNA LAN/WAN to DELSYS and BILLSYS, and X.25 dial-up to CREDSYS and AUDSYS.
8. All data entered into the PC at billing shall be successfully distributed (an "online" acknowledgment of transaction completion from the legacy system) to the legacy systems within 2 hours.

Attachment 2. Analysis of the ATCO RFP by R. Q. T. Writer

As you requested, I looked at the ATCO RFP for "CCPS." Since my colleagues and I are familiar with ATCO, we are confident that we can "read between the lines."

Current procedures in ATCO are very paper oriented. This has not been a big problem in the past, as their operations were fairly small scale. The growth they expect is likely to expose all the weaknesses of their manual system. Using their current process would be slow and error prone. In revenue-producing operations, such as those in ATCO, speed and accuracy are essential to early revenue acquisition and low cost of quality. What they want is the ability to fill out Form 106 (one page, many copies) on a screen and to have data distributed automatically. The original form has to be modified, updated, and so on, as the order progresses, for about 8 hours.

Below is an explanation of their deployment plans, as well as our projection of the opportunity for cost avoidance by using CCPS.

There will be 50 billing offices within ATCO, and the CCPS workstations will be physically located there. *Without* CCPS, there would be separate audits, credit, and delivery offices (one of each) associated with each billing office, where forms processing would occur. CCPS eliminates the need for these additional offices, as well as the manual form completion at billing. Overall, the average saving possible is $5000 monthly for each manual office not required, or $750,000 monthly in the final configuration (150 total offices eliminated times $5000 monthly per position.). We estimate that about $4000 is associated with billing and delivery, and $1000 with audits and credit (not used for all orders). The billing and delivery functions have much higher priority because of the economics.

ATCO plans to install the first system[13] for a 1-month soak. The deployment schedule *assumes* successful experience with the first application in the soak and *parallel* preparation for full deployment. Ten systems[14] will be deployed monthly, with the first 10 going online during the month following the 1-month soak period, the second 10 during the next month thereafter, and so on. The first site will serve as the training site.

The table on the next page shows the deployment (workstation at billing) scenario by month, with the approximate monthly savings during the deployment. (It accounts for start-up by decreasing the first month's savings.)

	Month 1	Month 2	Month 3	Month 4	Month 5	Month 6	Month 7
Offices required *without* CCPS	4	44	84	124	164	200	200
Offices *installed*	1	11	21	31	41	50	50
Offices *avoided*	3	33	63	93	123	150	150
Monthly savings	10	115	265	415	565	705	750
Cumulative savings	10	125	390	805	1370	2075	2825

I do not believe their announced schedule. It appears that expansion of their operations is *on schedule for billing and delivery* (bigger money here), that is, a 4Q10 start. My guess is that operations in *audits and credit will be delayed* until *perhaps* 2Q11. They expect to sign a contract with someone within 2 months. It gets very expensive if they cannot start implementation by December 2010.

Their "requirements" have the following implications, as we see it:

1. The existing systems AUDSYS, BILLSYS, CREDSYS, and DELSYS are legacy systems, very complicated. It's unreasonable to touch them. However, each of those systems has an existing *terminal* interface that can be emulated.

2. There is no X.25 software in the PC operating system, and there is no commercially available IBM bus-compatible X.25 input/output board. We will have to acquire that I/O board and software.

---

[13] One billing office, four legacy computers, *but no* associated audits, credit, and delivery offices that *would require data entry without CCPS.*

[14] Note that each new system will include another four legacy computers, *not linked* to any other CCPS offices.

3. The protocols for the data links are poorly documented and are probably not correct.

4. The command sequences to the various systems as currently used by the clerical staff are documented and are probably correct.

5. The peak transaction rate at billing is 10–15 transactions per hour. It occurs during the 10:00–11:00 a.m., and 2:00–3:00 p.m. hours on business days. Having a short queue extending into the next hour is probably all right, as that happens now.

6. The average data entry time at billing is 4 minutes.

7. An installation request is typically completed by a technician 8 hours after the work request.

8. Technicians usually start reporting completion at about 11:30 a.m. and 4:30 p.m.

It looks like there is a potential profit stream available to MSDS from ATCO of about $4–5 million yearly. This is based on the amount of work similar to CCPS that we estimate they will generate in the future and assumes a modest penetration into their overall market. It is no wonder that your management wants to do this. We have also heard that ATCO expects lots from their vendors, and is not shy about changing vendors if they do not deliver as promised.

Should you have questions, please contact me.

R. Q. T. Writer

Attachment 3. Analysis of X.25 Board by T. A. Edison

I looked for shops that could build a CCPS board. All inquiries point to "BoardTech." This is a small outside vendor with the best credentials for this kind of work.I talked with Ido Bords, the owner. (I have worked with him for years, and so could talk pretty freely.) His informal quotation was as follows:

1. Models can be available 9 months after contract signing.

2. First production boards can be available in *about* 12 months.

3. Boards in the quantities needed can be available starting 1 month after first production board.

4. Cost for design and development—$550,000.

5. Cost per board (prototype or production)—$900.

My sources and experience say this is the vendor of choice. However, their estimates for production boards have always been optimistic. Their model estimates are excellent. They usually have trouble with the first production boards because they are understaffed. After that, production is smooth, and the quality is superb. We think the 12-month estimate has about a 50/50 chance of happening. We are sure that they could deliver the first production board at 15 months.

If you need the 12-month production board, I suggest an incentive. I think a performance bonus for the first production board at 12 months would get his attention, and he would get extra staff. This should improve the probability a lot. (Note that less than 12 months is not really possible.)

If you have questions, give me a call.

T. A. Edison

REFERENCES

GLASS R., J. ROST, and M. S. MATOOK (2008) Lying on software projects. *IEEE Software* **25** (6), 90–95.

HURST P. W. (2000) Threads of control. In *Software Engineering Project Management*, ed. R. H. Thayer, pp. 410–422. Los Alamitos, CA: IEEE Computer Society.

Chapter 3

Estimation

One of the most difficult parts of the planning process is the part associated with developing estimates of the size of the project, the effort that will be required, the schedule, and the cost. In this chapter, we will attempt to develop an understanding of the estimation methods that are available to help and the pros and cons of each. We will discuss several estimating methods, parametric models, function points, plan-based methods, and task duration estimation. Finally, we will have a few words to say about how the project manager can and should respond to stakeholders' sometimes unreasonable demands regarding costs and schedule.

We will start with an assumption that the project manager has the primary responsibility and accountability for estimation. The project manager, who we described in Chapter 1 as a person who has the ability to negotiate the scope, the schedule, and the budget, can never blame someone else for inaccurate estimates. That person needs to insure that the estimates are as good as they can be and that the stakeholders understand the degree of risk associated with the estimates. That is the project manager's responsibility. The accountability portion of the statement implies that if the estimates are not as good as they can, or should, be, the project manager will suffer the consequences and will be held accountable, not only for technical failures but also for inaccurate estimates.

The managers of software-based development projects are usually asked to make estimates at two major points in the project life cycle. These are during the project's feasibility phase when a preliminary business case is being developed, when a preliminary project plan is available, and when a draft of the architecture document has been completed. We will call this estimate the early sizing estimate. The second point is near the end of the definition phase when a baselined business case, a final project plan, a baselined architecture document, and at least some of the detailed requirements are available. We call this the plan-based estimate. Figure 3.1 shows where in the development life cycle these estimates usually need to be made.

The early sizing estimate is usually expected to be a very rough estimate and is frequently used as part of the feasibility evaluation to determine if the time and cost for the project are within reasonable limits. These estimates can be as far off by as much as plus or minus 100% of the actual cost and time if the technology being used is reasonably well known. If the technology is new or is unknown at the

Managing the Development of Software-Intensive Systems, by James McDonald
Copyright © 2010 John Wiley & Sons, Inc.

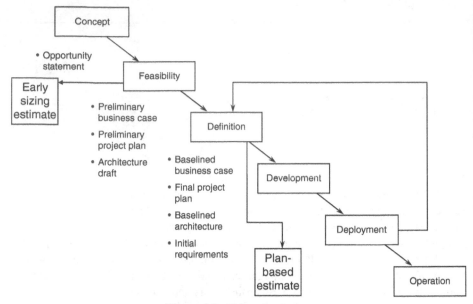

Figure 3.1   Types of estimates.

time the preliminary estimate is being made, we would expect the early sizing estimate to be even further from their actual values. When we develop a plan-based
estimate, we should be able to produce much more accurate results, typically within
plus or minus 10% of the actuals. During the time from preparation of the early
estimate to the time we produce a plan-based estimate, we would expect to learn
much more about the project in terms of its scope and its architecture. As we
approach the point where plan-based estimates can be made, we should update our
early sizing estimates and we would expect that by the time our plan-based estimates
are made, the early sizing estimate should be close to the plan-based estimate.

During this interval, the manager of the project needs to have close and continu-
ous contact with the project's stakeholders so that, first, they understand well the
large expected variability in the early sizing estimates. Then as we move through
the interval, the stakeholders need to be kept up to date on how the expected time
and costs are changing and the reasons for the changes. When the development
manager allows long periods of time to go by without updating the stakeholders on
the most recent versions of the expected cost and schedule, the stakeholders will
almost always express surprise and disappointment when the plan-based estimates
are developed. The reason for this is that as the development terms learn more about
the requirements and the work involved in implementing those requirements, the
expected cost and schedule usually increases. Unfortunately, it is virtually impossible to make good, firm delivery commitments based on the early sizing estimates
unless the stakeholders are willing to use the plus 100% estimates when doing their
financial and operational analyses. The good news is that when we have developed

plan-based estimates, we are usually in good shape to make firm delivery commitments that can frequently be within plus or minus 10% of the expected values.

3.1   ESTIMATING METHODS

There are several types of estimating methods. The three most frequently used methods are: experience-based methods, parametric methods, and plan-based methods.

Experience-based estimates are estimates made by individuals who have developed similar products or functionality many times in the past. As an example, in my last industrial job, I had a technical manager reporting to me who was responsible for the development of specific software-based features for a very specific purpose. His group had developed the original product 3 or 4 years prior to the time my experience with them began, and since that time, they had spent most of their time adding capabilities to the product in response to customer requests. When a customer came to me with a request for an additional feature, I would ask them to describe in a short paragraph what they were looking for. Then I would go to the manager in my organization and ask how much time and effort would be required to add that feature to the product. He would typically respond by saying something like, "It will probably take a systems engineer about a month to develop detailed requirements, a software developer about 6 months to design and implement the software. Then it will take another person about 4 months to develop functional tests, execute those tests and 2 more months working with the software developer to fix any problems found during testing. So, in total I would estimate that it will take about a total of 15 staff months and a total interval of about 11 months from start to customer delivery." By knowing the average cost per staff month for the organization, I could provide the customer with an estimate of the cost for the addition of the new feature.

It is very difficult to teach someone how to do experience-based estimating. However, sometimes we are fortunate enough to be in a position where we have previously developed similar products or applications. When we are, we can feel reasonably confident about developing those kinds of estimates. However, we need to be careful about making experience-based estimates for anything beyond the addition of new individual features to a product. When the application is new, when the architecture is new, or when the work is complex involving more than a very few people, experience-based estimating does not usually work well. So, in this book, we are not going to have much more to say about experience-based estimates other than saying that we hope the reader is occasionally in a position to feel competent using them.

The second type of estimating method involves the use of parametric models. These models are based on first estimating how many lines of code will need to be produced for a specific application or how much software functionality will need to be produced. Functionality in this context is usually measured in terms of function points. We will discuss what we mean by function points shortly. Parametric models are used most frequently for developing early sizing estimates, sometimes also called top–down estimates.

The third type of estimating method involves the development of a work breakdown structure, estimating how much time and effort will be required to complete each task, linking those tasks in a network of task precedences, assigning resources to tasks, and developing a detailed project schedule similar to the one that we discussed in Chapter 2. This method is used for developing the plan-based estimates discussed above and is sometimes called bottoms-up estimating model because it is based on the details of the work that must be accomplished to complete the project.

3.2 PARAMETRIC MODELS

Since the mid-1970s, many different parametric models have been developed for estimating the effort and cost required for the development of software applications. They have names like SLIM, PRICE, SEER-SEM, COCOMO II, and KnowledgePLAN®. The best known, and most widely documented, of these models is COCOMO II. It has been developed by a team led by Dr. Barry Boehm at the University of Southern California's Viterbi School of Engineering. In its simplest form, the model estimates the required effort, the length of the schedule (interval), and the size of the required staff with three equations:

$$\text{Effort} = 2.4\,(\text{KLOC})^{1.05} \qquad \text{Staff Months}$$
$$\text{Interval} = 2.5\,(\text{effort})^{0.38} \qquad \text{Months}$$
$$\text{Staff} = \text{effort}/\text{interval} \qquad \text{Employees}$$

If we know how many thousand lines of source code we need to produce, we raise that number to the 1.05 power and multiply the results by 2.4 to get the expected effort in staff months. We then raise that effort to the 0.38 power and multiply the result by 2.5 to produce an estimate of the interval from the beginning of requirements writing to first customer delivery measured in months. Then we simply divide the estimated effort in staff months from the first equation by the estimated interval from the second equation to get an estimate of the average number of employees who will need to work on the project.

For example, if we will be developing 32,000 lines of source code, we would raise 32 to the 1.05 power and multiply the results by 2.4 to get an estimate of the effort, 91 staff months in this example. Then we raise 91 to the 0.38 power and multiply the result by 2.5 to get an estimate of the interval, 14 months for this example. Then we divide the effort (91 staff months) by the interval (14 months) to get the average number of staff (6.5 employees) who will work on this project. The actual COCOMO II model used by serious estimators is much more complex than indicated by this example. It includes additional parameters called scale factors that account for differences among projects and things like whether this project is similar to or very different from other works that have been done by the organization, whether the requirements are very rigid or tend to be flexible, and other parameters called effort multipliers that account for things like the product's complexity and required reliability, development team capability, and tightness of the development schedule.

The constants that appear in these models were determined by the creators of the models by fitting the mathematical equations that describe the models to data from large numbers of actual projects for which they were able to obtain descriptive data. The models have been shown to be quite accurate when they were applied retroactively for real projects, even for those that were well beyond those included in the developers' initial project databases. However, there is one serious problem when we try to use these models to estimate the effort and interval for projects that have not yet been developed. That problem arises because most of them are based on one key parameter, which is the quantity of software (measured in source lines of code) that will be produced. In reality, we are seldom able to predict in advance with any degree of accuracy how many lines of source code we will need to produce to achieve the project's objectives. So, the parametric models that we have just discussed are not directly useful in developing early sizing estimates.

3.3 FUNCTION POINTS

An alternative approach is to first develop an estimate of what are called "function points" for each software application or product. Function points were invented by a group led by John Albrecht at IBM in the 1970s as a method for measuring the productivity of software application development groups (Albrecht and Gaffney 1983).

The first step in using function points as input to a parametric model is to count them. Methods for counting function points are specified in the *Function Point Counting Practices Manual* published by the International Function Point Users' Group (IFPUG).[1] That manual specifies how to count function points. The process can be briefly described as in Fig. 3.2.

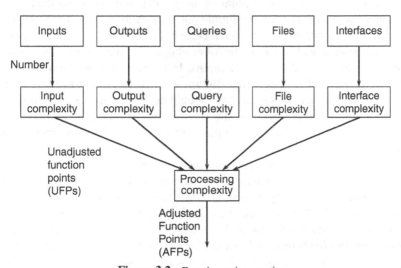

Figure 3.2 Function point counting.

---

[1] Available for purchase from the IFPUG, 191 Clarksville Road, Princeton, NJ 08550.

First, we count the number of inputs, outputs, queries, files, and interfaces required for the application. Then for each of these categories, we evaluate their complexity to determine the total number of unadjusted function points (UFPs). Finally, we evaluate the overall processing complexity of the application to determine the total number of adjusted function points (AFPs).

Then we will use the results as input to a parametric model to estimate the size, schedule, and cost for development of the software.

The IFPUG's *Function Point Counting Practices Manual* is a large document. In hard copy format, it is about 1¼" thick. I have done some magic and compressed the very detailed and extensive content of the manual to a few paragraphs and figures to provide a flavor for its content. First, the manual tells us that we need to count the total number of external user inputs using the following guidelines:

- Count all the screens (or dialog boxes for a graphical interface) used to input each transaction.
- Count all other unique inputs.
- Count change, add, and delete transactions separately.
- The same screen or dialog box used for inputs and outputs should be counted separately.
- Do not include inquiry screens in this category.

The first bulleted item above says that we should count each block of data that the user can see simultaneously as one distinct input even though the corresponding transaction might require several blocks of input to complete that transaction. So, the rule says that we should be expansive and count all of those blocks separately. The second item says that we should count all unique inputs as separate inputs. For example, if we are working with a point of sale system and one of the inputs to that system comes from a card reader, we should count that card reader as a unique input. Next, we need to be sure that inputs which enter new data into the application, inputs that change the data within the application, and inputs that delete data from the application are all counted as separate inputs. If a screen or dialog box is used for both inputting data and for displaying output, we will count that as both an input and as an output. The last one says that we should not count queries as an input even if the query requires some input from the user to produce an output in, perhaps, the same or a different format. The user's input in that case is counted as part of a query function point count.

We do the same for outputs, queries, files, and interfaces to other applications using similar guidelines. For each category, we next go to a unique table that looks similar to the input complexity weighting table shown in Table 3.1.

The number of UFPs that we assign to each input will depend upon the number of internal logical files into which the input data need to be placed and the number of attributes or data fields that are input by the user or by the input device as part of this input. The number of function points that will be assigned to each input can be 3 for simple inputs that access only one or two internal logical files and input from 1 to 16 data items, 4 function points for inputs that are of average size, touching

Table 3.1 Input Complexity Weighting

Input Complexity	1–4 Attributes	5–15 Attributes	16+ Attributes
0 or 1 files accessed	3	3	4
2 files accessed	3	4	6
3+ files accessed	4	6	6

Simple → 3, average → 4, complex → 6.

Table 3.2 Processing Complexity Factors

Data communications
Distributed functions
Performance requirements
Heavily used configuration
Transaction rate
Online data entry
End-user efficiency
Online updates
Complex processing
Code reusability
Conversion/installation ease
Operational ease
Multiple site installation
Facilitate change
Total degrees of influence (TDIs): 0–70

more internal files and providing more data attributes, or 6 function points for even more complex inputs. We do the same thing for all other inputs and for each output, each query, each internal logical file, and for each interface. The IFPUG counting standards manual contains tables similar to, but different from, the one shown in Table 3.1 for each of the other function types. When we complete all of these counts, we will have both the number of functions of each type, their complexities, and the total number of UFPs.

Then, we look at the entire application and evaluate the processing complexity of the overall application by rating a series of complexity attributes on a scale of 1–5. The complexity attributes are shown in Table 3.2. There are 14 complexity attributes. If we score each on a scale from 0 to 5, the sum of the complexity attribute scores, called the total degrees of influence (TDIs) (of complexity), will be a number between 0 and 70. As an example, suppose we are looking at the data communications complexity of an application that will be developed for use on a PC and we know that this application will never have to communicate with anything other than the local user, who will provide all inputs from the keyboard and the mouse and will see all of the results on the PC monitor. We would give that application a data communications complexity score of 0. On the other hand, suppose are developing a software application intended to drive a telecommunications switch that would create connections among users who are connected by telephone or by a wireless connection to the switch and to both other users who are connected directly to that switch as well as to external users who could be reached either via the Internet or by traditional data or voice trunks via another similar switch at another location. In addition, that switch would probably need to be monitored via a telemetry or TCP/IP link to a remote monitoring location. We would probably give the data communications attribute of that application a score of 5. Again, the IFPUG counting standards manual describes a range of complexities for each of these 14 application complexity attribute scores primarily via examples like the ones that we have just used. When we have calculated the TDIs for the entire application, we calculate the AFPs for the application by inserting the number of UFPs and the TDIs into the following equation to calculate the AFPs:

$$AFP = UFP \times (0.65 + (0.01 \times TDI))$$

The result of this adjustment is shown graphically in Fig. 3.3. It says that, depending upon the TDI, the raw function points or the UFPs are adjusted upward by up to 35% for a very complex application with TDI = 70 or downward by as much as 35% for a very simple application with TDI = 0. We will now use the AFPs as input to an early sizing parametric model.

If we were really using function points as a measure of the size of our application, we would probably complete a spreadsheet like the one shown in Table 3.3 to show all of our calculations.

In this table, you would enter the number of simple, average, and complex inputs; outputs; files; inquiries; and interfaces and multiply the number of each shown in the weighting column. These are added across the rows then summed down the right column to get the total number of function points for each category of functionality and the total UFPs.

In the bottom portion of the form, you would rate each of the complexity on a scale from 0 to 5 then sum these numbers to get the TDI. Then, insert the UFPs and the TDI into the equation at the bottom of the chart to calculate the total AFPs for the application.

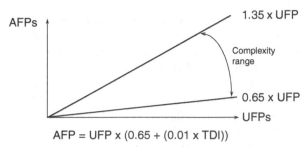

Figure 3.3   Adjusted function points. AFP, adjusted function points; UFP, unadjusted function points; TDI, total degree of influence.

Table 3.3 Function Point Worksheet (from J. Brian Dreger, Function Point Analysis, Prentice Hall, 1988)

Business Function	Number	Complexity	Weight	Line Total	Type Total
Inputs		Simple	×3		
		Average	×4		
		Complex	×6		
Input total					
Outputs		Simple	×4		
		Average	×5		
		Complex	×7		
Output total					
Files		Simple	×7		
		Average	×10		
		Complex	×15		
File total					
Inquiries		Simple	×4		
		Average	×5		
		Complex	×6		
		Complex	×7		
Inquiries total					
Interfaces files		Simple	×5		
		Average	×7		
		Complex	×10		
Interface total					
Total unadjusted function point:					

Processing complexity				
Factor	Value	Factor		Value
1. Date communcications		8. Online update		
2. Distributed function		9. Complex processing		
3. Performance		10. Code reusability		
4. Heavily used configuration		11. Conversion installation ease		
5. Transaction rates		12. Operation ease		
6. Online date entry		13. Multiple site instillation		
7. End-user efficiency		14. Facilitate change		
Total degree of influence:				
Adjusted function point				
Adjusted function point = unadjusted function point × (0.65 + (0.01 × total degree of influence))				

So, now that we have the number of function points associated with an application, what can be done with it? The researchers who have developed the parametric models have collected data, including function point data from hundreds, and sometimes from thousands, of software development projects, and have analyzed that data. To provide an illustration of what they have done, let us look at a few of the results obtained by one of those researchers, Capers Jones, founder of Software Productivity Research, Inc. and developer of the KnowledgePLAN model. Mr. Jones first looked at the productivity of software development teams, measured in function points per staff month, as a function of the size of the application measured in function points. He plotted this data on a chart like the one shown in Fig. 3.4. Of course, when he plotted that data, he produced a scattering of points, one for each project that was observed. Then, he fit a line to these points using statistical techniques and produced the results shown in Fig. 3.4. It says that for relatively small projects producing 10–20 function points of capability, the productivity was in the range of 15 function points per staff month. For projects as large as 10,000 function points, the productivity was only about 1 function point per staff month. To calibrate ourselves, a project producing 20 function points would typically be done by one person within a couple of months. A 10,000-function point project would probably involve at least a few hundred people and would take 2–3 years for completion. So, the first thing that we see is that productivity greatly decreases with the increasing size of the application being developed.

A second factor that Jones observed was that productivity was very different for different kinds of software. Figure 3.5 shows the overall distribution ranging from about 1 function point per staff month to approximately 64 function points per staff month with an average of about 5 function points per staff month. In addition,

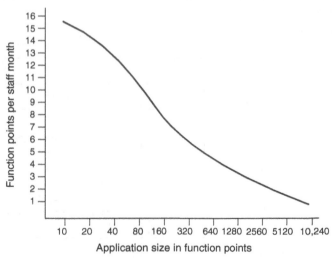

Figure 3.4   Relationship between application size and productivity (from Capers Jones, Applied Software Measurement, McGraw-Hill, 1991, reproduced with permission of McGraw-Hill Companies, Inc.).

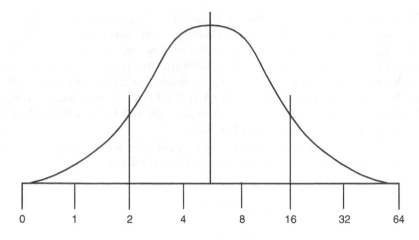

Figure 3.5 Distribution of productivity (from Capers Jones, Applied Software Measurement, McGraw-Hill, 1991, reproduced with permission of McGraw-Hill Companies, Inc.).

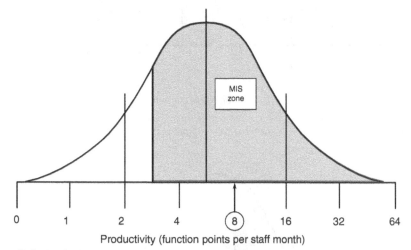

Figure 3.6 Productivity for projects in the MIS zone (from Capers Jones, Applied Software Measurement, McGraw-Hill, 1991, reproduced with permission of McGraw-Hill Companies, Inc.).

he found that if projects were classified as management information system projects, those projects, such as payroll and accounting applications, spreadsheet projects, statistical packages, and word processors, usually had an average productivity of 8 function points per staff month and tended to fall in the upper portions of the distribution as shown in Fig. 3.6.

Projects that he classified as belonging to the system software zone, such as operating systems, process control applications, telecommunications software, and similar applications, had an average productivity of 4 function points per staff months and generally fell in the lower part of the distribution as shown in Fig. 3.7.

Finally, he looked at software projects that he classified as being in the military zone. These were projects like avionics software, fire control applications, and embedded real-time software, which were constrained to follow military specifications. He found that the average productivity for those projects had an average productivity of 3 function points per staff months and fell in the lower tail of the productivity distribution as shown in Fig. 3.8.

So, now we know that both the size of the application and the type of software can greatly impact the productivity of the team developing the application. Jones,

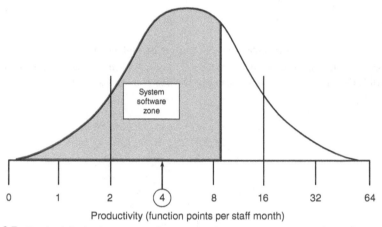

Productivity (function points per staff month)

Figure 3.7   Productivity in the system software zone (from Capers Jones, Applied Software Measurement, McGraw-Hill, 1991, reproduced with permission of McGraw-Hill Companies, Inc.).

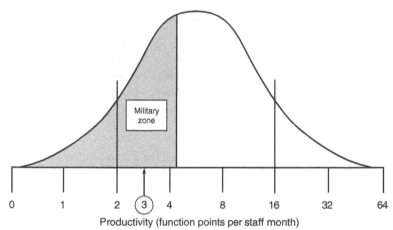

Productivity (function points per staff month)

Figure 3.8   Productivity for projects in the military zone (from Capers Jones, Applied Software Measurement, McGraw-Hill, 1991, reproduced with permission of McGraw-Hill Companies, Inc.).

as well as the creators of other popular parametric models, went on to identify many other characteristics of software development projects that impacted software development productivity. They have incorporated those findings into the commercial estimation tools that they have made available. The use of those tools is illustrated in Fig. 3.9. Both KnowledgePLAN and COCOMO II are software packages that run on a PC. KnowledgePLAN can be purchased commercially[2] from Software Productivity Research, Inc. in Hendersonville, NC. Sources from which the COCOMO II software can be downloaded, at a modest cost, can be found at the University of California Software Research Center's web site.[3] When we use parametric models to produce early sizing estimates for our projects, we first count function points as briefly described in the function point section of this chapter and enter them onto a form similar to the one shown in Table 3.3. We also answer several questions about the project type and the environment in which the development work will be done. The tools produce estimates of the required staff months of effort, the average project headcount, the schedule duration, and the cost if the user provides an expected cost per staff month. The tools also provide upper and lower bounds on these estimates to give the user a feeling for the possible ranges of the differences between actual and estimates.

If you plan to use this technique to develop early sizing estimates for a real project, it will be important to get at least one of the team members educated about the details involved in applying the content of the IFPUG function point counting standards. One way to do this is for that person to take a commercially available function point counting course then for that person to seek certification as a function point counter from the IFPUG organization. Alternatively, you might consider hiring a function point consultant. I prefer the former because then you have someone who is knowledgeable about function point counting, who also knows the application well, and who is likely to be available throughout the interval from the time of the early sizing estimate until a bottoms-up estimate can be produced.

Use of the automated tools is fairly straightforward, and a user can probably learn enough about the tools from the documentation provided with the tools to make appropriate use of them.

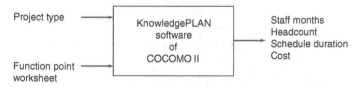

KnowledgePLAN is a proprietary product from Software Productivity Research (SPR), Inc.

COCOMO II, available free of charge from the USC Software Center, has a function point-based estimation capability.

Figure 3.9   Using commercially available parametric modeling estimation tools.

[2] Available for purchase from Software Productivity Research, Inc., Hendersonville, NC.
[3] http://sunset.usc.edu.

3.4 BOTTOMS-UP ESTIMATING

Developing bottoms-up estimates involves one major estimating effort having to do with how long it will take to accomplish each task in the work breakdown structure (WBS). In Chapter 2, we estimated the duration of each task in the WBS shown in Fig. 3.10 by asking the core team member who was going to be executing each task how long that task would take to complete if they worked on that task full-time. Each person responded with a task duration (and an implied commitment that they would complete the task in the time they had estimated), which we added in the lower-right corner of each task box. However, that is not the usual situation. Normally, the people who are going to be assigned to each are not members of the core team and they are not in the room when task durations are being estimated. So, we need an alternative method for the core team to use when they are estimating task durations. For that task, we recommend that the core team use what is called the wideband Delphi technique.

To use that technique, the manager assembles the core team in a room where they first develop the work breakdown structure as we discussed in Chapter 2. Then each person on the core team is asked, for each task, to individually estimate the shortest amount of time (the optimistic estimate) in which the task could possibly be done, the most likely time that the task will take, and the longest time (the pessimistic estimate) that the task might take if it were assigned to a member of the organization who specializes in that kind of task and that the person works on the task full-time from the time the task is started until it is completed. The estimates provided by each member of the core team are displayed to the whole team. Then team members are asked to discuss the assumptions that they made and why they came up with their estimate, particularly for those that are very different from the estimates of other members of the team. After a brief discussion, members are allowed to modify their original estimates if they want to do that based on the discussion. The leader looks at the data and discards any outliers. Then the averages

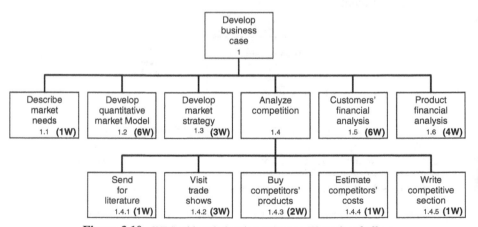

Figure 3.10 WBS with task duration estimates. W, weeks of effort.

of the optimistic, likely, and pessimistic estimates are calculated. Let us look at an example.

Figure 3.11 shows the data from one task for a project for which I was the development manager. There were seven people on the core team for this project, and I was the person with the marker in my hand when the optimistic, likely, and pessimistic estimates for this task were developed. Each member of the team independently estimated the three times. We displayed them on a whiteboard as shown in the figure. Then, the team had a brief discussion and some members of the team changed their estimates. Others stayed where they were.

After the changes, we had seven optimistic estimates (1, 2, 3, 3, 1, 2, and 5), seven likely estimates (3, 6, 6, 10, 4, 5, and 6), and seven pessimistic estimates (12, 13, 16, 18, 20, 23, and 24) with all durations measured in full-time weeks of effort. Now it was my job as the leader to eliminate the outliers. I decided that the 5-week optimistic estimate was very different from the other optimistic estimates, so I crossed it out. I decided that the 10-week estimate was very different from the other likely estimates, so I crossed it out. I could not find an outlier among the pessimistic estimates so I did not eliminate any of those estimates. Then, we averaged the remaining optimistic estimates to get an average optimistic estimate of 2 weeks. We averaged the remaining six likely estimates and got an average likely estimate of 5 weeks. And, finally, we averaged the seven pessimistic estimates to get an average pessimistic estimate of 18 weeks. What do we now have?

Figure 3.12 shows our results for this task. It says that almost no one believes that this task can be accomplished in less than 2 weeks as indicated by the zero value of the graph for durations less than 2. Members of the core team think that it is most likely that the task will take about 5 weeks as indicated by the peak of the graph at a duration of 5, and most think that it would never take more than 18 weeks to

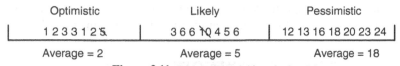

Optimistic	Likely	Pessimistic
1 2 3 3 1 2 5̶	3 6 6 1̶0̶ 4 5 6	12 13 16 18 20 23 24
Average = 2	Average = 5	Average = 18

Figure 3.11   Using the Delphi method.

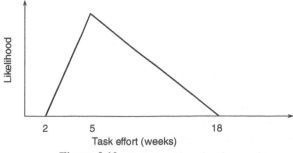

Figure 3.12   Task duration estimation.

complete this task. However, as input to our scheduling tool, we need a single number for the duration of each task.

To get an expected value from the optimistic, likely, and pessimistic estimates for the task duration, we add the optimistic estimate to four times the likely estimate to the pessimistic estimate and divide that total by 6 according to the following equation:

$$\text{Expected duration} = \frac{\text{Optimistic} + 4 \times \text{likely} + \text{pessimistic}}{6}$$

For the values in the example given above, this becomes

$$\text{Expected duration} = \frac{2 + 4 \times 5 + 18}{6} = 6.7 \text{ weeks}$$

And we will use 6.7 weeks as the duration for this task when we schedule the project. This might look like black magic. However, there is some theory behind what might look like an arbitrary calculation. If we assume that the actual time for the task is a random variable and the probability density of the task's time duration is a beta distribution with a lower value of 2, a most likely value of 5, and an upper limit of 18, and if the shape parameters of that probability have specific values, then the expected value of the task duration is given by the equation described above. We will return to the more theoretical aspects of this calculation in Chapter 8 when we talk about risk management. However, for now, we will simply use this calculation to determine the task's expected duration.

Intuitively, what we are doing with this calculation is looking at the upper and lower apexes of the triangle in Fig. 3.12 and adjusting the expected value upward or downward from the likely value depending upon which tail of the triangle is longer. In the case of the example given here, the right tail of the triangle is longer than the left tail, so the expected value is set to be 6.7 weeks as compared with the likely value of 5 weeks. If the left tail of the triangle were longer than the right tail, the expected value would be set to a number that is smaller than the likely value.

3.5 ADJUSTING THE EXPECTED VALUES

After we have expected values for all of the task durations, we have to adjust them to account for the assumption that we made when we started doing our estimates. We asked members of the core team to make their optimistic, likely, and pessimistic estimates assuming that the person doing the work would work on the task full-time, uninterrupted, from the time the task starts until it finishes. In reality, most development team members do not work that way. They spend some of their time on vacation and holidays. They spend time working with other team members on activities related to other team members' tasks. They participate in the inspection of others' works. They are interrupted by telephone calls and emails. They attend organizational meetings and tend to administrative duties. They sometimes have to wait for information from other team members and, if they are working on more than one task, they will require some "switch time" to move between tasks. To the author's knowledge, there are no public domain studies that would indicate how much time team members are likely to spend on these tasks, but during the past several years, I have seen three proprietary studies that have indicated that development team members typically spend 30–50% of their time on these other tasks. That means that we can count on only about a 24-hour work week from most developers when they are working on a nominal 8 hour per day schedule.

It implies that before we use our expected task duration estimates, we have to scale them up by a factor of 1.67. When we do that and enter the results into our scheduling tool, we will have an excellent estimate of the time required to complete the project. It will almost always be longer and more expensive than stakeholders have assumed that it will be. So, what do we do when we first expose our bottoms-up cost and schedule to our customers and other stakeholders? Usually, we do not have to do anything. They usually react first by saying that the cost is outrageously high and the schedule is much too long. Then we do need to have something to say.

One thing we can consider to respond is to have some alternatives available that will reduce the cost and schedule. The first is to reduce the scope of the project and, possibly, to phase deliveries of additional features to be delivered in later releases if the customer still wants them when we get to that point. A second thing we could do is to split some tasks between two team members into two tasks and to overlap work on them if that will reduce the total time required for the initial tasks. That will shorten the schedule but will almost surely result in overall project costs that are higher than the initial estimate. The team could consider reusing designs and codes that they have previously developed or incorporating open source freeware into the product, but these are things that they should have looked at when the product architecture was being developed, so it will probably not help at this point. Some readers might suggest planning to have the team work overtime. This is a reasonable option for short periods of time, but if overtime is extended for more than a few weeks or a couple of months the productivity of the team will surely deteriorate. I learned this when I was associated with a very large project in the late 1980s and early 1990s. Customers for the product were continually complaining that it was taking too long to get new features added to the product. So, the management of the development organization put a plan together that required all team members to work a minimum of 60 hours per week. That meant that they needed to work at least two extra hours each day plus a whole day on the weekend. They were well compensated and were paid at higher rates for their overtime hours. Initially, this seemed to work well. However, after about 6 months, there was a noticeable decline in productivity and, after a year, productivity went to zero. After the management realized they had a serious problem, they returned to normal work hours. But it took the team 2 years to return to its former levels of productivity. The message here is that once a detailed project plan is developed and scheduled, there aren't many things that can be done to reduce costs or schedule other than modifying the requirements with a concurrent change in the schedule.

My advice is that the team should prepare some alternative scopes and schedules before beginning final commitment negotiations with customers and management.

The project manager should be ready and willing to consider and present alternative scope, delivery date, costs, and resources.

If the job cannot be done within the negotiated constraints, the project manager should consider not doing the job at all. I have been involved in four different projects over the years for which I have been unable to reach an initial agreement with the customer on the scope, schedule, and budget for the project and where the customer has said that they need to look elsewhere for a solution to their problem. In all four cases, I encouraged them to look elsewhere. In all four cases, they eventually came back and reluctantly agreed to one of the alternatives that I proposed.

A rule of thumb that can be used to help remind us of these trade-offs is an equation that says that once a detailed plan has been developed, we are bound by an equation that looks like this:

$$\frac{\text{Features}}{\text{Budget} \times \text{time}} = \text{constant}$$

In this equation, *features* is a measure of the product's functionality, in number of features, function points, or some other convenient measure; *budget* is the amount of money being spent per unit of time; and *time* is the time to customer delivery of the product. Depending upon the units that we choose for measuring these variables, the *constant* on the right side of the equation can be any positive number, but once this relationship has been developed by putting together a bottoms-up schedule, there is little that can practically be done to change the relationship. The equation says that when we are negotiating scope, budget, and schedule with customers, we have little flexibility, but we do have some. When the customers say that they need additional features, it means that the budget (in dollars per unit of time) or the time, or both, must increase. If they say that the schedule needs to be reduced, that means that the functionality must decrease or the time must increase. If they say that the time must decrease, then the functionality or the budget, within limits, must increase. There is little or no theoretical justification for this equation. It is just a simple memory-jogging device to remind us that once we have a baseline plan, one of the plan variables cannot be changed independently of the others.

We should be very willing to talk frequently with our stakeholders during the planning process to keep them up to date on the estimating process and to help them understand both what we are doing and why the project is costing what we have estimated and is taking longer than they probably wished that it would.

Finally, we should never count on inventions coming along during the course of a project that will significantly reduce the cost and the schedule. During the past 40 years, there have been only seven or eight new technologies that have significantly changed the productivity of development teams. That means that they appear on the average only once every 5–6 years. That interval is much longer than most development schedules. So, we should never count on our teams or anyone else creating a new technology that might reduce schedules or costs during the development interval. On the other hand, you should never stop looking for improved technologies. You might be lucky enough to find one at just the right time.

3.6   SOME THINGS TO REMEMBER

The most important things we have discussed in this chapter are the following:

1. The manager of the project must accept both responsibility and accountability for estimating.
2. Try to use function points and one of the parametric tools for initial cost and schedule estimates.
3. Use early sizing estimates only as approximate indicators of schedules and costs.
4. Recognize the large uncertainties in early sizing estimates and be sure your stakeholders also understand.
5. Use the Delphi technique (or expert opinion) to estimate task durations.
6. Base deliverable commitments only on detailed bottoms-up estimates.

CASE STUDY 3   *Negotiating Budgets and Schedules*

Purposes

1. Practice skills that the project manager needs to use with the project's stakeholders to reach agreement on project scope, cost, and schedule.
2. Understand how project management processes might help in a difficult negotiation.
3. Learn what could go wrong when using these techniques in a negotiation.

Background 1

The following paragraphs describe the background information that is available to you. You will be negotiating budgets and schedules with your marketing manager peer. A second background section for this case, which describes the information that is available to him, follows this section. Please read both before beginning your activity for this case study.

You are the project manager for a development project that is intended to produce a new customer product. It was proposed at the business unit level in your company about 6 months ago that you be the "champion" for this project. The product is needed to respond to customer requests for the functions it provides and to help generate new revenues for your business unit. The job involves a significant amount of both new hardware and software development.

Immediately after you were asked to be the product champion, you requested your peers, who were responsible for systems engineering and market management, to make a person or two in each of their organizations available to develop requirements and a business case for the product. They were both able to provide that support. You were able to make part of the time of a software development manager from your organization available to work along with them in developing these documents. The systems engineer, who was very highly rated and knowledgeable about the application, took the lead in developing both the business case and the requirements. Shortly after work started on the requirements and the business case, hardware and software developers, as well as system testers, began to roll off the last project on which they were working. You asked a few of the lead technical people to work with the manager, who was working on the business case, to develop the system architecture and a project plan for the development work.

The team had been working in that mode for a few months. By January 2010, they had developed an excellent set of requirements, a solid architectural design for both the hardware and the software, and a draft of a business case that looked favorable—even with very conservative market assumptions. However, the team had not made enough progress, in your opinion, on the project plan. To address this problem, you decided to take the six managers, each of whom had at least one of their people slated to work on the project, off-site for 3 days to develop and write a project plan. This session produced spectacular results. A very credible plan was developed during the off-site meeting. All that remained after returning to the office was the detailed editing and distribution of the plan.

By the time the plan was completed, in February 2010, approximately 15 people had been freed up from the earlier project, and you expected that there would be 5 more people available within the next few months. The development plan that you put together matched this availability schedule very well. It called for a peak staff of about 20 people halfway through the development period, continuing at that level until shortly after the second customer delivery. The first release was planned for May 2011 and the second release at the end of 2011. These releases would contain the features listed in the attachment. You have recently heard that your competitor is starting a field trial of a prototype of their product that competes with yours.

It is now February 2010. Your current view of staffing and funds required to deliver the features described in the requirements are

Year	Average Staff	Cost (U.S.$ million)
2010	17	2.9
2011	18	2.8
2012	3.5	0.5
Total	38.5	6.2

Unfortunately, these estimates are somewhat higher than the preliminary estimates you gave to your market management peer about a year ago when customers began to ask about this product. At that point, and during budget discussions last fall, you were working with the following estimates, which were subject to revision when detailed requirements were known and a project plan was developed. Those earlier estimates were

Year	Average Staff	Cost (U.S.$ million)
2010	14	2.4
2011	10	1.6
2012	5	0.6
Total	29	4.6

The expected development interval, when these initial estimates were developed, was about 2 years, with a delivery at the end of 2011.

The differences between the two estimates were caused by the following factors:

- The original estimates assumed that a hardware prototyping effort that was under way last year would produce some hardware that could be used in the production product. This did not work out because the work was stopped as the result of a 20% reduction in the size of your development workforce during 2009. It raised the estimate by 2.9 staff years.

- The original estimate assumed that 25,000–30,000 lines of new software would have to be developed. Based on the requirements and architecture that are currently available, it looks like it will require about 40,000 lines of new software. This has increased the estimate by 3.6 staff years.
- The original estimate assumed that one mechanical designer would be sufficient to do all of the physical design work over a 2-year period. In order to meet international physical requirements for the markets into which the market management organization would like to sell this product, we now estimate that a little more than two people will be required for approximately 14 months, increasing total staff requirements by 2.5 staff years.
- Finally, the technical supervision for the nine additional headcounts will be approximately 0.5 staff years.

Your official budget this year (2010) for this project is U.S.$1.2 million. Your marketing counterpart, who was heavily involved in allocating budget dollars, said that he simply did not have the U.S.$2.4 million that you felt was required in this year. He suggested that you proceed with the development work for the first half of this year, then, if at midyear the work appeared to be on track, you could jointly try to get an additional U.S.$1.2 million of funding. Your concern has been that if you are not able to get the additional funding at midyear, you would be faced with having to find jobs for approximately 20 people on very short notice. In your opinion, you have done a thorough job of minimizing the features that will be delivered in each of the first two releases of the product, and you have worked closely with the systems engineers in prioritizing the importance of each feature. The systems engineer has assured you that the business case still looks positive, even with the higher development costs.

You feel that it really is time that you and your market management peer had a private face-to-face discussion of this issue and you have called his secretary to arrange a date. The date was set for next week.

In the discussion, your objective will be to impress on your product manager the necessity of increasing the current year's budget from U.S.$1.2 million to U.S.$2.9 million. You believe that if you cannot get close to that amount, the combined results of a real staff reduction for the second year in a row and the resulting morale problems will be a very long extension of the project schedule. In order to have any hope of making the product available in a timely way, you must reach agreement on a higher budget level before you leave this meeting.

New Product Features Contained in Each Release

Release 1—May 2011	Release 2—December 2011
PABX interface	Change pairs
Test system interface	Continuity check
Local terminal interface	Autoload site-dependent data
Maintenance position interface	Scan performance
DS1 access	Retrieve scanned data
Change DS1 access	Enter/read scan site-dependent data
DS1 release	Insert errors
DS1 measure	
DS1 transmit	
Set date and time	

Continued

Release 1—May 2011	Release 2—December 2011
Set maintenance state Enter/read site-dependent data Read equipage Software download	

Background 2

You are the marketing manager for a line of customer equipment products that has been reasonably successful during the past several years. You are responsible for coordinating sales activities and allocating R & D funds to your product development organization. Last year's (2009) sales were considerably below your objectives. You managed to survive by reducing the amount of product development expense in 2009. This caused your development project manager peer to reduce the development staff by about 20% during the course of the year. You know he was not pleased to do that, but he managed to end the year within the budget that you had allocated and met all of the necessary customer commitments.

In the spring of last year, several customers asked their account teams if we would be manufacturing and selling a new piece of equipment which one of our competitors was beginning to market to their customers to meet an emerging need. In addition, your sales teams were forecasting a continuing decline in revenues for your products unless you brought some really new products to market in the near future. When these requests began to appear, you asked your product development counterpart to provide you with an estimate of the cost of developing the new product, its approximate time of availability, and its manufacturing cost. His estimate of the development cost, given to you in July of 2009, was U.S.$4.6 million, spread over 3 years, with a first customer delivery near the end of 2011. He felt that he would need about U.S.$2.4 million of development funding in 2010 to meet that schedule.

You asked one of the people in your organization to begin testing the waters among your customers and your sales teams concerning their needs. You also asked your systems engineering counterpart to make someone available to help with this exploration. Unfortunately, he did not have anyone available to address the question seriously when you asked, but he agreed that he would try to make one of his very best people available later in the year. Your market planner, working on his own, was not able to make much progress in estimating the size of the market. He did find, however, a considerable amount of information about your competitor's product, which was already on trial with one of your major customers. It contained the features listed at the end of this background section. In September, one of the best systems engineers in the development organization became available and started to work on the requirements. He jointly worked with your planner and one of the managers in the development organization to complete the business case. They developed a business case that, even with very conservative market assumptions, showed a favorable return on investment. They have assured you that the business case is consistent with the most recent version of the development project plan that was recently updated by the development organization.

It concerned you, though, that it would be the end of 2011 before your development organization would be able to deliver a product to market.

It also concerned you that the development expense in 2010 would, when combined with other planned work, keep the development cost essentially flat. You suspected that the development estimate may have been worked from the assumption that the development staffing should remain flat and not from the needs of the product that was wanted by the customer. You had previously had experiences with product development organizations that led you to the conclusion that this was a widespread practice in the R & D part of your company. Among your market management peers, it had become known as "protecting technical headcount."

You have had recent discussions with your market management bosses concerning this phenomenon and you feel that they generally support your perception on this issue. You and they feel that if sufficient pressure is brought to bear on the development organization, they will reduce their estimate of the costs to develop the new product. You feel that you really do need a product to market for the application, but you have some doubts about the development organization's ability to deliver the right product at the right time. When you reviewed a draft of the business case with your management a short time ago, the only comment you got on it was that the case lacked "excitement" and it would need to look more favorable to generate significant interest at higher management levels. In 2010, you were allocated a total of U.S.$18.3 million for development of all of the products in your product line portfolio. You have heard that there might be an additional U.S.$10 million available at the business unit level as a contingency and as a source of development funding to be applied to promising projects throughout the year. You allocated U.S.$1.2 million of your 2010 development budget (out of the total of U.S.$18.3 million) to this project, hoping that both the total development cost could be reduced and that you could get some of the U.S.$10 million contingency funding if it were required.

It is now February 2010. This afternoon, your secretary received a call from your development project manager counterpart. He asked that you be available for a discussion next week concerning the product and the budget. You hope that he is coming with a proposal that will reduce the cost of development and also meet your customers' needs. If he does not present the expected proposal, you want to be prepared for a discussion that will impress upon him the importance of getting to the market quickly, the financial risks that you face in the current year, and your belief that if the development team is challenged, they can accomplish almost anything—after all, that has been your experience in managing high-performing sales teams for the past 5 years.

Features Provided in Competitor's Product

Test system interface	DS1 access
Local terminal interface	DS1 release
Maintenance position interface	DS1 measure
Change DS1 access	DS1 transmit
Enter/read site-dependent data	Read equipage
Change pairs	Continuity check
Scan performance	Retrieve scanned data

Activity and Output
After reading both the development manager's and the market manager's background information given above, you should prepare an analysis for each of them that will help them get ready for the meeting. Assume that each party to the discussion has only the information available in their specific background description and that neither knows the content of the other's background section. Your recommendations for each, which should follow the analysis, should outline the approach that they should take to the discussion and should be written in a way that they could almost use it as a "script" for the discussion.

In preparing these recommendations, you should think about the following:

1. What the communications style of each is likely to be
2. How openly should each person share the facts that they have?
3. How well do you expect that each will listen to the other?
4. What is likely to go well during the meeting and what might go not so well?
5. How you think the participants will feel during the discussion?
6. What appears to be the basic cause of issues that are brought to light by this case?
7. What can be done by the project manager to address the mistrust that sometimes exists between employees with his responsibilities and employees with profit/loss responsibilities?
8. What can be done by both stakeholders and project managers to better integrate the working relationships between marketing/sales functions and product or system development functions?
9. Could you use a project audit at this point in the negotiations to help reduce uncertainty as well as any mistrust that might exist?
10. Would it be appropriate for the project manager to agree to the currently available budget with the hope that he would be able to find a way to do the job for significantly less cost?
11. Would it be appropriate for either the marketing or the project manager to suggest discontinuing the project now and finding new jobs for the staff?

REFERENCE

ALBRECHT A. J. and J. E. GAFFNEY (1983) Software function, source lines of code and development effort prediction: A software science validation. *IEEE Transactions on Software Engineering* **9** (6), 639–648.

Chapter 4

Planning for Verification and Validation

In Chapter 3, we discussed one of the important activities that must take place during the planning phase of a project, that is, estimating. In this chapter, we will discuss the planning that must be done during the planning phase for verification and validation. The reason for doing special planning for these two activities is that unless they are planned well, they are unlikely to be done very well. In the author's experience, the development of requirements, architecture, coding, and hardware design are processes with which team members are usually very familiar and for which they understand the need. However, activities associated with verification and validation, specifically inspections and testing, do not seem to come naturally to developers, and many of them would rather not be involved in those activities. They are two activities that, if done properly, can consume a significant part of a project's resources. So, in planning, we need to give them special emphasis. First, we will describe what each of these activities is. Then we will discuss what planning needs to be done to insure that they are implemented well.

4.1 INSPECTIONS

In this chapter, we want to develop our ability to properly use and manage inspections on our projects. Let us start talking about what we mean by inspections, what should be inspected, the planning that needs to be done by the project manager, and of what value they can be to the project manager's ability to monitor the status of the project.

Inspections are rigorous examinations of documents that contain work products produced by the development team. They are sometimes called in-process inspections. The purposes of an inspection are to find errors, to provide improved communications among the functional specialists who are working on a project, and to improve the development process. Of particular relevance to readers of this book is the fact that the project manager can also use them to help monitor the status of the project. The inspection process was created by Michael Fagan (1976) in the 1970s

---

Managing the Development of Software-Intensive Systems, by James McDonald
Copyright © 2010 John Wiley & Sons, Inc.

at IBM. The value of inspections has been documented by many authors, for example, Brykczynski and Wheeler (1993) and Porter et al. (1997). Historically, they have been used to review requirements specifications, architecture documents, software code, and test scripts. However, in the author's experience, other inspections of other documents, such as logical hardware designs, circuit designs, very large scale integrated (VLSI) designs, and wiring diagrams are also valuable (Gilray 1996).

The format of an inspection is a small formal meeting of peers, typically with three to six participants, led by a moderator who is specially trained to lead the inspection team. The process stresses the need for adequate preparation, active participation in the inspection meeting, and follow-up, usually by the author of the document and the moderator. It produces data for process and project monitoring. Figure 4.1 is an illustration of the inspection process.

Figure 4.1 shows the flow of work through an inspection. The input to each work task is usually a specification of what the output of the task should be and a standard describing how the project team does that kind of work. The individual responsible for the task does the work and produces a draft of the work product. That draft is distributed to the meeting participants well before the inspection, and each participant reviews it carefully, making notes on what they believe to be errors. At the meeting, the document is reviewed; errors are identified; and a decision is made about whether the draft is OK to be baselined, or if it needs to go back to the author for additional work before baselining. When it is baselined, it becomes the final output from the work task. If it is not OK for baselining, it goes back to the author for additional work and review by either the author and the moderator or by the entire inspection team. This cycle repeats until the draft is OK for baselining.

I have used the word "baseline" several times here. The reader may not be familiar with the precise definition of that word. By baseline, we mean the depositing of the document in a repository, or a library of documents, after which any additional changes in the document require a formal process involving approval for the change, possibly a reinspection after the change, and approval for redepositing the document into the repository.

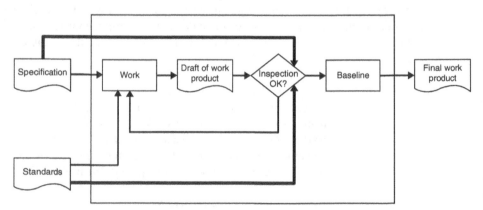

Figure 4.1   The inspection process.

Work products that typically get inspected on a software development project are responses to requests for information, requests for quotes, and contracts with the customer. This does not necessarily include the "boilerplate" legal portions of those documents but rather concentrates on portions of those documents that list expected deliverables, dates for delivery, perhaps performance specifications, and, sometimes, cost to do the work. Requirements and detailed design documents, for both hardware and software, should always be inspected. Sometimes, depending upon the experience of the project team and the team member doing the work, code and detailed circuit and device specifications should be inspected. Test plans and, sometimes, test cases should be inspected. Finally, user documentation, deployment plans, and training course materials should be inspected.

Let us discuss what actually goes on inside the inspection meeting. The moderator starts by announcing the purpose of the meeting and by asking each participant for the reason that they are participating and how much time they spent preparing for the meeting. The recorder notes their responses. Typical participants in an inspection meeting of the design for the module of the software might include the person who wrote the requirements that will be implemented by the software, a person who is developing a different module that will need to communicate with the software being inspected, a person who has developed similar modules in the past, and the person who will be testing the application after all of the necessary software has been integrated. The author and, of course, the moderator will also participate as inspectors. One of these people will take on the role of the reader and another will serve as the recorder. All participants look for errors in the document and describe those errors to the other members of the inspection team, answering their questions until they understand the cause of the problem. Then the recorder records and classifies the type of error.

Similar inspections can be done for hardware. For the inspection of the design of a circuit module into which a VLSI device will be integrated, the participants will probably include the author, another person who has some expertise in module design, the designer of the VLSI device that will be added to the module after it is prototyped, a mechanical designer who is interested in the module's heat dissipation capabilities and its structural integrity, and a software developer whose software will be loaded and run on the module when all of the designs have been implemented. And finally, the moderator, who may or may not be a hardware developer, should be a person who understands the discussion that takes place during the meeting. This inspection meeting is similar to the software meeting in that the rolls of the reader and the recorder are filled by participants in the meeting.

As a result of the activities of the recorder and other members of the inspection team during the meeting, several reports are produced. They include a detailed error list that goes to the author and the moderator. An error summary, specifying the numbers and kinds of errors found, goes to the organization's inspection coordinator or analyst who is responsible for the overall inspection process on the project or in the organization in which the work is being done. The inspection report, which is a very short document identifying the work unit, its author, the date of the inspection meeting, the meeting participants, and whether or not the work was approved for

Figure 4.2   Inspection reports and their distribution.

baselining, goes to the project manager and to the manager to whom the author reports. Figure 4.2 shows the reports and their distribution.

As you can imagine, fully implementing a rigorous inspection process on a typical software/hardware development project can consume a significant amount of time and effort. To insure that appropriate resources are available for doing this work, the project manager needs to insure that several things need to be a part of the project plan. They include a listing of which tasks in the work breakdown structure will end with an inspection of the document created by that task; sufficient time scheduled at the end of the task to allow for the inspection to occur; assignments of moderators with and authors for each task that will end with an inspection; an estimate of the total number of inspections that will need to be conducted; an estimate of the total number of staff hours that will be required for authors, moderators, and other inspectors, taking into account the need in a design inspection, for example, to have requirements developers, designers, programmers, testers, and, perhaps, deployment support people involved; and a comprehensive inspection staffing plan that answers the following questions: What will be inspected? How will those items be inspected? Who will do the work? When will it be done? And how much will it cost?

That inspection staffing plan needs to include the time of the inspection coordinator, the authors, moderators, inter- and intragroup inspectors and the time for inspection training. Some rules of thumb for estimating the amount of effort that will be required are about 10 staff hours per thousand non-commented source lines of code for code inspections and about a half hour of staff time per page for other documents like the project plan, requirements, and test cases. Hardware inspections are particularly time-consuming, typically requiring approximately 50 staff hours for a VLSI device and approximately the same amount of effort for inspections of a moderately complex circuit module.

The typical costs of inspections range from about 5% to 15% of the project's total cost when they are done well. That seems like a lot, and some project managers will say, "There is no way that I can increase the overall project budget by that amount." This estimate does not mean that you will increase the project's budget by that amount. It does mean that if you spend 5–15% of the budget doing inspections, you will reduce the overall project cost by more than that amount. We are not going to show all of the logic behind that reasoning here, but virtually all economic studies that have been done on that subject support that conclusion (Brykczynski et al. 1993; Porter et al. 1997). For example, you will save more time and cost during development, testing, and initial field support than you spend on doing the work associated with inspections.

I once worked in an organization where I and the people in the department that I was managing decided to start doing these kinds of inspections. We struggled for about 2 years to get the level of inspection work up to about 3%, but we had little impact. At about that time, I got a new boss who decided that the whole larger organization was going to get seriously involved in doing inspections. He put a person in charge and gave that person full-time responsibility for developing the process, training employees, and analyzing results. We worked for several months and, finally, we were able to get up to 7% of our time devoted to inspections. Once we passed the 5% level, we could immediately see the results. While we were putting about 7% of our total effort into inspections the cost of development rework, testing, and field support decreased by approximately 15%, making the overall impact very positive across all of our projects.

We have just discussed what needs to be done by the development manager to assure that sufficient effort is available to do inspections. Now, what is in it for the project manager? Earlier, we looked at a figure like the one shown in Fig. 4.3. If I were the project manager, I would be able to see the results of business case development and requirements writing when those documents were finished. However,

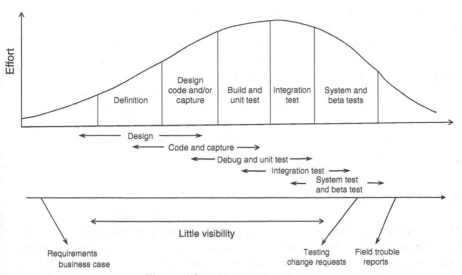

Figure 4.3 Period of little visibility.

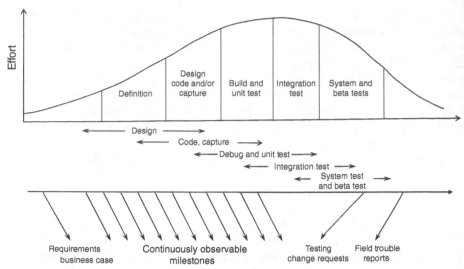

Figure 4.4   More visibility during design, coding, and capture.

from that point through the start of testing and the generation of change requests or failed tests, I would have very limited visibility of the status of tasks. I would have to depend on asking people who work on the project what the status of their work was. So, I would have really very little visibility of the end points of tasks during the long period from requirements approval through testing. When we put an inspection program into place and we inspect requirements, designs, and possibly coding and captured circuit designs, we have many more continuously observable milestones made up of the inspection report sign-offs by members of the inspection teams. If the availability of those inspection reports is used as visible end points for all of the tasks taking place during that time, I, as the project manager, will have much more information about the status of the project than I would otherwise have. Those extra task completions are shown in Fig. 4.4. Now I can react much more quickly and can take control when problems occur.

Like the cumulative task completion chart that we talked about during our planning lecture, it will be helpful if you prepare a chart like the one in Fig. 4.5 that shows as of each date on the horizontal axis how many inspections we plan to have completed. We will track and plot our actual results on this chart to see in an aggregate way how we are doing as compared to our plan.

4.2 TESTING

The second activity that requires special emphasis during the planning of a project is testing. It is sometimes considered by members of the development to be a second-rate specialty that requires little skill and technical knowledge. It is not and does require substantial technical expertise. In this section, we will explain how to

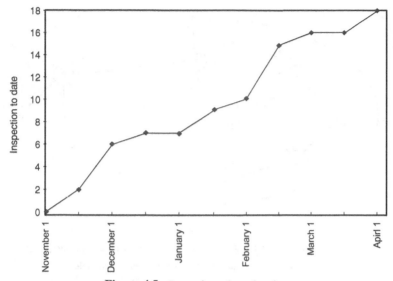

Figure 4.5 Inspections planned to date.

properly apply project management techniques to the testing portions of a project. We will provide an overview of testing, briefly discuss a variety of testing approaches and test types, talk about some testing principles and problems, and then discuss test monitoring.

When a problem is detected by a customer after the delivery of our work, the customer frequently asks, "Didn't you test the product before you released it?" When we explain that we tested the results of our work extensively, they might then respond by asking, "Well why didn't you test it completely?" The answer to that question is quite simple in that exhaustive testing is almost impossible. Let us look at a couple of examples.

In Fig. 4.6, we see a flow chart for a program with 11 control points. If we traced all of the possible paths through this program, we would find that there are 3×10^{10} paths. If each path could be tested in 1 second, it would take 976 years to exhaustively test this program. Similarly, for hardware, we have a simple example in Fig. 4.7. In that figure, we have a 40-pin random logic device. There are 2^{40} possible input/output states. Suppose we could execute one million tests per second. It would then take 300 hours to exhaustively test all combinations even if there are no sequential dependencies built into the device.

In the case of both hardware and software, we see that exhaustive testing of even these small parts of a typical system is virtually impossible. When we develop real pieces of hardware, we typically have circuit modules consisting of tens or hundreds of hardware devices at least as complex as the one shown in Fig. 4.7 and software running in that environment that is considerably larger and more complex than the simple program shown in Fig. 4.5. So, we have to admit that for real systems and applications that we develop, we can almost never do exhaustive testing.

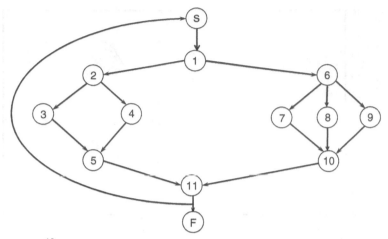

3×10^{10} possible paths at 1 test per second = 976 years!!!

Figure 4.6   Exhaustive testing is virtually impossible.

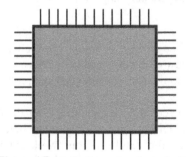

Figure 4.7   A 40-pin random logic device.

To make up for that lack of practicality, several systematic approaches have been developed which attempt to permit reasonably thorough, though not exhaustive, testing to be conducted in reasonable amounts of time. One of these approaches is black box or functional testing based on the functional specifications of an entire system or the parts of that system. Figure 4.8 illustrates what is meant by black box testing.

When black box testing is used to test a product, we use the functional specifications to determine what the system is supposed to do in response to input data when the initial state of the application is known. To use this method, we would set up its initial state, stimulate it by providing input data, then observe the actions taken and the changes in the state of the system. If the actions and the state transformations match what the specifications say that they should be, then we would declare that the test has been passed and no fault has been found. Black box testing is probably the most commonly used systematic testing approach. However, as shown in Table 4.1, there are many other approaches, some of which are shown in that figure and some of which are more appropriate than others for specific situations.

Stimuli   Responses

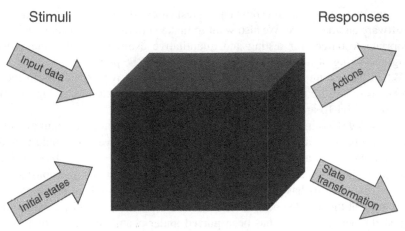

Figure 4.8   Black box testing.

Table 4.1   Some Other Systematic Approaches to Testing

Cause/effect
   Graphing
   Direct identification
   Good for nonsequence dependent testing
Transaction flow
   Useful for systems in which an input/output activity is part of a series of input/output
   steps
Syntax directed
   Effective for validation of input stream handling
State transition
   Best for validation of sequences of events
Equivalence partitioning
   To assist with choice of input, output, and state data
Boundary value analysis
   Using test stimuli at and around boundaries specified in requirements

---

We are not going to go into the definitions or methods used for each of these test methods. Rather, the point that we want to make here is that the theory available to assist with testing is extensive and, for a team member to do a good job of testing, he or she should be knowledgeable about this extensive theory and should be practiced in applying the theory to real applications. Very often, we find that the team members assigned to testing are the last people who happened to join the development team and are the least-skilled members of the team. This is usually done because of an assumption that testing will be done near the end of the project and that it requires the least knowledge and skill. In reality, that is not the case. Preparation for testing should start during the time that the project is being planned and when the requirements are being developed. This is so that lead testers can participate in project planning, so that they can participate in requirements and design inspections and so that they can spend time developing test cases while developers are designing the software and hardware. We also want to make sure that the project plan includes appropriate resources for testing and quantitative estimates of the rate at which testing and fixing of faults found can be included in the plan.

When the testing plan is being developed, the test representative on the core team needs to be sure that all stages of both internal and external testings as shown in Fig. 4.9 and 4.10 are included in the plan.

Figure 4.9 starts in the upper left part of the figure showing each unit of software or hardware being unit tested by its developer. The test coverage should include as many internal paths and states as practical. This is called white box testing, as opposed to black box testing, because it looks inside the units and considers how the units' functionality has been implemented. Some suggested entry criteria for unit testing are that the detailed design of the unit has been inspected by a team of peers and that the detailed design has been placed under change control. Some possible exit criteria are that test checklists have been created; unit test cases have been executed and passed; test results have been recorded; and a peer or the local team leader has approved the results of unit testing. When all test cases have been executed successfully, the implementation (code or circuit design/parts list) is placed under change control.

Pairwise and integration testing is done by either the individuals who have developed the units or by a separate integration group. Pairwise and integration

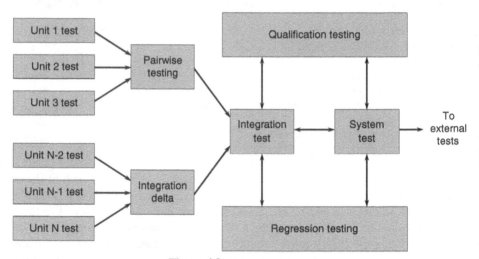

Figure 4.9   Internal test types.

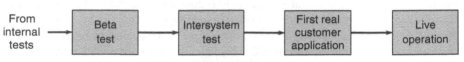

Figure 4.10   External test types.

testing are done to determine if the individual units communicate and operate properly with each other. Test coverage at these stages is sometimes just sanity checking of feature functionality and interunit interfaces. Some possible entry criteria for pairwise and integration testing are that unit testing has been completed and that all designs are under change control. Successful completion of integration test cases, resolution of all high-severity problems, and recording of unresolved problems in the change control system typically serve as exit criteria for these stages.

System testing must always be performed by testers who are different people from those who have developed the individual units and modules. Test coverage typically includes conformance to requirements, consistency with user documentation, ability to achieve capacity and reliability targets, and behavior under stress and error conditions. Some suggested entry criteria are completion of integration tests, system test cases placed under change control, and no outstanding high-priority change requests remaining from unit or integration testing. Exit criteria from the system test phase include the execution of all system test cases, no outstanding high-priority change requests, and completion of all regression tests with no outstanding change requests.

Regression testing is a part of system testing performed by system testers. The testing includes a determination of the effects of changes or additions to a previous version of the product. The entry criteria usually include the completion of integration testing and the baselining of regression test cases. The exit criteria should include passing of all regression tests and the recording of all regression test results.

Qualification testing refers to testing usually done by an outside agency, such as the Underwriters Laboratories, to confirm that the product adheres to specific safety standards if the product includes newly developed hardware and to radiation standards specified by the Federal Communications Commission for either commercial or residential use.

External testing, which means testing in the customer's environment, starts after internal testing has been completed with a beta test as shown in Fig. 4.10. It is the first test in the customer's environment. It is conducted jointly by the development team's system testers and customer representatives. Ideally, the test coverage would be the same tests that the customers will use to determine if the product is acceptable to them. The entry criteria should include the completion of system testing and no outstanding high-priority change requests due to faults found during internal testing. Exit criteria from beta testing should be all customer acceptance tests successfully run and no outstanding high-priority change requests.

If the application needs to interface with other applications in the customers' environment, there will typically be another stage during which interfaces to those other systems and joint operation will be tested. Testing during this stage is usually done jointly by the development team's system testers and representatives of the customer. The types of testing, entry criteria, and exit criteria are similar to those used for beta testing.

After beta testing and intersystem testing are complete, the application is usually turned over to the first real customer and, perhaps, other customers who put the product into live operation. The person on the core team who represents the testing function needs to insure that the project plan contains a description of what testing will be done and how it will be done, who will be doing each phase of testing, when it will be scheduled, and how much it will cost. Testing on large projects typically requires 20–30% of the project's overall budget.

4.3   REQUIREMENTS FOR SUCCESSFUL TESTING OPERATIONS

In addition to including appropriate processes and resources for testing, it is also necessary that a configuration control system, including source control, for both hardware and software, a method for recording test failures and resolutions of change requests initiated by test failures, and a maintenance review board to assign and prioritize faults and to change requests be in place. Detail test plans should be developed for all stages of testing. Adequate computing resources (computers and test environments) separate from those used by developers should be available. And a mechanism for monitoring testing progress must be in place. This includes a description of planned test cases, a quantification of test cases developed, the number of test cases executed, the number of test cases passed, the number of change requests opened, the number of change requests closed, and the severity of open change requests.

All testing, including unit and integration testing, must be planned. System testers should be made available as early as possible at the start of the project to both participate in the planning and to start developing test cases. Independent testers, separate from those doing development, must be used. Test plans and, in some cases, test cases should be inspected. Effective regression testing facilities must be provided after the first release of a new product. System test results should be demonstrated to the project manager and to the entire development team frequently. And rigorous configuration management, including a change control board and a change request process and system, must be in place.

Problems associated with testing that commonly appear are that at the time tests are scheduled for execution, requirements documents and user documentation are not available. Without requirements and without the user's instructions, testers cannot be expected to do their job. Some projects attempt to use testing as a substitute for high-quality designs. Sometimes system test time is compressed to make up for lost time during development of requirements and development. Very frequently, the difficulty of fault correction is underestimated or is not planned at all. Regression testing is sometimes overlooked, and stress, reliability, and error testing are omitted. When all of these problems occur simultaneously, system stability is usually never achieved and the project is likely to be canceled before its completion.

If, on the other hand, adequate test planning is included in the project plan, the project manager now has an additional view of the project in support of the monitoring process. In the first part of this chapter, we showed how an inspection process could be used to provide additional visibility of task completion during the design, code, and capture phases of the project. Likewise, during the unit, integration, and system testing phases, a comparison of testing results with the testing plan can fill the gap in Fig. 4.11, where more visibility is desired.

If the test plan contains quantitative estimates of the number of test cases developed, the number of test cases executed, and the number of test cases passed as shown in Fig. 4.12, it can be used as a basis for monitoring progress during the test phases of the project. When that is done and progress is monitored against these estimates, we have filled the gap where more visibility is desired as shown in Fig. 4.13.

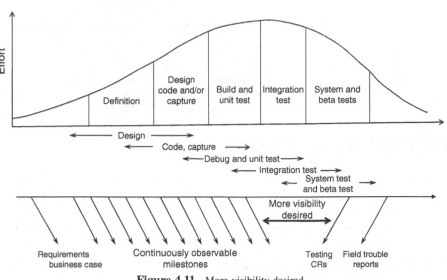

Figure 4.11   More visibility desired.

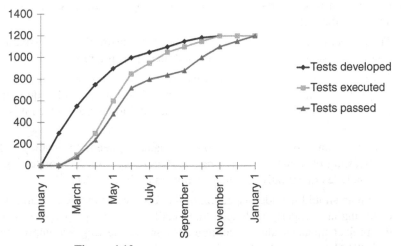

Figure 4.12   Quantitative estimates of testing progress.

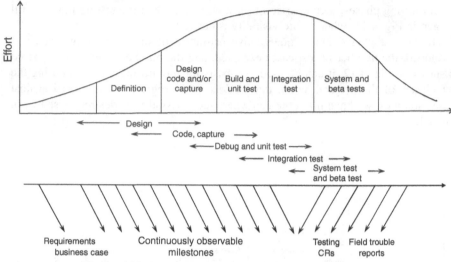

Figure 4.13   Task completions available throughout the project.

4.4   SOME THINGS TO REMEMBER

1. The project manager should plan inspections of responses to requests for information and proposals that involve the development of new software and/or hardware, customer requirements, designs, sometimes code, test plans, sometimes test cases, user documentation, deployment plans, and customer training course materials.

2. If these inspections are not planned and monitored, it is unlikely that they will get done well, or perhaps not get done at all. In that case, the project will incur higher costs and the project manager will not have sufficient status information to know the true status of the project until it is too late to do anything about it.

3. The project manager and the core team needs to insure that the testing function is represented on the core team and that appropriate testing is planned.

4. Testers need to be assigned somewhat earlier than they normally would be assigned, not only to help with planning, but also to assist with requirements and design inspections, to develop test cases and to be ready when it is time to execute the tests.

5. The test team, working with the project manager, needs to develop a thorough testing plan that includes adequate resources for integration testing and also includes quantitative profiles as illustrated in Fig. 4.11.

6. That plan should include inspection of the test plan to insure that all aspects of testing are properly included. And, finally, after the project gets started, the project manager should continually compare testing accomplishments with the plan.

CASE STUDY 4

Spend 20 minutes reading the following requirements document for a gas station control system (GSCS).

If you are working with other people, organize into groups of four or five and hold an inspection meeting. Each group will need to have a moderator, a recorder, a reader, and one person who will volunteer to play the part of the author of the document. Take approximately 45 minutes to conduct the inspection meeting. If you are working by yourself, read the document carefully and note any items that you believe to be defects.

Please look for the following classes of defects:

1. Ambiguous information
2. Extraneous information (E)
3. Inconsistent information (II)
4. Incorrect fact (IF)
5. Miscellaneous defect (MD)
7. Missing information (MI)

The recorder should record the page and requirement number for each defect, the defect class, and a short description of the defect on the Defect Report form that follows.

Defect No.	Page No.	Requirement No.	Defect Class	Description
1				
2				
3				
4				
5				
6				
7				
8				
9				
10				
11				
12				
13				
14				
15				
16				
17				
18				
19				
20				
21				
22				
23				

Defect No.	Page No.	Requirement No.	Defect Class	Description
24				
25				
26				
27				
28				
29				
30				

Source: From Basili et al. (2000). Reproduced with permission from IEEE © 2000 IEEE.

Requirements Document for a GSCS

Overview

This is an *excerpt* from a requirements document that describes a GSCS. The gas station allows customers to purchase gas (self-service) or to pay for maintenance work done on their cars. Some local businesses may have billing accounts set up so that the business is sent a monthly bill, rather than paying for each transaction at the time of purchase. There will always be a cashier on duty at the gas station to accept cash payments or to perform system maintenance as necessary.

The requirements in this document concern how the system receives payments from the customers. Customers have the option to be billed automatically at the time of their purchase or to be sent monthly bills and pay at that time. Customers can always pay via cash or credit card.

Glossary

Credit Card Reader.   The credit card reader is a separate piece of hardware mounted at each gas pump. The internal operations of the credit card reader and the communications between the GSCS and the card reader are outside the scope of this document. When the customer swipes his or her credit card through the card reader, the card reader reads the account number from the credit card and sends it to the GSCS. If the account number cannot be read correctly, an invalid token is sent to the GSCS instead.

Credit Card System.   The credit card system is a separate system, maintained by a credit card company. The internal operation of the credit card system and the communications between the GSCS and the credit card system are outside the scope of this document. The GSCS sends an account number and purchase amount to the credit card system in order to charge a customer's account; the credit card company later reimburses the gas station owner for the purchase amount.

Gas Pump.   The customer uses the gas pump to purchase gas from the gas station. The internal operations of the gas pump and the communications between the gas pump and the GSCS are outside the scope of this document. The gas pump is responsible for recognizing when the customer has finished dispensing gas and for communicating the amount of gas and dollar amount of the purchase to the GSCS at this time.

Gas Pump Interface.   The gas pump interface is a separate piece of hardware mounted at each gas pump. The internal operation of the gas pump interface and the communications between the gas pump interface and the GSCS are outside the scope of this document. The gas pump interface receives a message from the GSCS and displays it for use by the customer. The gas pump interface also allows the customer to choose from a number of options and communicates the option chosen to the GSCS.

Cashier's Interface. The cashier's interface is a separate piece of hardware mounted at the cashier's station. The internal operations of the cashier's interface and the communications between the cashier's interface and the GSCS are outside the scope of this document. The cashier's interface is capable of displaying information received from the GSCS. The cashier's interface is also able to accept input from the cashier, including numeric data, and to communicate it to the GSCS.

Functional Requirements
1. After the purchase of gasoline, the gas pump reports the number of gallons purchased to the GSCS. The GSCS updates the remaining inventory.
2. After the purchase of gasoline, the gas pump reports the dollar amount of the purchase to the GSCS. The maximum value of a purchase is $999.99. The GSCS then causes the gas pump interface to query the customer as payment type. The customer may choose to be billed at the time of purchase or to be sent a monthly bill. If billing is to be done at the time of purchase, the gas pump interface queries the customer as to whether payment will be made by cash or by credit card. If the purchase is to be placed on a monthly bill, the gas pump interface instructs the customer to see the cashier. If an invalid or no response is received, the GSCS bills at the time of purchase.
3. If the customer has selected to pay at the time of purchase, he or she can choose to pay by cash or by credit card. If the customer selects cash, the gas pump interface instructs the customer to see the cashier. If the customer selects credit card, the gas pump interface instructs the customer to swipe his or her credit card through the credit card reader. If an invalid or no selection is made, the GSCS will use the credit card option, which is the default.
4. If payment is to be made by credit card, then the card reader sends the account number to the GSCS. If the GSCS receives an invalid card number, then a message is sent to the gas pump interface asking the customer to swipe the card through the card reader again. After the account number is obtained, the account number and purchase price are sent to the credit card system, and the GSCS and gas pump interface are reset to their initial state. The purchase price sent can be up to $10,000.
5. If payment is to be made by cash, the cashier is responsible for accepting the customer's payment and for making change, if necessary. When payment is complete, the cashier indicates this on the cashier's interface. The GSCS and the gas pump interface then return to the initial state.
6. If payment is to be made by monthly bill, the purchase price is displayed on the cashier's interface. The cashier selects an option from the cashier's interface, alerting the GSCS that the payment will be placed on a monthly bill. The GSCS then prompts the cashier to enter the billing account number. The customer must give the billing account number to the cashier, who then enters it at the cashier's interface. If a valid billing account number is entered, then the billing account number, purchase price, and a brief description of the type of transaction are logged. If an invalid billing account number is entered, an error message is displayed and the cashier is prompted to enter it again. The cashier must also have the option to cancel the

operation, in which case the cashier's interface reverts to showing the purchase price and the cashier can again either receive cash or indicate that monthly billing should be used.

7. To pay a monthly bill, the customer must send the payment along with the billing account number. The cashier enters monthly payments by first selecting the appropriate option from the cashier's interface. The GSCS then sends a message to the cashier's interface prompting the cashier to enter the billing account number, the amount remitted, and the type of payment. If any of these pieces of information are not entered or are invalid, payment cannot be processed; an error message will be displayed; and the cashier's interface will be returned to the previous screen. If the type of payment is credit card, the credit card account number must also be entered, and then the paper credit card receipt will be photocopied and stored with the rest of the year's receipts.

8. Unless otherwise specified, if the GSCS receives invalid input, it will send an error message to the cashier's interface. The cashier will be expected to take appropriate action, which may involve shutting the system down for maintenance.

Nonfunctional Requirements

1. The system must always respond to customer input within 1 minute.

2. The system should be easy to extend, so that if necessary, another payment option (e.g., bank card) can be added with minimal effort.

REFERENCES

BASILI V., F. SHULL, I. RUS, and O. LAITENBERGER (2000) Improving software inspections by using reading techniques. International Conference on Software Engineering (ICSE) Tutorial, June 2000.

BRYKCZYNSKI B. and D. A. WHEELER (1993) An annotated bibliography on software inspections. *ACM SIGSOFT Software Engineering Notes* **18** (1), 81–88.

FAGAN M. E. (1976) Design and code inspections to reduce errors in program development. *IBM Systems Journal* **15** (3), 192–211.

GILRAY J. J. (1996) Applying the code inspection process to hardware descriptions. *Hewlett-Packard Journal* **48** (February), 68–72.

PORTER A, H. SIY, C. A. TOMAN, and L. G. VOTTA (1997) An experiment to assess the cost-benefit of code inspections in large scale software development. *IEEE Transactions on Software Engineering* **23** (6), 329–346.

Chapter 5

The Organizing Process

The topic of this chapter is the second of the major project management processes—organizing. It will discuss a variety of structures that are available for organizing development work and will outline some of the advantages and disadvantages of each. Then it will provide some suggestions for getting a new project started and for managing the ongoing execution of the work. Finally, it will present one of the most common problems faced by managers of software and hardware development work, conflicts among members of the development team and conflicts with and among stakeholders, and some methods for resolving these conflicts.

Figure 5.1 shows a high-level view of the organizing process. Like the planning process, the process looks quite simple at a high level. Inputs to the process are the business case, or contract, which defines the contributions to the business that will be made by your project; the project plan, which answers the questions "What are you going to do?" "How are you going to do it?" "Who is going to do it?" "When will it be done?" and "How much will it cost?"; and the architecture document, which helps answer the question "What are you going to do?" The output of the process is a well-oiled, fully functioning, high-performance team. That looks simple, but it typically requires even more effort and time than the planning process requires.

Let us start by defining what we mean by a high-performance team. High-performance teams are frequently discussed in the literature related to the organizing process. Most authors, when defining high-performance teams, say that the team needs to have interdependency among its members. The members of the team need to have a good reason for working together and understand that reason well. The team members have to have a commitment to work together, and they need to be willing to accept accountability for the team's results. They also need a moderate, but not a destructive, level of competition among the members of the team. It would be nice to always develop a high-performance team as an outcome of the organizing process. However, when we really look for high-performance teams, we find that it is very difficult to find them.

Those reported in the literature typically include only five or six members and usually have a very short-term objective. It is very difficult, if not impossible, to find high-performance teams that have 10, 20, or 30 members, which are typical for

Managing the Development of Software-Intensive Systems, by James McDonald
Copyright © 2010 John Wiley & Sons, Inc.

software development projects and teams. But producing a high-performance team is a good objective for a project manager.

5.1   TYPICAL ORGANIZATIONAL STRUCTURES

Let us discuss the three typical organizational structures that are commonly seen in organizations.

The first is called a functional structure, a diagram of which is shown in Fig. 5.2. In this structure, people who supervise, or manage, each of the functions carried out by the organization report to the business leaders of the organization. They, in turn, supervise all of the people in the organization who perform that function. For example, function 1 might be requirements engineering; function 2 might be software design and coding; function 3 might be testing; and function 4 might be hardware design.

In this structure, there are no project managers. Projects work their way through the organization. There are frequently conflicts related to project priorities, and many of the decisions about which person should work on which project go to the business leader for resolution. The emphasis in functional organizations is on becoming the best they can be at performing their functional specialties. This is because the person

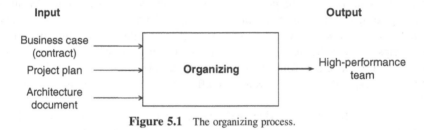

Figure 5.1   The organizing process.

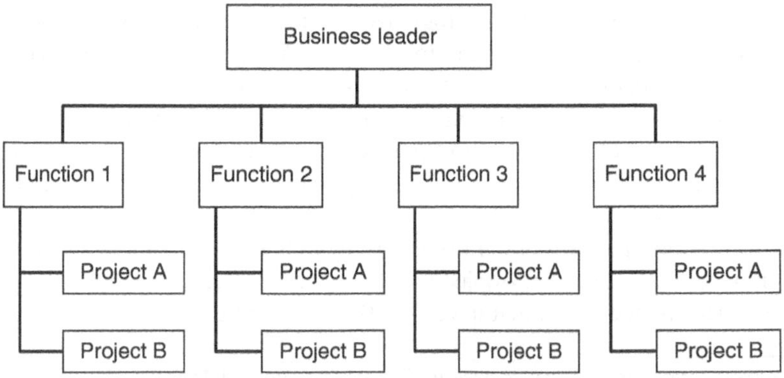

Figure 5.2   Functional organization structure.

to whom they report, and who evaluates their performance, has primary responsibility for that same function. This structure is frequently used in manufacturing organizations.

The second structure is called the project structure. It is illustrated in Fig. 5.3. In this structure, the primary responsibility of the people reporting to the business leader is for the projects being done by the organization. In this case, they are projects A, B, C and D. The people performing each of the functions required for each project report to the person who is responsible for that project and the person filling the project boxes are the project managers. So, for project A, the people responsible for functions 1, 2, and 3 all report directly to project A's project manager. Those working on project B report directly to project B's project manager. This structure shifts emphasis from the functional specialties of the functional project structure to the projects. It improves project communications because the path for serious and important communications is shorter than it was in the functional structure. However, on the downside, it makes less efficient use of resources. For example, in Fig. 5.3, all four projects require function 3. Suppose that each project requires only one-fourth of a function 3 person's time. However, according to the theory of this structure, there would be four different people doing that function even though only the time of one person doing function 3 is required. The people in the function 3 boxes will spend three-fourths of their time either doing nothing or performing other functions for which they do not have any particular expertise. This structure also encourages both project members to work themselves out of a job. When we defined a project, we said that a project has a limited duration and a definite end. So, as projects are finishing, the manager either needs to find a new project that makes use of the skills of the team or to find jobs for himself or herself, as well as for members of the team, on other projects. This structure is common in the construction industry.

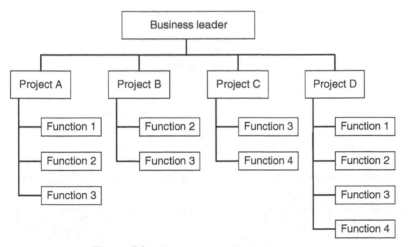

Figure 5.3 The project organizational structure.

The third common organizational structure, shown in Fig. 5.4, is called the matrix structure. It is a combination of the functional and project structures. In the matrix structure, we have managers who are responsible for the functional specialties reporting to the business leader and project managers who are responsible for projects also reporting to the business leader. People performing the various functions report to both the functional manager and the project manager. This structure is usually used when projects being done by the organization require all the functional specialties. It is used when resources cannot be duplicated for each project. On the downside, employees have two bosses and individual employees frequently have conflicting demands on their time. Use of the matrix structure requires very clear specification of the roles and responsibilities of everyone in the organization.

This structure, sometimes with variations, is often used by software and hardware development organizations. It has many variations. In the last industrial organization that I managed, we used a structure like this, with a twist, in that the same people who filled the functional managers' positions also filled project managers' positions. We had eight projects under way, each employing between 5 and 15 people, with 6 functional managers, each of whom managed one or two projects, and I, as the organizational manager, managed one of the projects.

The chart in Fig. 5.5 (Youker 1977) shows the amount of authority that the project manager has in each of these organizational structures. On the horizontal axis, we are plotting the authority of the project manager, and on the vertical axis, we are plotting the percent of the people in the organization who are working in a functional structure. By authority of the project manager, we mean the amount of authority that the project manager has for assigning individual resources to tasks on the project. It does not mean his or her ability to crack a whip to get the tasks or projects finished on time. At the left we have a functional organization structure with no project manager and 100% of the employees working in a functional structure and, of course, no authority resting with the project manager. Through the middle of the chart, we move from a part-time project manager to a full-time project manager to a project office, with a project manager and a support team using a

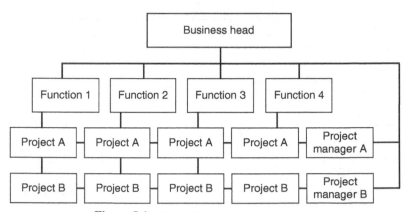

Figure 5.4 The matrix organizational structure.

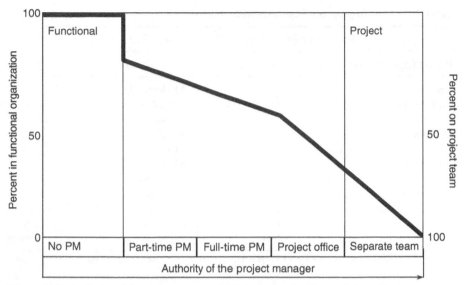

Figure 5.5   Authority of the project manager (PM) (reproduced with permission of Project Management Publications from Youker (1977)).

variety of matrix organizations, fewer of the members of the organization working in a functional structure until we get to the right edge with separate project teams, no one working in a functional structure and maximum authority for the project manager to assign resources to tasks. So, we see that as we move from left to right, the authority invested in the project manager increases.

Now, let us look at which organizational structure is best for which projects. Table 5.1, which comes from the same source as Fig. 5.5, shows several characteristics of projects in the first column and levels of those characteristics across each row. So, for example, if the uncertainty associated with your project is low, a functional structure is best. If uncertainty is moderate to high, the matrix organization is best. And, if uncertainty is clearly high, then a project organizational structure is best. The way you would use this chart is to classify your project based on each characteristic, and for each characteristic, put a check mark in the column that best matches your project. When you finish doing this for uncertainty, technology, complexity, and so on, determine which column contains most check marks. That will be the best structure based on the nature of your project. If you get approximately equal numbers of check marks in two or three of the columns, then it probably makes little difference which structure is used. As we indicated earlier, project structures are common in the construction industry. Suppose our project was not a software/hardware project but was the construction of a high-rise building. That project would typically have a high degree of uncertainty, relatively new technology, which in this case would be based on the construction materials, high complexity, long duration (typically 3–4 years for high-rise buildings), large size, with probably several thousand different people and resources being required, usually important, at least to the developer who is footing the bill, usually one customer, high dependency within the

Table 5.1   Most Appropriate Organizational Structure

Project Characteristic	Most Appropriate Type of Organizational Structure		
	Functional	Matrix	Project
Uncertainty	Low	Moderate–high	High
Technology	Standard	Complex	New
Complexity	Low	Medium	High
Duration	Short	Medium	Long
Size	Small	Medium	Large
Importance	Low	Medium	High
Customer	Diverse	Few(three to four)	One
Interdependence within	Low	Medium	High
Interdependence between	High	Medium	Low
Time criticality	Low	Moderate	High
Differentiation	Low	Low–high	Medium

Source: Reproduced with permission of Project Management Publications from Youker (1977).

project and usually low dependency with other construction projects, usually very critical time constraints, and, finally, a medium amount of differentiation from buildings that have been built in the past. With all of our check marks in the far-right column, the project structure would probably be the best structure for this project.

So, the most appropriate organization structure for a project depends upon the nature of the project. It also depends on the management style of the parent organization and the personal capabilities of people in the organization who might be available to manage projects. If the upper management is not willing to turn complete responsibility for projects over to one person, we would be unlikely to see project structures in that organization. If there are no people with the ability to manage all aspects of projects available in the organization, we would probably not see matrix structures or project structures. The project manager's job is typically most difficult in a matrix organization. So, organizations that want to use that structure need to be sure that their project managers are well trained and suited for working in a complicated environment.

5.2   TEAM BUILDING

Now, let us shift gears and spend some time talking about building teams. To build a good team, and maybe even to approach a high-performance team, the project manager needs to recruit team members, set the climate for team development, negotiate appropriate goals, clarify team members' roles, facilitate, and sometimes make, appropriate decisions, and monitor and control all of the tasks being done by the team. Team building should include active participation by all managers and technical contributors who will contribute significantly to the project. It should include part-time and full-time members of the team and should include representation from other parts of the organization who will provide support to the team.

The project manager needs to negotiate to obtain members of the team. If you are the project manager, you should not settle for "second best." However, unless your team is very small in size, like two or three, do not expect to get everyone that you want. You need to develop a detailed project plan. You need to organize the team by assigning tasks to people or groups as specified in your project plan. You need to circulate a task–responsibility matrix so that everyone knows who is responsible for each task. The project manager should hold a kickoff meeting, at which you should try to get the team members to know each other, establish working relationships, review what you will be doing, and identify problem areas.

The project manager needs to obtain commitments from team members to complete the tasks to which they have been assigned on schedule. This is absolutely necessary, although it is sometimes a slow process. On almost every project for which I have been the project manager, there has been at least one person who says, "I don't think I can complete that task in the time you have allocated to it." And, even after I have done some cajoling, they have not been willing to commit. I normally handle a problem like this by asking the person to start working on the task and to get back together after a week or two to discuss how they feel about it then. Usually, after they have gotten more deeply involved, they will finally agree to commit to the date, and they usually do make that date. However, if they cannot agree, they need to be placed somewhere else, either on another project or on another task.

Project managers need to build lines of communication, both inside and outside the team. They need to insure that team members understand and pay attention to each other. I have occasionally been running a project meeting when I have noticed someone dozing at the far end of the room when one of their team mates is speaking. When I see that happen for the first time, I make sure that I address a question to the person who is not paying attention by saying something like, "Josh, what do you think of what Carmen just said?" If I get a response that does not answer the question, I simply repeat the question and allow the dozers to respond, if they can. If they say that they do not have a response, I will repeat what their teammate said and perhaps suggest a possible response. One incident like that usually fixes the problem for everyone on the team for the entire duration of the project.

The project manager is directly responsible for communications with higher management and other stakeholders. That does not mean that he or she is the only member of the team who can or should talk with higher management, but the project manager must insure that higher management receives all the information that they need to have. One way to insure this is to ask stakeholders in advance what they would routinely like to know about the project and when they would like to know it. Then routinely provide written answers to their questions or arrange face-to-face meetings during which the necessary information is exchanged.

If you have been asked to manage a team and you find that you are not personally able to get the team to jell, you might want to get professional help to conduct some team-building exercises. People who do that kind of consulting work are usually very good and usually do not charge exorbitant amounts for their services.

5.3 TEAM MAINTENANCE

Once you get the team started, there are some ongoing things that need to be done to maintain the team. Here are some suggestions:

1. Keep team members informed about recent developments, both in the project and in the surrounding larger organization as well as about customer plans or actions. There is nothing worse for team morale than to have things happen in either the customer's organization, the parent organization, or in the project that comes as a major surprise to members of the team.

2. It is a good idea to occasionally have an external speaker come to a project meeting to emphasize the importance of the project to the organization.

3. The project manager can provide exposure for team members by giving them major roles in each project meeting. For example, if there are five people working on the project whose major role is testing, you can rotate responsibility among those five team members for providing an update on the progress of work related to testing.

4. Publicize the team's work in any way that you can.

5. Finally, try to remove roadblocks that the team is experiencing. Here is one example of roadblock removal. A few years ago, I was working with a team that needed some Sun workstations and a particular release of the Sun Solaris operating system to start the next phase of the project. This happened at a point in time when the larger organization started to have year-end financial problems. So, the word went out from on high that nothing could be purchased until after the end of the fiscal year. The team was stymied and could not continue its work. Fortunately, I had a friend with whom I had gone to college 20 years earlier who had just gotten a job with a Sun reseller. I called him and explained our problem. After I assured him that we would be able to make the purchase shortly after the end of the year, he said, "I have four of the workstations in my car. Which version of the operating system do you need?" He stopped by the next day to deliver two systems to the team, and their work continued, uninterrupted. That is a good example of what I mean by helping to remove roadblocks.

5.4 MANAGING CONFLICTS

Sometimes, after you have built your well-oiled fully functioning high-performance project team, you see symptoms of poor teamwork such as frustration, conflict or unhealthy competition among team members, unproductive meetings after which you hear members of the team say, "That was a waste of time. I don't know why we continue to have meetings at which nothing gets done," or, sometimes, lack of trust or confidence in organizational management.

All of these are really symptoms of conflict either within the team or between the team and the project stakeholders.

We can do several things to address conflicts. The first and easiest is avoiding conflict before it begins. Here are a few ways to do that:

1. By really understanding the customers' needs and expectations

2. By insuring that team members understand both their parent organization's business needs as well as the team's internal or external customers' needs. By our parent organization's needs, we are referring to the parent organization's need to make a profit every quarter and every year, or, if it is a government or nonprofit organization, the need to stay within a specified budget. I have frequently heard team members say things like, "We really need to do more or do things better to get this job done right." When you hear those comments, it is usually worth digging into their meaning to determine if they mean that the organization should put more effort into the project. That presents a good opportunity to remind them of the organization's overall profit or budget needs or constraints.

3. Finally, by having a comprehensive and detailed project plan that is understood by all members of the project team, we can go a long way toward helping team members understand how and why we are doing things as we are.

5.5 RESOLUTION OF CONFLICTS

If you find that, in spite of all you have done to avoid conflict, it still occurs, there are five very standard ways to resolve conflicts. By resolution, we mean the removal of the underlying causes of a conflict. The first two methods that are listed in Fig. 5.6, withdrawal and smoothing, are only temporary fixes that delay resolution. Compromising, forcing, and problem solving offer the potential for really resolving the source of conflicts.

Withdrawal means trying to avoid the conflict entirely. This style is typified by delegating controversial decisions, accepting default decisions, and not wanting to hurt anyone's feelings. It can sometimes be appropriate when victory is impossible, when the controversy is trivial, or when someone else is in a better position to resolve the problem.

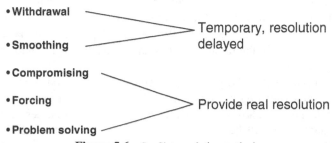

Figure 5.6 Conflict resolution methods.

Smoothing is basically making the assumption that the controversy does not exist. For example, if your project team has a conflict with another team, you might say, "Let's assume they don't exist. We need to get through only a couple of more weeks to complete this project. Please don't respond to them or request anything of them." This technique is sometimes effective when the issue will go away shortly without any overt action.

Now let us talk about the other three methods, all of which hold some promise of permanently resolving conflict. They are compromising, forcing, and problem solving.

Compromising is a search for alternatives that provide some satisfaction to both parties in the conflict. For conflicts within the project team, the manager should ask the parties to first privately discuss the issues. To make this work, both parties to the conflict must be able to understand the issue and to describe them to the manager. Then, if the conflict is not resolved, the manager should offer to help. Frequently, this is the only way to resolve what we might call personality conflicts. As an example of this, several years ago, I had a male member of a project team come to me to complain that a female team member, Patricia, who happened to be very pretty, would not pay any attention to him on either technical or other matters. I asked if he had discussed the issue with her. He answered, "No, this isn't something that I would feel comfortable talking with her about." So, I made a deal with him. I said that if he would agree to have a private conversation with her to determine if they could resolve the issue, and if the problem could not be resolved, I would intervene and try to help. He reluctantly agreed.

About 2 weeks later, I saw him and asked if they had the conversation. He reported that they did. My next question was "Do I need to become involved?" He said that they had resolved the issue and that my involvement would not be necessary. Being a curious person, I asked if he would be willing to describe the problem again and the resolution they reached. He, somewhat sheepishly, explained that Patricia had a hearing impairment and the resolution was simply that when he passed her in the hallway, all he needed to do was say "Hello" to her at a sufficient volume so that she could hear him. This is a great example of the kinds of issues that sometimes, because of unknown information, cause interpersonal conflicts.

The next method is forcing. It basically means punching the other party out, purposely not paying attention to them, and pushing your own point of view. This sometimes provides a permanent resolution but seldom works for conflicts within the team because remember that the members of a high-performance team need to be dependent on each other. It will also sometimes work for conflicts outside the team when you are very sure that you will never be dependent on that other party or group for assistance in the future. It is not an approach that I would recommend under most circumstances.

Problem solving is the third effective method. This method treats the conflict by examining and evaluating the alternatives. If it is a conflict inside the team, the manager should get the parties to logically discuss the alternatives and the measures of goodness that will be used to make the decision with each other in the presence of the manager. The manager would list the alternatives on the left side of a whiteboard or a flip chart. Across the top, he or she would list the measures that we plan to use to evaluate the alternatives, such as cost, reliability, and ease of implementation. Then, we would fill in the impact of each alternative on each of those measures. Sometimes, the resolution becomes obvious when this has been done and the issue gets resolved with little further discussion. However, if there are differences of opinion about the impact of alternatives on the measures or about the importance of the various measures, the project manager might need to make an arbitrary decision about which alternative to select. When this happens, project managers need to be careful that they do not give the impression that they are playing favorites among the members of the team. If there is no clear answer and the manager needs to make an arbitrary decision, he needs to explain what decision he made, and why, so that no one feels offended or left out of the decision making. For simple decisions where there were only two alternatives, I sometimes just flipped a coin in the presence of the parties and made the decision based on whether heads or tails were showing after the flip.

5.6 SOME THINGS TO REMEMBER

The most important things we have discussed in this chapter are the following:

1. The project manager needs to get the team organized and to lobby for the right structure.
2. He or she needs to recruit a strong team and get it off to a good start.
3. When symptoms of conflict appear, the project manager needs to act to resolve those conflicts quickly.

CASE 5   *The Shared Office*

Purpose

1. To think about, and perhaps to discuss, how to resolve personality conflicts that sometimes arise among members of a project team

Background

Victor and Dennis, who are members of your team, share an office. It is not a very big office, but it is the only space that is available in the current space crunch. These two people could not be more different. They seem to be at each other's throats all the time and you wish that you could separate them, but the fact is that there is no place to put them. The latest thing that happened is that Victor just came into your office to complain that Dennis threw all of Victor's books on the floor that were on the top shelf of the common book case. Victor is extremely upset.

Victor's View of the Situation

You have had just about enough! You are EXTREMELY UPSET. It is bad enough that you have to share offices with Dennis, a nosy and messy idiot, but now he is purposely messing up your things. You came into your office and found that Dennis had thrown on the floor all the books that you had carefully placed on the top shelf of the shared bookcase. This is enough! You told him that next time he does something like that, he is going to be sorry. He is also a pig. There are pieces of half-eaten fruits and sandwiches all over his desk. But he probably cannot see them due to the piles of junk on his desk. He is always taking things from your desk and you even suspect that he has been going through your drawers, although you have not caught him. The day you do you will......!!@*!! But in the meantime, you want your manager to make Dennis stop taking your things or else you are going to take things into your own hands. You have to talk with your manager about it right now!

Dennis' View of the Situation

You share an office with Victor. Well, it is really more like a closet than an office. Victor is a real idiot and has all these personal friends at work that are not at all connected with your project. They hang around Victor's desk like flies. It is hard to concentrate with people coming in and out and talking there all the time. You would say something about it, but Victor is hypersensitive. As it is, you have put up with a lot and you just about had enough. The latest thing that happened is that this morning, you were looking for a document that you needed (and which one of Victor's "visitors" probably threw away like they have done in the past). You are sure that you had put it on the top shelf of the shared bookcase so you started looking for it. Since you could not find it at first, you decided to look very thoroughly. So you took everything that was on the top shelf and you put it carefully on the floor (given your crowded quarters, there was no place else to put them) while you looked for the missing document. Just then, the phone rang and you answered. While you were on the phone, Victor came in the room and starting yelling and screaming obscenities at you. Well ... you are simply not going to take that kind of talk from anyone. As soon as you finish on the phone, you are going to go to your boss and tell him exactly what you think of Victor and ask him to make Victor stop talking to you that way and to get his "friends" to stay out of your things. YOU ARE VERY UPSET.

Activity

This an obvious case of interpersonal conflict and one that you will need to address immediately. Put yourself in the role of the manager of this team. How will you go about resolving this conflict? We talked in this chapter about several ways of resolving conflicts, some of which were likely to be successful for interpersonal conflicts, and some of which were not. First, select the approach that you would like to use. Then, plan how you are going to implement that resolution.

You will probably need to consider the following things:

1. Should you have your first discussion with Victor and Dennis together or talk to them separately?
2. If you decide to talk with them separately, what should you do and what should you try to accomplish during that discussion?
3. If you have chosen to start by talking with them separately, should you follow up by having a discussion with both of them together?
4. When, and if, you get them together, how should you start the conversation?
5. What should you try to accomplish during a conversation with both of them?
6. Should you suggest how they need to behave and provide them with "office rules" that they need to follow?

7. Should you get them to brainstorm some alternatives and get them to agree on a resolution?
8. At the end of the conversation with both of them, what do you want to achieve?
9. What follow-up should you do after such a joint meeting?

Output

Prepare an analysis of this dilemma and write a recommendation to the manager about how he or she should approach this conflict. If you are in a class and you are doing this exercise as a group, you should develop a brief presentation to describe to other members of the class how this situation should be managed.

REFERENCE

YOUKER R. (1977) Organizational alternatives for project management. *Project Management Quarterly* **8** (1), 18–24.

Chapter 6

The Monitoring Process

The subject of this chapter is monitoring. As shown in Fig. 6.1, the inputs to the monitoring process are the detailed project plan, a well-oiled, fully functioning project team, and information about the status of the project from inspections and other reporting mechanisms. The outputs from the monitoring process are deviations from the plan. The purpose of monitoring is to find those deviations then to exercise the fourth project management process, control, which is aimed at fixing problems. The monitoring process is the easiest of the four major project management processes to implement. However, the control processes is much more difficult, often requiring creativity and extremely close monitoring of its implementation.

The basic concept of monitoring is making a comparison of progress against the projections contained in the project plan. To do this, we need to have a detailed project plan with planned frequent, specific, and visible task completions. We need to be able to quantify our expectations and our progress. We need to have a time and place to share those results with the project team and a standard way to report the results to all stakeholders. Therefore, the monitoring process requires a detailed plan with frequent, specific, visible milestones (task completions). The visible task completions that we have previously discussed provide us with a basis for quantifying the status of the project. There needs to be a forum where the plan and the actual progress can be reported and discussed with the team. And there needs to be a standard reporting process to deliver this information to stakeholders beyond the development team.

Project audits and reviews, which we will discuss in Chapter 9, are also a part of the monitoring process.

6.1 PROJECT MEETINGS

We have previously discussed how a detailed plan can be produced and the importance of visible objectives (task completions). The forum that we will use for sharing results with the project team is the project meeting. We want to define what we mean by a project meeting, talk about a typical agenda for that meeting, show some

Managing the Development of Software-Intensive Systems, by James McDonald
Copyright © 2010 John Wiley & Sons, Inc.

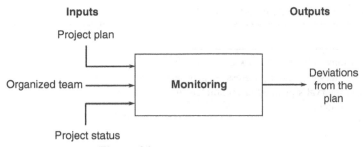

Figure 6.1   The monitoring process.

examples of what gets reported and discussed, the documentation that should be produced, and a few warnings about what can go wrong during project meetings.

Project meetings are periodic meetings of the project team to discuss project goals, progress against those goals, the general status of the project, and issues that are bound to occur along the way. They are usually held every 2–4 weeks after the project gets under way. Sometimes, when a new project is getting started, they need to be held every week. The important thing is that they should be held on the same day, at the same time, and in the same place every time.

Everyone who is participating in the project should attend. That includes the project manager, who should chair the meeting, all of the members of the team, and, occasionally, guests, such as senior management, customers, and marketing or sales representatives.

In preparation for the meeting, the project manager needs to let everyone know what the agenda will be, what data will be discussed, what action items are pending, and anything else of significance that will be discussed. For large projects, it is helpful if the project manager gathers most of the data that will be presented in advance so that the agenda can be shaped to match the needs of the project and the meeting completed as efficiently as possible.

Table 6.1 shows a typical agenda for a project meeting. The meeting starts with a review of the tasks that were scheduled to be completed since the last meeting followed by a review of the status of those tasks. Hopefully, most of them would have been finished during that interval. Then, the task completions for the next interval and the team members who are responsible for them are reviewed. This serves as a warning to those responsible for those tasks that they should be prepared to discuss those tasks during the next project meeting. Next, any action items that were pending for resolution from the last meeting are reviewed and new items, usually having to do with tasks that have not been successfully completed since the last meeting, are added to the list along with the name or names of team members who are responsible for resolving them. For pending action items from the last meeting, those team members who were assigned responsibility for them are expected to report on their status.

Then the project manager and the team review the major current project risks and give members of the team an opportunity to add additional risks as part of this

Table 6.1 Typical Agenda for a Project Meeting

Agenda
Review last interval's planned task completions.
Review last interval's actual progress → generate new action items.
Review next interval's planned task completions.
Review action items.
Review risks.
Review appropriate project data.
Highlight most significant issues.
Demonstrate progress.

discussion. It is important that contingency or mitigation plans for major risks have been developed and updated as necessary.

The project manager then reviews data related to the project schedule, the inspection program, testing, quality, and cost/staffing. Data on those topics are shown in Figs. 6.2 through 6.9 and in Tables 6.2 and 6.3.

From our planning discussion, schedule items are usually related to tasks, their durations, and their completion dates as we have shown on the Gantt chart in Fig. 6.2. We also talked about the need for monitoring task completions. In Fig. 6.3, we have plotted the cumulative number of planned milestones, as shown by the dashed line and the actual number of completed milestones or tasks, shown by the solid line. This project started in July of 2009. It got off to a slow start as illustrated by the actual line being below the planned line. They caught up in December and January, but started to fall behind again in February. Charts like this one are good overall indicators of progress. However, to really know where you stand, you need to go to a detailed list of tasks as shown in Table 6.2.

That table shows a typical list of tasks with the initials of the person who is responsible for each, the planned or target date, what I call the current working view (CWV in this table), and the actual completion date. What we really need to see in this detailed view is whether any of the tasks that have not been completed on time are tasks that are on the critical path, because remember that if a critical path task is not completed on its planned schedule, the completion of the entire project is delayed. So, the project manager needs to pay special attention to the critical path tasks.

Another set of data that the manager wants to review at project meetings is the data flowing out of the inspection process. In Fig. 6.4, we see the preparation rate and inspection rate for inspections during the months of October through January. For this project, we see that the inspection rate is approximately the same as the expected rate. The preparation rate is a little low as compared with the expected preparation rate. This, by itself, does not indicate that anything is wrong with the inspection process, but the project manager will probably also want to look at the actual fault found rates as compared to the expected fault found rates to determine if the process is working as it should.

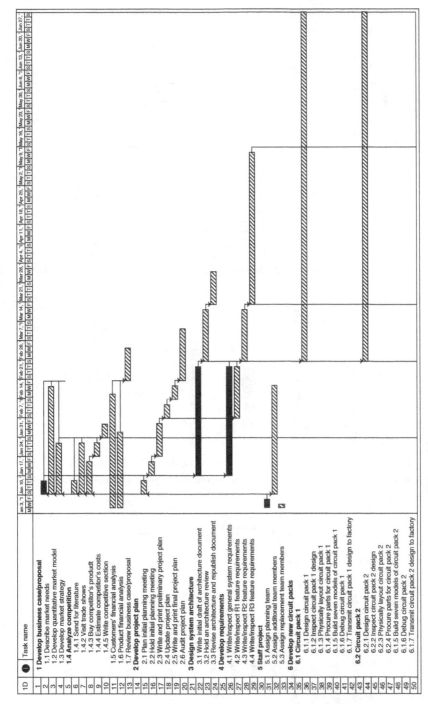

Figure 6.2 Gantt chart developed during the planning process.

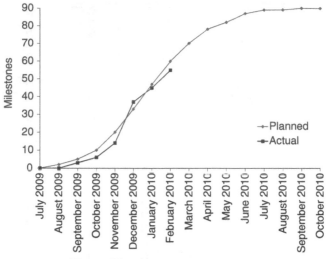

Figure 6.3   Monitoring task completions.

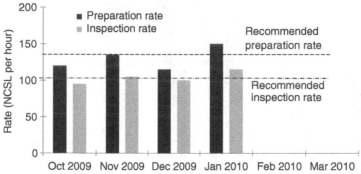

Figure 6.4   Preparation and inspection rates for inspections. NCSL, noncommented source lines.

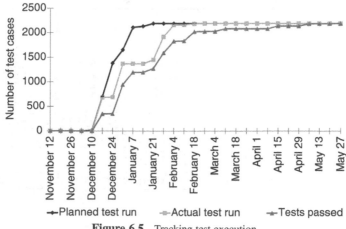

Figure 6.5   Tracking test execution.

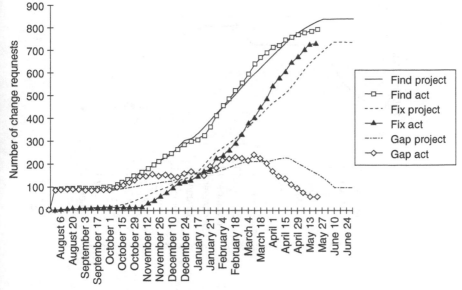

Figure 6.6   Measuring resolution of change requests.

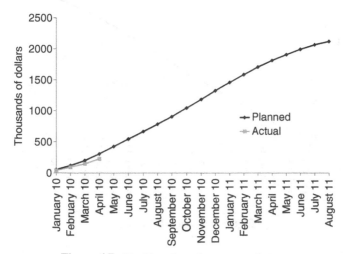

Figure 6.7   Tracking planned versus actual costs.

Figure 6.5 provides an example of testing data that might be reviewed at the project meeting. The red line shows the number of test cases we had planned to execute as of each date on the horizontal axis. The yellow and white lines show the number actually run and the number passed as of each date. The relationships shown in this chart are not all that unusual. The reader might wonder about why tests passed might be running so far behind the tests executed between the beginning of January and the end of February.

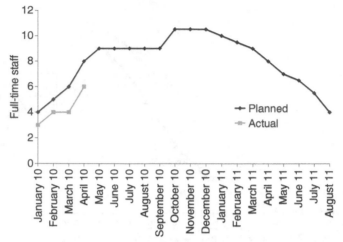

Figure 6.8   Monitoring the number of people working on the project.

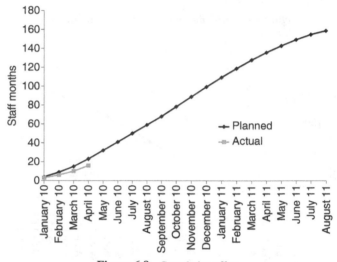

Figure 6.9   Cumulative effort.

The answer is that some time along the way, after some testing has been done and some change requests have been issued, the testers usually end up waiting for developers to fix the problems that have been reported, while the developers are still trying to finish development and integration of the code that is necessary to complete the current release. Eventually, they do finish and the fixes catch up with those reported.

Figure 6.6 is a chart from a real project that I worked on several years ago. It tracks the planned finding of faults during testing versus the actual number found, the number of planned fixes completed versus the actual fixes completed, and both the projected gap versus the actual gap.

Table 6.2 Detailed Task List

SLC-2000 ITH Hardware Development					
Circuit	Description	Resp	Target	CWV	Actual
THC	Stocklist to OCW	mc	5/29		4/24
	V1 design to EID (routing)	dbh			7/10
	V1 assembled CP available	mc		9/27	10/1
	Debugged V1 model to SW	dbh		11/8	11/4
	95% stocklist to OCW	mc	11/22		11/22
	V2 design changes to EID	dbh	11/22	3/4	3/4
	100% stocklist to OCW	mc	1/24	3/9	3/21
	V2 available CP available	mc	1/10	4/22	4/30
	Debugged V2 model to SW	dbh	1/31	5/19	5/19
	Artmaster to RG	mc	2/28	5/21	5/20
	Certified focus prime data	mc	4/9	6/10	6/15
	Final firmware OCW	dbh	4/13	7/16**	7/20
	CP/func. test to OCW***	dbh		8/31	4/92
	PSR ship	ocw	8/3	9/11	
PCU	Stocklist to OCW	mc	5/29		4/24
	V1 design to EID (routing)	dbh	5/15		5/31
	V1 assembled CP available	mc		9/16	9/16
	Debugged V1 model to SW	dbh		11/8	11/4
	95% stocklist to OCW	mc	11/22		11/22
	V2 design changes to EID	dbh	11/22	3/4	3/4
	100% stocklist to OCW	mc	1/24	3/9	3/21
	V2 available CP available	mc	1/10	4/20	4/20
	Debugged V2 model to SW	dbh	1/31	4/3	5/21
	Artmaster to RG	mc	2/28	5/1	5/5
	Certified focus prime	mc	4/9	6/5	6/5
	Final firmware OCW	dbh	4/13	N/A	
	CP/func. test to OCW***	dbh		8/17	4/92
	PSR ship	ocw	8/3	9/11	
AMU	Stocklist to OCW	mc	5/29		5/15
	V1 design to EID (routing)	dbh	6/1		7/12
	V1 assembled CP available	mc		10/9	10/9
	Debugged V1 model to SW	dbh		11/22	11/22
	95% stocklist to OCW	mc	12/6		12/6
	V2 design changes to EID	dbh	12/6	3/9	3/10
	100% stocklist to OCW	mc	2/5	3/9	3/26
	V2 available CP available	mc	1/24	5/22	5/21

Table 6.3 Action Item Register

ITH Project Meeting Action Item Register						
Open Items						
Number	Who	Action	Status	Open	Due	Closed
220	jrk tle rjf	Codec accuracy issues across local access hardware	5/27 > Trying to get together and understand issues 6/10 > Will test when setup exists in lab 9/30 > No status as yet—very low priority 10/14 > Still low priority	3/4		

The three charts in Figs. 6.7 through 6.9 are typical of the charts used at project meetings to track staffing and cost. Since for most software development projects most of the cost is related to staffing, we will usually look at them together. In Fig. 6.7, we compare the planned cost with the actual cost and find that actual expenses are running somewhat below expected costs. If we look at Fig. 6.8, we see that the actual staff working on the project is below the planned levels. And, as shown in Fig. 6.9, the cumulative effort is running behind the planned effort. We do not have the milestone chart for this particular chart available, but if we did, we might expect that the task completions are running behind the planned profile, so it would be quite obvious that the project manager needs to recruit another person or two and to get them to work on appropriate project tasks to get the project back on schedule.

The next thing that we want to look at is our action item register that should be kept as a running total for the entire project. In Table 6.3, we see one action item, number 220, for which people with the initials jrk, tle, and rjf are responsible. Given its status, it looks as though it is a relatively unimportant issue. It was opened at a project meeting on March 4 and as of October 14, it is still being reported as a low priority. But the action item list is a good way to remember to get back to items like this before the project is finished. Of course, there will also be some high-priority items on a typical action item register, and these usually come and go much more quickly than the example we have shown here.

Shortly after the project meeting has been completed, the project manager needs to document the discussion. He or she should prepare a written synopsis of the meeting. All of the handouts, slides, and other materials used during the meeting should be attached. And an electronic copy of the package should be distributed to all project team members and possibly to other stakeholders as quickly as possible after the meeting. The documentation should not be distributed the day before the next meeting and certainly not at or after the next meeting. Distributing it quickly allows team members some time to get prepared for that next meeting.

When the formal part of the meeting is finished, the project manager should invite any of the team members who are interested to visit the work environment or laboratory with those who have reported task completions to observe the results of those task completions. This becomes more interesting when unit testing gets started. Its purpose is to avoid the reporting of task completions when they are "not quite there." The first few times I tried doing this, the person reporting those kinds of tasks was not able to successfully demonstrate what they had accomplished. The team quickly learned that they should not do that again, not because the project manager was watching, but because several of their peers were also observing the demonstrations.

6.2 SOME WARNINGS AND ADVICE

Here are a few warnings. Some members of the project team will probably want to talk endlessly about the issues that are raised. The project manager needs to politely end those conversations. Project meetings should not be the place where problems are solved. That gets done between project meetings. Problems and issues can and should be raised at project meetings, discussed for understanding, and then be assigned to team members for resolution. If team members try to solve problems at these meetings, they become too long and other team members will be bored before the meeting ends. Another factor that sometimes extends the length of project meetings is the number and duration of tasks. Ideally, the duration of tasks should be longer than the interval between project meetings and not longer than the time between three project meetings. There can always be exceptions, but if there are too many short tasks, the meetings are likely to drag on. The project manager needs to insure that the team follows the agenda and that the group does not get distracted by too many side issues. And, finally, we need to keep the meetings interesting and participative to insure appropriate attendance and to continue team building.

To help make project meetings successful, they should be held regularly, scheduled well in advance, should be structured and well controlled, and, most important, should be as short as possible.

To make the monitoring process work well, the project manager needs to insure the team has a good project plan. He or she needs to personally lead all project meetings. He or she needs to track and to analyze the metrics specified in the project plan and should take action to address deviations from the plan.

6.3 SOME THINGS TO REMEMBER

The most important things we have discussed in this chapter are the following:

1. The project plan defines what will be monitored.
2. Regularly scheduled project meetings at the same time and location each time provide visibility to team members and, sometimes, to management outside the team.

3. Deviations from the plan trigger control activities, typified by things recorded in the action register.

4. Meeting notes record the project's status and action items and answer stakeholders' questions.

CASE STUDY 6   *Customer Expectations*

Purposes

1. Learn to anticipate unstated customer expectations.
2. Learn how to plan for inevitable unanticipated customer requirements.
3. Develop methods for coping with those requirements when they arise.

Background

Here is a situation, based on an actual experience, that will give you an opportunity to address issues related to "missed" or unanticipated customer expectations (requirements). It is a somewhat simplified version of the actual situation, but it illustrates the same points that were learned by the participants in the real project.

After the development of a new telecommunications testing capability had been completed and that functionality had been integrated into our most modern switching and distribution system, an opportunity came available to market a stand-alone version of the same features with some of our older telecommunications systems that were being installed in the local network in Beijing, China.

During a 6-month period when system and beta testing of the integrated features were being completed, our sales team in Beijing and a marketing person on the development team began to negotiate a contract for installation of the stand-alone features in Beijing.

This was an excellent opportunity developed by our sales representatives in Beijing and a Chinese-speaking member of the development team. The contract was signed more quickly than the team anticipated. It called for the first delivery to four test sites within 6 months of contract signing.

Because of the rapidity of the negotiations, the text of the contract, which was written using traditional Chinese characters, was not translated into English for review by the project team before contract signing. However, an excellent diagram of the proposed first installation, which was included as part of the contract, contained both Chinese characters and English phrases describing each block in the diagram. After the contract was signed, the sales person in Beijing, who was representing the team, summarized what he believed to be the most important points in the contract in English, attached the diagram, and circulated it to the development team.

The diagram was reviewed carefully by a systems engineer who was a member of the development team and who, while he did not develop the requirements for the integrated product, was quite heavily involved in the later stages of that development effort when he volunteered to help with system testing. The necessary development work for the stand-alone product was estimated and scheduled based on a brief set of requirements that he wrote. The diagram became part of his requirements.

When the software and hardware developers seriously began to work on the changes, they noted that in the lower-right portion of the diagram was a small box lettered "MTU," which stands for maintenance termination unit. "Whoops," they said, "We hope this does not imply that we need to interface with the MTU in Beijing. We were never able to make it work properly with the integrated version of the product, but, fortunately, it was not required in domestic applications." Unfortunately, it was a part of the Beijing contract and, because of the particular equipment configurations used in the most densely populated parts of the city, it was required there. It would require extensive effort to find a way to make it work.

Much later in the development cycle, when the team's customer support people were working with the sales team and the customer to put together a beta test plan, they discovered that the customer wanted to perform tests that would demonstrate whether those tests could be performed in 8 seconds as they required of all testing products used in Beijing. Unfortunately, a standard loop test done by the stand-alone (or the integrated) product took from 30 to 90 seconds, depending upon the sequence of artificial intelligence tests that the system determined should be actually run. The project team knew that there was no way that any competitive product could perform an equivalent analysis in 8 seconds. There were limits set by the physical and electrical properties of local distribution facilities that precluded that possibility. They then arranged to have the portions of the contract that specified these performance requirements translated into English. The contract contained a very clear statement that a test must be executed within 8 seconds.

Activity

The details behind all of the reasons why this particular project team got to this point are not the important part of this exercise, so please do not spend a significant amount of time trying to guess all of the reasons why. The results, however, are quite common. There are almost always requirements that were not obvious to the development team, but which the customer clearly expects to be met. And this was one of those cases.

To analyze this case, you should develop three charts. The first should contain a slogan that will you remember to be on lookout for similar situations in every project that you undertake. The second chart should contain your suggestions outlining how project teams should plan for handling similar unanticipated expectations. The final chart should contain a list of alternatives that might have been considered by the development team to respond to the two problems outlined above.

Output

If you are analyzing this case in a classroom setting with a group of other students, one of the members of your group should prepare a summary of your analysis in a form that can be shared with other members of the class. They should prepare a summary of your discussion in visual form and be prepared to make a short presentation (5–10 minutes) to the class when you reconvene. Your results will be compared with the results achieved by other groups.

During the readout session or in your summary analysis, you might want to discuss the following questions:

1. Should you, routinely, include in your estimates some contingency for unanticipated requirements?
2. Should the contingency effort be "buried" or made known to the entire project team and to all the stakeholders? What issues of integrity might each option generate?
3. How do you know how much contingency effort to include for what kinds of projects?

When you have not accounted for contingencies, what options do you have when you learn of the new requirement?

Chapter 7

The Control Process

In this chapter, we will discuss the fourth major project management process, control. There are two types of control with which the project manager needs to be concerned. The first has to do with control of the tasks, resources, and schedule defined in the project plan. We will call that kind of control "project control." The second kind of control is related to control of the artifacts being produced by the project. We will call that type of control "artifact control."

7.1 PROJECT CONTROL

Project control is closely related to monitoring. In the last chapter, we defined monitoring as the process by which the manager continually observes the status of the project and searches for deviations of the status from the project plan. When a deviation is identified, the manager uses the control process to respond to the deviation.

Figure 7.1 shows the relationship between the monitoring and the project control process. In this figure, we start with a project plan, an organized team, and the status of the project. The monitoring process detects deviations from the plan and passes them on to the controlling process. Using that process, the manager determines what, if any, changes need to be made to the plan to address the deviations. Then, if necessary, the manager changes the plan appropriately.

Sometimes we will find that the deviations are large and serious and that major changes must be made to assure successful completion of the project. Other times, we will find that the deviations are minor and we might conclude that no changes are required. Let us look at some examples to clarify what kinds of changes are typically required.

Suppose we find that midway through a project a task that should have been finished 3 days ago has not been completed. Our first step would probably be to determine what that task is. Then we need to know if it is on the critical path. If it is not, we can breathe a small sigh of relief and go on to determine how much slack is associated with that task, or how late can it be before it appears on the critical path for the project. If it has a slack of 14 days, we can breathe a second sigh of relief and conclude that we still have $14 - 3 = 11$ more days to complete the task.

Managing the Development of Software-Intensive Systems, by James McDonald
Copyright © 2010 John Wiley & Sons, Inc.

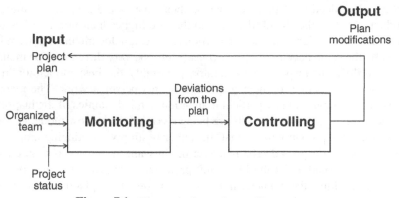

Figure 7.1   The monitoring and controlling processes.

Then we will ask who is responsible for the task and ask that person why the task has not been finished and how much longer will be required to finish the task. If they tell us that it is not finished because the person doing the work was sick for 4 days last week but is now recovered and has returned to work. They estimate that it will require two more days to complete the work. In this case, it is unlikely that any changes will need to be made because it appears that the work will be done well before that task joins the critical path. The project manager might offer some encouraging words and check regularly on the task for the next few days until they are able to confirm that it has been completed. However, the manager still needs to be careful that the person doing this task is not expected to start another important task during the time that they are finishing the first task. Hopefully, that will not be the case.

If we found that, instead of sickness, the person responsible for this task simply had been able to finish it on time, the manager might have taken a very different approach. If the responsible person was not able to articulately explain the cause for the delay, the manager might ask another team member to join the responsible person to assist in both understanding the cause of the delay and in helping to complete the task. In neither of these cases would a real change in the project plan be required.

Let us look at a different kind of deviation. Suppose the manager finds from inspection data that are regularly presented during project meetings that the rate of finding faults in design documentation is running much higher than expected. This could mean that the inspection teams are being overly aggressive in recording faults. It could mean that some of the developers are doing a poor job of documenting their designs. Or it could mean nothing and simply be a random variation on the fault-finding rate. The manager, in this case, would probably want to work with the inspection coordinator to examine the inspection data to identify the kinds of faults being found. If they determine that the cause of the high fault rate is because the inspectors were identifying numerous stylistic faults rather than faults that would cause the design to fail, they might respond by changing the inspection procedures to omit the identification of faults other than those that would cause real failures in the product. On the other hand, if they find that the higher-than-normal rates were caused by extremely high fault rates in two specific design documents that were both produced by the same developer, the response might be very different. The manager might ask a different inspection moderator, preferably the best moderator in the organization, to moderate the next inspection of this person's work. The manager might ask the moderator to pay particular attention to the dynamics of the inspection meeting to insure that only real faults are being recorded. If the new moderator finds similar results, it is probably likely that the author is simply introducing more faults into their work than expected. The manager might want to pair the person up with a colleague who could assist the high fault producer to improve the methods they are using. If that fails, the manager might want to consider replacing the person or at least assign them to a less critical role on the project.

Finally, suppose the day for release of the product has arrived and there is still a high-priority change request open in response to a fault that was found during functional testing. This is one of the more difficult control issues frequently faced by project managers. It is difficult because they are usually faced with a broad range of options. Some people might say that this is a simple problem and the answer is obvious. The day for release has arrived and the product must be released independent of the existence of a potentially serious problem. Others would take the opposite tack and determine that the product cannot be released until the problem is fixed. I have found from being involved in many similar situations that one of the options between these extremes is usually best. We might first ask, "If we release the product in its current condition, how likely is it that the customer will use the faulty feature before we can fix it?" If the customer uses that feature and it does not work, how serious would the impact be on the customer's business? And, finally, if we need to release the product a second time to fix the problem, or issue a risky patch, how much cost will we incur for that added effort? Depending upon the answers to these questions, a range of possible actions is likely to be revealed. These might include releasing the software as it is, releasing the software only after fixing the offending problem, and releasing the software as it is with a notification to the customers that this specific feature does not work properly and recommending that they try not to use the application or that specific feature until the problem is fixed. There is no solution that is always right to this problem. The best response will depend on a myriad of factors and can only be determined by considering all of those factors. There is one certain thing that we should point out. If the manager decides to release a product containing a known serious fault, he or she should always notify the customer that this is being done and should obtain concurrence from the customer that this is their preferred approach.

So, we see that project control actions can take a wide variety of forms. We have listed only a few examples here. Some of them will require no real change in the project plan. Others will require major changes in both the implementation and, infrequently, major changes in the plan itself. This is frequently where the judgment of the manager is most exposed. It requires the capability developed with experience and sound judgment to take appropriate project control actions.

7.2 ARTIFACT CONTROL

Artifacts of projects like those being discussed in this book are things like requirements documents, architectural descriptions, high- and low-level design documents,
software code and hardware/device logic and circuit diagrams, printed wiring board
layouts, test cases, and customer documentation. All of those artifacts need to be
under change control. That is the second type of control with which the project
manager needs to be concerned.

7.3 REQUIREMENTS CONTROL

One of the most difficult parts of managing the execution of a software-based project
is the problem created by changing requirements. To address this problem, the
manager needs to work very hard to assure that the requirements get documented
and baselined as early as practical. Baselining requirements means that they have
been documented using whatever format the organization and the development team
have decided they are going to use for this project. It also means that the requirements have been inspected and agreed upon by both members of the development
team who have participated in the inspection of the requirements and by the customer
who is paying for the work, and those who will be using the product when it becomes
available. Sometimes, the funder and the user will be the same person, but other
times, they may be different people. It is important to get the agreement of both.

I have found that sometimes, it is difficult to get funders or users to spend the
time required to review requirements thoroughly enough to actually sign a piece of
paper saying that they agree with the requirements as specified in requirements
documents. Sometimes, they find it easier to view a prototype of the product and,
based upon that review, agree that what they have seen will meet their needs. In
either case, it is imperative to get their agreement on the description of the product
being developed. If possible, it is preferable to get their agreement in writing and to
then incorporate that agreement and the requirements specification either as an
addendum to the contract that the development organization has with the customer
or, if the project is one being done for an internal customer, the agreement between
the funding organization and the development organization.

Once this has been accomplished, the requirements should be baselined. That
does not mean that the requirements cannot be changed after that point. However,
it does mean that in order to change the requirements, a formal process needs to be
followed to make a change in the requirements. Figure 7.2 outlines a process that
might be used to achieve this initial baselining.

In that figure, the developers of the requirements, who might sometimes be
called business analysts or sometimes systems engineers, first study the problem
system that we discussed in Chapter 1. They then describe in a requirements document what solution they believe will most appropriately solve the problem. They
review these proposed requirements with both the customer who is funding the
work and the ultimate users, if they happen to be different from the funder, and

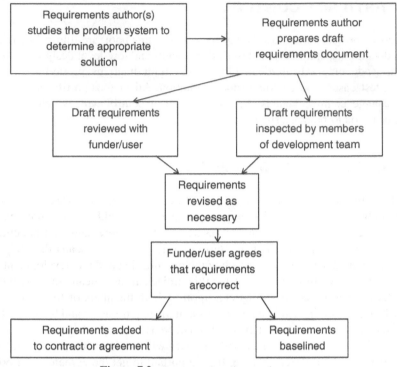

Figure 7.2   Process to baseline requirements.

have the requirements inspected by members of the development team. They make revisions resulting from the customer review and the inspection. Then, the requirements document is added to the agreement between the customer and the development organization and the requirements are baselined.

The manager should work with the legal, sales, marketing, or internal administrative people who develop the customer agreement to insure that a description of the process that will be used to modify and respond to requests for changes in the requirements is developed. This description should specify how changes should be requested, how the impact of those changes will be evaluated, and how estimates of costs of making those changes will be incorporated into the customer agreement. It should then call for a decision to be made by the customers or their representatives, particularly if the requested change will change the cost of the project.

7.4 ARCHITECTURE, DESIGN, CODE, AND TEST CASE CONTROL

The other artifacts that need to be controlled are the architectural description of the product, the high- and low-level designs of both hardware and software, the actual software code, and test cases that will be used to qualify the product for use. The generic title of the activities related to control of these artifacts is configuration management. The use of configuration management can be traced back as early as the 1950s when the methods that were used initially used for hardware development started being applied to software development. Since that time, a large number of software applications have been written and made available to assist development teams with controlling the documents describing their designs.

We are all very familiar with one of the results of the techniques used by software development teams to control their code. That is the version numbering that we commonly see with releases of the software that we use. Version numbers are those like 1.1, 1.06.531, and 6.2.2 that we frequently see associated with the software on our personal computers. There are many different schemes for numbering the versions of software and documentation. And there are many different software packages used for controlling the versions of software and documentation that our teams are working on and the numbers to them. A few of the packages that this author is familiar with are BitKeeper, ClearCase, CVS, DesignSynch, Perforce, and SCCS (Rochkind 1975), which is virtually obsolete now, but which was the first commercial application made available for this purpose in the mid-1970s.

The point of this discussion is that the project manager needs to keep changes under control. Team members cannot be allowed to independently make changes in the requirements, the design, or the testing of either software or hardware.

The systems for tracking and controlling changes do not, by themselves, control change. As a part of the project plan, the team needs to specify what change control tools will be used, how the tools will be managed, and how the team will manage the changes that are inevitably necessary during the course of development. I have found that it is usually best to assign operation and administration of the chosen change control software to a technically oriented member of the team, sometimes to someone whose primary responsibility is verification or validation. For larger teams, this usually means someone who works in a system test group. In addition, there needs to be a relatively small group of team members that I refer to as a change control board. Their responsibility is to review proposed changes, either in requirements, in designs, or in code hardware designs; to prioritize the importance of those requests; to give permission to team members to check out appropriate artifacts and make changes; then to schedule changes into appropriate releases of the product.

7.5 SOME THINGS TO REMEMBER

The most important things that we have discussed in this chapter are the following:

1. Project control is the process of promptly responding to deviations from the plan identified by the monitoring process.
2. Control actions can include a wide variety of methods, ranging from a broad revamping of the overall project plan to doing nothing at all other than following an issue carefully.

3. Control actions necessitated by findings of a deviation from the plan sometimes require the most creativity on the part of the project manager. The manager can sometimes benefit from consulting with a variety of the team's members before deciding what action should be taken.

4. Artifact control can be broken into two parts, one of which is not exclusively under the control of the team, that is, the content of the requirements, and the other of which is primarily under the control of the team, that is, control of architecture, the design of hardware and software, and the content of test cases.

5. In the case of controlling requirements, it is important to get the change control process defined in the customer agreement under which the work is done and then to involve the customer in evaluations and decisions concerning any proposed changes and the cost of those changes.

6. Artifact control can be done primarily by the team members. However, it is important to insure that individual team members are not continually making independent changes. A small, but strong, change control board, supported by appropriate change tracking software, can ease the project manager's responsibilities for this aspect of control.

CASE STUDY 7   *Controlling a Small Project*

Before reading the background for this case, please read the *activity* and *output* sections. That will make it easier to read the background section. Note that there is an organization chart that follows the case description. If you look at it while reading the case, you will find the material easier to follow.

Purposes

1. Think about the appropriate team structure.
2. Manage unexpected difficulties.
3. Consider how to resolve internal team conflicts.

Background

The Interactive Voice Systems organization has been doing exploratory development work for several years to determine if new digital signal processing devices and the latest software algorithms that have been developed by researchers would allow them to add advanced voice recognition capabilities to their mainline product at a price that customers would be willing to pay. The work has been done at a low level of effort during these years, with various highly qualified technical employees moving into and out of the work. There were usually only one or two people involved at any point in time.

In 2007, a prototype circuit pack, based on the device technology that was available at that time, was designed by Jim Wong, a circuit designer in the organization. Before he finished debugging the prototype design, he was offered a promotion, which he accepted, to manage one of the software development groups in the organization. One of the other members of the circuit design group, Will Yousef, attempted to complete the debugging but was never able to get the performance of the hardware to the point that would be necessary for a production product. Will eventually moved onto another "hot" project and became deeply involved in that project, which was expected to continue throughout 2008 and 2009. One of the members of the software group, Aaron Ginzberg, continued to work on the board's software throughout 2008 and, by the end of the year, was able to demonstrate enough capability to generate sufficient interest with an external customer so that the customer indicated a willingness to fund the development of a production product during 2009 and 2010.

This opportunity presented a problem for the organization. While Aaron was available and currently involved, everyone else who had worked on prototype versions of the product had either left the organization or was deeply involved in other high-priority work. The systems engineering manager, Marc Getrouwe, suggested that they investigate the possibility of purchasing hardware and associated software from an external supplier and concentrate the organization's development resources on integrating the purchased capabilities into the existing system. He undertook a study with an outside vendor at the beginning of 2009 to determine what capabilities could be provided by that method and what kind of partnership arrangement could be agreed upon with the vendor. It was clear that the external vendor would, at a minimum, have to redesign its processing board to make it physically compatible with the existing Interactive Voice System.

In the fall of 2008, the internal hardware and software development managers, Drew Hardgrave and Graham Harvey, started to put together broad estimates of the effort and interval that would be required to develop, integrate, and test the necessary hardware and software. Based on their personal experience, and with the assistance of Aaron Ginzberg, they estimated that the hardware would require about 2.3 staff years of effort spread over approximately 18 months and the software would require 4 staff years of effort spread over 24 months. Systems engineering, testing, and customer support would require an additional 4 staff years. Based on those estimates, total development cost would be approximately $1.7 million. The external customer was willing to pay for the development and would purchase the hardware if the product could be delivered to a beta site in August 2010 and put into service in January 2011. Denart Lomax, the product manager, negotiated an agreement with the customer that outlined a payment program and a delivery schedule.

After extended discussions within the Interactive Voice Systems organization, a decision was made to go with the internal development option. This implied that a new circuit board with more modern devices would have to be designed. The team recognized that they had a problem, because it was then April of 2009. No strong experienced circuit designer was available to get started on the hardware, and the customer wanted the beta product in 16 months.

On the positive side, a second software developer had become available in January of 2009. He was "CJ" Lee. He was familiar with the development of software for digital signal processors and microprocessors, which would be required for this job, but he had no experience with speech interpretation algorithms. He began to work with Aaron in January and by April, they had developed the first draft of a software architecture. Graham Harvey was pleasantly surprised that they appeared to be working well together. Their personalities and their capabilities were quite different. Aaron was articulate, somewhat quiet, and very good with customers. Unfortunately, he had no experience with the development of production products. All of his experience had been in exploratory work. CJ, on the other hand, was very talkative. In fact, he talked so fast that others sometimes had difficulty understanding him. He had several years of production software development experience and had a fairly strong mathematical/analytical background. He was, however, not a person whom you would normally let loose with a customer.

A third software developer, Erik Jongerden, would become available in April. He had joined the organization in mid-2008 and had been involved in helping with a feature of the last release of the Interactive Voice System, which needed to be completed by April. His work on that project was quite straightforward and he completed it on schedule with reasonably good quality. However, he had spent several late nights and weekends meeting his deadlines. Prior to joining the organization, he had been involved for several years in supporting people in the corporation's research organization who developed speech processing algorithms. In that assignment, he designed, laid out, and debugged boards containing digital signal processor devices that were used by the researchers for testing their algorithms. He was also responsible for setting up and maintaining the researchers' software development environment. The managers believed that he would be a good addition to the speech interpretation team since he was familiar with the hardware and had been associated with the algorithm developers. However, he had never designed a board that would be manufactured nor had he developed any software from scratch. Based upon informal conversations with him, they were very impressed with his knowledge of digital signal processors and the breadth of his interests.

Now for the difficult part. The only circuit designer who could be made available in the short term was Guy Bainvol. He was a less experienced employee who had some experience in board design but was not the kind of person who would be the strongest contributor to an important project. Drew Hardgrave, the circuit design manager, believed that it would be reasonable to get started with Guy on the team, and later, when he completed his current work, he would add Will Yousef to the team. He expected that Will would become available around the middle of 2009. It appeared that the board design could be partitioned into two parts. One portion would be designed by Guy, the other portion by Will. Will had become quite good by now and was one of the most efficient circuit designers in the organization. Not only was he fast but he was also careful and was usually able to design a complex board with only two iterations, when other designers usually required three or four iterations. Both Guy and Will were extremely quiet.

According to Marc Getrouwe, no systems engineer was available to develop detailed requirements. All were working on higher-priority projects. He felt that because this opportunity had been developed as a result of exploratory work, the developers would be able to develop requirements as well as any of the systems engineers in his group. He was able to get Graham's and Drew's agreement on this issue. So there was no systems engineer explicitly assigned to the team.

Finally, Darlene Rodriguez, who was in the system test group, was designated as the lead system tester. She would not be heavily involved in the beginning of this project but would available part-time during 2009 and full-time in 2010. No customer support person was identified. Greg Pierpoint, a member of the Physical Design group, would dedicate about 20% of his time to the project during the next year.

Robert McCrae, who was the business leader of the Interactive Voice Systems organization, asked Graham Harvey to organize the team, serve as its leader, and develop a project plan. Graham had never developed a formal written plan before, but Drew Hardgrave had recently led teams that did develop formal project plans to kick off their projects. Robert assumed that Graham, who was an experienced software development manager, with some assistance from Drew, would be able to put together a plan and lead this relatively small team with little involvement by him. The team had its first meeting in April and decided to meet every 2 weeks. Graham asked CJ Lee to take on responsibility for organizing those meetings, developing a project schedule, and issuing meeting notes. The organization structure as of April 2009 is shown in the organization chart which follows this case description (Fig. C7.1).

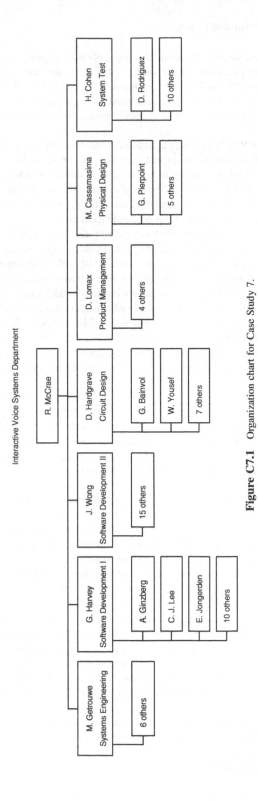

Figure C7.1 Organization chart for Case Study 7.

During the next few months, the team met regularly and, after each project meeting, CJ issued the meeting notes. From a review of each set of notes, Robert concluded that the project was moving along reasonably well. One set of notes in April 2009 had a copy of a Microsoft Project Gantt chart attached showing both tasks and the assignment of individuals to tasks. Later notes contained a block diagram of a circuit pack, which indicated that it was being circulated for review.

In June, just before Will Yousef was scheduled to become available to work on the team, Robert decided to sit in on one of the project meetings. He observed two things. First, there were extensive technical discussions of low-level details about the amount of memory and the input/processing capacity that would be required for the application. Second, the team seemed to be saying (to itself) that they did not know enough about how the customer would use the product to make decisions about the performance requirements of the product. Robert asked some polite questions during the meeting to show his interest and received reasonable answers. Afterward, he discussed the meeting format with Graham, suggesting that it be turned into a traditional project meeting with reporting of status and issues and assignment of action items to be followed up after the meeting with minimal technical discussions taking place during the meeting. Second, he consulted with both Graham and Drew Hardgrave, as well as with Marc Getrouwe, to help them resolve what performance would be required. Marc, who still had no one in his group to make available for this project, indicated that he thought it would be sufficient to provide enough capacity for one speaker at a time. All four agreed on the reasonability of this assumption. Graham and Drew agreed to relay this information to the team so that they could move along. Again, the team met regularly and Robert sat in on a few more meetings.

About 2 months after the time of the incident described in the paragraph above, Robert again heard a discussion at a project meeting about the amount of memory and input/output capacity. He questioned whether or not these issues had not been resolved approximately 2 months ago. Aaron Ginzberg responded for the hardware people, indicating that he had asked them to visit the issue again because he felt that future capabilities that would be required by the customer would need significant amounts of additional software that simply could not fit on the board if a minimal memory configuration were implemented. Erik Jongerden said that he had asked them to look at the I/O capacity again, because any more than one incoming signal would greatly overload the existing I/O design.

Guy very quietly replied that increased memory and processing power could be added, but the additional functionality could not fit on one board, and a prototype of the revised board could not be available by October 2009 as required by the development plan. Will Yousef did not speak up. Erik Jongerden very authoritatively said that the prototype circuit board could not be available, under any circumstances, by October. This exchange was redirected by the managers who were present to a review of the status of both hardware and software designs. Software developers all indicated that they were on schedule as compared to the plan. Guy reported that he was about 2 weeks behind the plan in delivering a circuit schematic to the support group that would be doing the physical layout of the board. However, he thought he would make that delivery before the next project meeting and he would ask the layout people to work overtime to reduce their normal 8-week interval to 6 in order to deliver a prototype of his portion of the board to the software developers by the end of October.

At the end of this meeting, Robert indicated to the team that he was disappointed with the progress being made, particularly with their inability to pin down the basic issues related to memory and capacity requirements. He said that they were going to have to get serious about this important project and to take the customer's requirements and due dates seriously.

Afterward, he spoke to both Graham and Drew about the team's apparent inability to resolve some very basic issues and to move briskly along.

When the meeting minutes were issued, they contained no reference to the discussion that had taken place about memory and I/O capacity. They indicated that software development was on schedule and that circuit design was 2 weeks behind schedule.

Robert was unable to attend the next project meeting but noted in the meeting notes that a decision was made at the project meeting to have Erik Jongerden develop the hardware diagnostic software, which would normally be developed by the circuit designer. This change in responsibility was made to free up Guy and Will Yousef so they could concentrate on the circuit design and get a model of the first production board made available to the software developers by February 2010.

At the next project meeting, which Robert was able to attend (in October), Guy reported that a prototype version of his portion of the board was in the final stages of debugging and would be available to the software developers by the end of the month. During the status reports given by the software developers, all reported that they were on schedule. Robert noted that he had not seen any inspection meeting notices from the team and asked how the software inspections were going. The software developers indicated that they had not yet conducted any design or code inspections.

Aaron and CJ said that it would be reasonable to schedule inspections of the software that they had developed to date. There were about 20,000 new lines of code to be inspected, and they thought that could be done during the next 6 weeks. Erik had a problem with this suggestion. He had about 50,000 source lines of code, most of which had been lifted from the speech processing algorithms supplied by the research organization. He had spent most of his time integrating the pieces, but he could not quite see how he and his two counterparts could inspect all of his code. Graham agreed that he would work with the software developers to plan a reasonable program of inspections.

The inspections began. Several weeks later, Graham reported that the inspections were moving along, that Aaron's and CJ's code was in reasonable shape, but that some serious rework was required in portions of the code that was developed by Erik. One of the inspectors from the other software group in the organization, who had been helping with the inspections, noted that when he asked questions about the software configuration control system, he found that no configuration management software structure had yet been set up. This had been CJ's responsibility.

At the end of October, when a model of the prototype circuit pack became available, Guy and Erik Jongerden spent a day or two in the lab attempting to load Erik's software onto the board. Jongerden, unfortunately, reported that he was not able to spend any more time helping Bainvol debug his board because he had a considerable amount of work to do on his software as a result of the inspections program. However, based on his extensive experience with boards like this one, he provided several simple suggestions about what needed to be done to debug the board to the point where it would be usable by the software developers.

Guy wrote some small software routines that would help to debug the board, but he felt that he needed full hardware debugging software as well as some applications code to debug the board. He made no changes in the board for the next several weeks but devoted most of his time working with Will on the final design of the production board. During the period from November through January, the software developers spent most of their time completing their inspections and doing the necessary rework. During that period, project meeting notes indicated that all software and hardware work was on schedule. However, the work on the hardware diagnostic software was not getting done. Drew Hardgrave reported that it was not unreasonable to delay development of this software until Will Yousef completed his part of the board design. Then he could spend time developing those diagnostics. The model boards could be debugged manually and by building special loads of the application software.

In February 2010, project meeting notes indicated that the hardware would be available 1 week after the planned availability date. At that point, CJ started to work with Will Yousef to load the first portions of the application software onto the board. They quickly discovered that in order to load CJ's software, they needed some key portions of the software that Erik Jongerden was developing in order to compile and load CJ's software on the board. Unfortunately, Erik had just discovered that he needed to make some major changes in one of his software modules. In fact, he still had to develop about 5000 lines of new code. He reported that he was unable to get to developing this code because he was spending most of his time in the lab helping Will and Guy debug some particularly nasty problems that they were having with the first models of the board. During this period, very little was heard from Aaron. He could build and test most of his software on a local Linux system and, at least initially, he could work independently of the hardware. Both Erik and CJ had to get their software working on the board before Aaron could put his software into the system. Because his applications could run on a Linux PC, he was able to give customers demonstrations with a simulated version of the product. He was frequently called upon to support customer presentations by Denart Lomax and Marc Getrouwe. He was very good in that role and apparently appreciated being away from other members of the team.

Robert attended a project meeting in mid-March and found that Erik Jongerden had "about another month" of work to do on his new modules before he could get into the lab to start integrating with the hardware. Graham decided that during this period, he would assign CJ to getting the configuration management environment setup. Along the way, CJ reported that he was unable to get the entire set of existing software to build, no matter how he structured the system. Robert, again, asked Graham to dig into the causes of the software build problems and to get a good status report on the quality of the hardware and the software that was under development. He suggested that Graham enlist Jim Wong (remember he was the circuit designer who had been promoted over a year ago) to help with this investigation since Jim knew what had worked and what did not work the last time around. Graham, Drew, and Jim spent the next 2 weeks talking with the team members about their status and problems. The circuit developers have been struggling with the same, few nasty problems since February. They reported little progress and believed that they could not make much progress until Erik's application software could be loaded onto the board to assist with the debugging. Aaron was difficult to track down. He spent several days during these 2 weeks on trips to customer locations supporting marketing and sales presentations. He did report by e-mail that most of his software was completed and tested in his Linux environment. He was simply waiting for a circuit pack with base software operating on it in order to integrate his software into the system. He also noted, incidentally, that in reviewing the project schedule so that he could report his status, he noticed that they had included no task (or time) for software/hardware integration.

Erik Jongerden reported that he would be able to work in the lab again with Guy and Will Yousef in about 2 weeks to begin loading his software onto the hardware. However, to do this, it would be necessary that the hardware be completely debugged before he started. Graham, Drew, and Jim reported the results of their investigation to Robert in early April. Jim was of the opinion that unless the integration happened within a few weeks, there was no way the team could meet the August beta date, which had been promised to the customer. He said that the last time they attempted to integrate software and hardware for the prototype application, it took him and Aaron about 8 months to get all of the software working on the board and to get most, but not all, of the bugs out of both the hardware and software. He also had dug into the configuration control structure that had been set up by CJ and was of the opinion that it would never work properly unless it was rebuilt from scratch. Robert indicated his concern and arranged to have Graham and Drew meet with the team every other day for a brief status report and problem solving session. He asked them to report to him once a week on progress.

Graham and Drew reported the following week that they had not seen Aaron. Erik was now available to work in the lab with CJ, Will, and Guy. During their first few days of work, Erik reported that he had discovered several new hardware problems and that he had given Will and Guy suggestions for fixing them. But he thought he and CJ would be wasting their time in the lab until the hardware was debugged. He and CJ were now back in their offices working on the configuration management setup and in unit testing Erik's new code.

It is now the second half of April 2010. Darlene has just started to develop a test plan but has no requirements from which to work. The user documentation people are ready to start writing user documentation but have no source material. The customer is expecting a delivery in August, which is only 4 months away. The schedule called for a 3-month test interval, which means that the hardware and software developers have only 1 month to integrate and debug all of their hardware and software. Robert, Graham, and Drew have concluded that the current team cannot do the job. They are looking for your advice on what they should do.

Activity

Review the background of this case. Then, consider three topics: the structure of the team, the technical problems being faced by the project, and the teamwork and communications issues. Briefly review all of these issues then select one of them for in-depth analysis.

Because the background section of this case is so long and complicated, it might be advisable that you first select the topic that you are going to analyze in depth before studying the background so that you can concentrate on the issues that are most related to your selected issue.

Outputs

If you choose team structure, you should prepare an analysis and recommendations on how they should now address the issues related to team structure that should have been considered at the time the project was started. What might have been done, by whom, to avoid the current situation? Who should have been the project manager? What should that person have done to assure that an appropriate structure was implemented? And, finally, what should they do now?

If you choose to address the technical difficulties, you might want to analyze the underlying technical issues and to make some recommendations concerning who should take control of what and what they should do to insure that customer expectations will be met.

If you choose to address teamwork and internal conflicts, you should analyze the content provided in the background section related to this issue and provide some recommendations about what, if anything, the project manager could do to resolve these difficulties.

As part of your analysis, you might want to address some of the following questions:

1. When is the optimal time to address the problems faced by projects like the one discussed here? How does the lateness of action impact the options that are available?

2. What project variables that could address these issues are available to the manager early in the project versus later in the project?

3. Why are such issues frequently not addressed at the optimal time?

4. How can a manager find the root causes of the problems of a team like this one? That is, what problems are development process issues and which are caused by working relationships among team members?

5. Given the current situation, can anything be done to make the project successful, that is, completed on time with appropriate functionality within the budget of $1.7 million? Why or why not?

REFERENCE

ROCHKIND M. J. (1975) The source code control system. *IEEE Transactions on Software Engineering* **SE-1** (4), December, 364–370.

Chapter 8

Risk Management

In this chapter, we will discuss technological and operational risks associated with our project. Technological risks are those related to the technology that we are using including unknowns related to those technologies or mistakes that might be made by members of our team when they use those technologies. Operational risks are those associated with operating the project, for example, the time that it will take an individual to complete a specific task.

Our objective will be to develop an understanding of what is really meant by risk and risk management. To do that, we will discuss risk in the context of planning and managing projects. We will discuss an overall risk management process. Then we will discuss the costs and benefits of risk management and, finally, we will examine two different quantitative techniques that can help us manage risks—simulation and event analysis.

Risk always involves uncertainty. The uncertainty is usually because there is some information lurking in the background that we do not know. The uncertainty involved in software development projects can affect us in either a negative way, in which case we will call it a risk, or it can affect our results in a positive way, in which case we will call it an opportunity. Managing risk involves analyzing the uncertainties inherent in executing a project, making decisions based on that analysis, and taking actions that capitalize on the opportunities and reduce the risks.

Almost everyone who is managing a software development project feels that they are dealing with a high-risk job. We want to help those project managers turn problems into successes and help them quantify what they mean by tight schedules and optimistic budgets. By planning in advance for managing risks, we can simplify later parts of the project by making replanning easier when we find that something has not gone according to our plan rather than raising false alarms and scurrying to fix problems when negative things happen.

We can use risk management to improve customer satisfaction by reducing the risks on projects that we are doing for our customers and provide additional information that they can sometimes use to help reduce their risks.

Using risk management explicitly also helps to improve project communications by using a common vocabulary concerning risks and by improving our ability to monitor the status of the project.

Managing the Development of Software-Intensive Systems, by James McDonald
Copyright © 2010 John Wiley & Sons, Inc.

The traditional methods used to manage risks are identifying them, estimating their severity, developing a plan for managing them, and then acting upon the things that are called for in your plan. The methods that are used to analyze the risks typically depend upon what kinds of risks are being considered. There are three different kinds of risk that we typically need to consider during a software development project. The first is statistical variability. These are things like the precise amount of time that it will take to complete each task, the probability that the customer will ask for major requirements changes during the first development cycle, and the number of test cases that will fail during system test. The second consists of events that might happen that we can anticipate, like a member of the development team getting a fabulous job opportunity in another company and leaving our team. And, finally, there may be things that we have overlooked. These might be tasks that should have been included in our work breakdown structure but were not included because members of the core team simply forgot to include them or did not know that they were needed.

Here is a mundane example that can be used to illustrate these kinds of risks. Every day, I complete a project when I drive from my home in Middletown, NJ, where I live, to West Long Branch, NJ, where I work. On my way to work, I usually start by driving for a couple of miles on local roads then get onto the Garden State Parkway. In Eatontown, I get off the Parkway and onto NJ Route 18. After a couple of miles on Route 18, I, again, take some local roads to West Long Branch. During that stretch of my trip, I usually stop at a local coffee shop to pick up a cup of coffee. Some of the statistical events that affect my time to get to work are things like the length of the cashier's line at the coffee shop, traffic at the several traffic lights that I encounter on local roads, delays caused by school buses during the school year, and occasional road repair or construction work.

There are also anticipated events like a snowstorm , which usually occurs about two or three times each year in central New Jersey, accidents that occasionally cause traffic delays, and one that has not happened to me for several years, getting a flat tire on my car.

Then there are overlooked events. For example, one morning a couple of years ago when I was leaving Route 18 and getting onto the local roads around West Long Branch, it was raining lightly. The intersection at which I leave Route 18 includes a jug-handle turn. A jug handle is supposed to be designed so that as you drive through the turn, the radius increases. At the Route 18 exit, however, that is not the case. The radius gets smaller as you drive through the turn. It ends in an uphill grade as the exit ramp joins the local road. As I was exiting the ramp, I accelerated very slightly and the rear end of my car spun out and I hit the guardrail on the right side of the road. Fortunately, neither my car nor the guardrail was damaged, but I did arrive about 10 minutes late for work because I had to sit in my car for several minutes until my heart rate returned to normal levels and the quantity of adrenalin in my bloodstream returned to normal levels. That is an example of an "overlooked" event that I would have never planned for.

In everyday life, we deal with statistical events, almost without thinking about them. Figure 8.1 shows a map surrounding the route that I normally use to get to

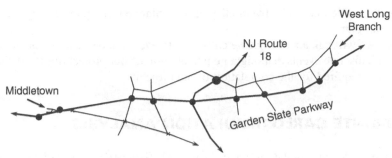

Figure 8.1   Your author's daily commute.

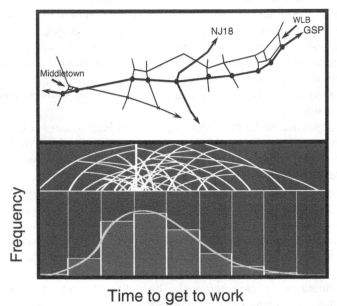

Figure 8.2   My choices and the distribution of time to get to work.

work. On my way from Middletown to West Long Branch, I have lots of opportunities to make decisions about taking alternative routes based upon what has happened and what I have observed up to that point. Each time I deviate from my planned route, I will change the time required to get from home to work. Figure 8.2 shows a probability distribution of the time to make my morning drive. From experience, I know that the minimum driving time is about 20 minutes. The most likely time is about 30 minutes, and the maximum time is about 45 minutes.

So, where are we? We are going to look at two methods for analyzing risks on our software development projects. The first will be risk modeling, in which we will simulate the uncertainties related to the duration of tasks on the project and develop a probability distribution of the amount of time required to complete the project. Then we will be better able to mitigate the risks associated with an uncertain time to project completion either by modifying our planned completion target or by revising our plan.

Then we will talk about what we call discrete event analysis, which is intended to deal with discrete events that might negatively impact our project like the delivery of hardware required for the completion of the project.

8.1 MONTE CARLO SIMULATION ANALYSIS

For Monte Carlo, or simulation, analysis we will first develop a network of task precedences as we have done in Chapter 2. Then we will use the Delphi method to estimate the ranges of task durations. We will use a tool called Risk+, a commercially available add-on for Microsoft Project, to run a Monte Carlo simulation that will help us determine the probability of completing our project over a range of dates. If the results are unacceptable, we can restructure the network and cycle through the analysis again or add some time at the end of the project to absorb some of the uncertainty associated with the variability of task completions. Working through these analyses with the core team helps with team building and helps to build a robust schedule.

Use of simulation or Monte Carlo analysis will help us answer questions like "What is the probability of completing this project in X months?" We then have a more solid basis for negotiating delivery commitments with our customers and our own upper-level management.

To use the Risk+ simulation tool, we need to provide the optimistic, most likely, and pessimistic task durations for each task. Risk+ selects a random task duration for each task chosen from a probability distribution that matches our estimates. Microsoft Project, with the help of Risk+, determines the project's critical path and comes up with an end date for the project using the end date of the critical path. Then it goes back and does this again, each time with a different set of randomly chosen task durations, for many iterations. The tool finally plots the results in terms of a probability distribution showing how often each of many possible end dates was achieved.

Let us look at a very simple example. Figure 8.3 shows a project involving four tasks, each with an icon showing the optimistic, most likely, and pessimistic task durations.

If we use the most likely times for this project, we find that the critical path will require 16 days as shown in graphical form in Fig. 8.4 and in the form of a Microsoft Project Gantt chart in Fig. 8.5.

When we put this same data into Microsoft Project, we see that the time required will actually be 22 days because Microsoft Project has taken nonworking days on Saturday and Sunday into account. The start date is April 1 and the completion date is April 22. This would be the nominal completion date if we used traditional methods for analyzing our project schedule.

Now, suppose that instead of using the most likely task durations we enter into Microsoft Project and Risk+ the optimistic, the most likely, and the pessimistic task

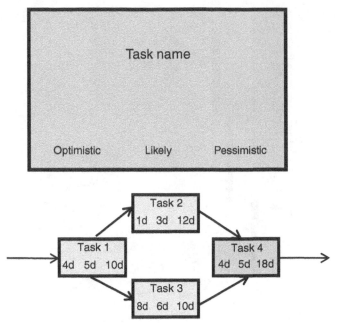

Figure 8.3   A simple four-task project with planning icons.

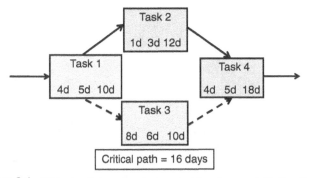

Figure 8.4   Critical path for a four-task project based on most likely estimates.

durations for each task. We then run the risk analysis, repeating the critical path calculation 1000 times, and obtain the results shown in Fig. 8.6.

With the assumptions used in this analysis, we find that instead of 22 days being required to complete this project, there is a range of project durations from 16 to 32 calendar days with the project ending as soon as April 16 if all tasks are completed on their shortest possible schedule or as late as May 14 if all tasks require the pessimistic duration for completion. However, it is very unlikely that all tasks would be completed within their optimistic times or that all would require their pessimistic times. The histogram in Fig. 8.6 indicates that approximately 50% of the time, the

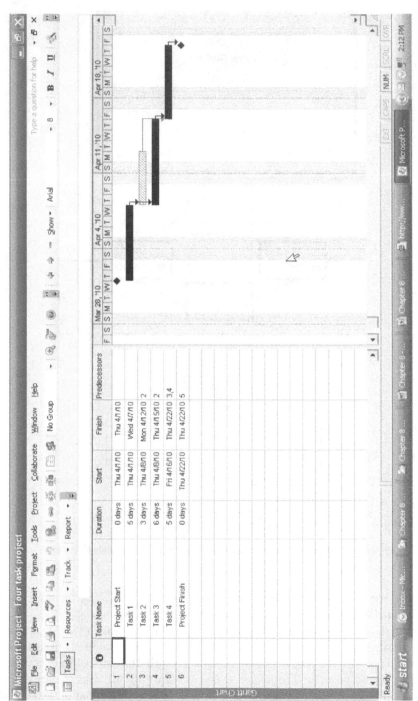

Figure 8.5 Gantt chart view of a four-task project.

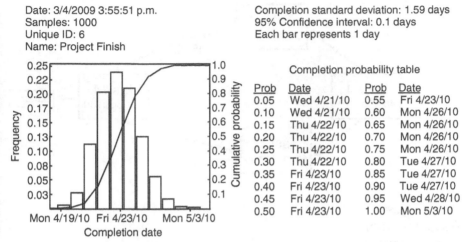

Date: 3/4/2009 3:55:51 p.m.
Samples: 1000
Unique ID: 6
Name: Project Finish

Completion standard deviation: 1.59 days
95% Confidence interval: 0.1 days
Each bar represents 1 day

Completion probability table

Prob	Date	Prob	Date
0.05	Wed 4/21/10	0.55	Fri 4/23/10
0.10	Wed 4/21/10	0.60	Mon 4/26/10
0.15	Thu 4/22/10	0.65	Mon 4/26/10
0.20	Thu 4/22/10	0.70	Mon 4/26/10
0.25	Thu 4/22/10	0.75	Mon 4/26/10
0.30	Thu 4/22/10	0.80	Tue 4/27/10
0.35	Fri 4/23/10	0.85	Tue 4/27/10
0.40	Fri 4/23/10	0.90	Tue 4/27/10
0.45	Fri 4/23/10	0.95	Wed 4/28/10
0.50	Fri 4/23/10	1.00	Mon 5/3/10

Figure 8.6   Results provided from a simulation analysis of the four-task project.

project would finish on or before April 23, but there is a 10% chance that the project would not finish until April 27, or later. If we were making a customer commitment to deliver our results by a specific date, we probably should not use the April 21 date, or even the April 23 date, because we would expect to meet those commitment dates less than about half of the time. However, we probably would not want to stretch the completion date all the way to May 14 when we would be 100% sure of meeting our commitment. A good compromise might be a commitment date of April 27 when our simulation analysis says that would have a 90% chance of delivering on time.

So, how should we handle these uncertainties when initially planning our project? Eliyahu Goldratt (1997) has developed a methodology called the critical chain, a set of rules based on what he calls the theory of constraints. This methodology recommends using what are called buffer tasks in the network to help protect against uncertainties in times required for completion of each task and the project completion date.

This methodology specifies a set of rules which say that you should always insert a dummy task, or a buffer, at the end of the project to account for uncertainties in the overall project completion date. That is buffer 1 in the example shown in Fig. 8.7. For the four-task project data that we just looked at, it should probably be about 5 days long to account for the difference between our April 22 deterministic completion date and the date of April 27, which we have a 90% probability of meeting.

A second buffer should be placed at each location where a noncritical path joins the critical path. The purpose of this buffer is to help insure that uncertainties along the noncritical path minimize the probability that its tasks will become critical path tasks. The duration of this buffer should be as large as possible without affecting the overall duration of the project. In the case of our four-task project, it should be 3 days long because that is as long as it can be without changing the project's critical

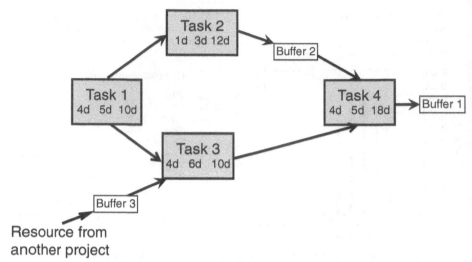

Figure 8.7   Buffer placement in a four-task project.

path. Finally, a third kind of buffer should be inserted just before a resource, or person, who is working on another project, joins our project. This one is to help avoid delays when that resource's availability gets delayed because of their work on the other project. The duration of the buffer should be determined based on the uncertainty associated with the start date of task 3 and the completion date of the task on the other project on which that person is working.

To summarize where we are on the probabilistic analysis project schedules, we can say the following: Start by developing a network based on the project's work breakdown structure, its task precedence relationships. Develop estimates of optimistic, most likely, and pessimistic task durations using the Delphi method. Enter the data into Microsoft Project and Risk+ to do a Monte Carlo analysis and use the results of the simulation to determine the sizes of the buffers that should be added according to the critical chain rules.

8.2   DISCRETE EVENT ANALYSIS

Now, let us talk about discrete event analysis. On my trip to work, an event might be something like an accident on the Garden State Parkway. Event analysis is a method for identifying risky discrete events, developing consistent measures of severity, quantifying the value of the risk by determining the expected loss, and then following a set of response rules to determine what to do. The process involves first establishing criteria for the severity of the risk and for responding to the risk. We identify the events, quantify their impact, determine the expected loss, follow our response rules, document the plan, then track and act when necessary.

We are going to use several levels of risk severity. The lowest level is none, in which case we take no special action. Next is low, which means that we simply track the potential risk; then medium, which means that we develop a contingency plan that we will take if the risk comes to pass; and finally, high, which indicates that we need to develop a mitigation plan to avoid the risk or to exercise counter-measures immediately.

To use this method, we first develop a risk profile for the organization or business we are working in. For most software-based projects, we are concerned with two measures of risk: time and cost. Of course, we could add a third measure, quality, but that would complicate the discussion that follows. To start this kind of analysis, we need to describe how the management of the organization that we are working in, and perhaps its customers, feels about the relative importance of schedule delays and cost overruns.

Figure 8.8 shows a risk profile for an organization in which I have worked. It was developed by asking a cross section of managers in that organization a series of questions about trade-offs that they would make between time and cost if they were faced with either schedule delays or cost overruns. These were questions like "On a typical project in your organization, would you be willing to incur a cost of $50,000 to avoid a 1-month delay in the project's schedule?" and "Please rate the severity of overrunning the budget for a specific project by $100,000 as negligible, low, medium, or high." After asking several questions like this of a cross section of managers, the risk profile chart shown in Fig. 8.8 was produced.

These severities were then converted into a set of rules describing how a project team should react based upon the impact of the risk on time lost and money lost. These actions can be summarized as follows:

1. If the impact is *negligible*, take no action.
2. If the impact of the risk is *low*, simply track the risk.
3. If the impact of the risk is *medium*, develop a contingency plan or counter-measure and track its status regularly.
4. If the impact of the risk is *high*, develop a new approach to mitigate the risk or institute immediate countermeasures.

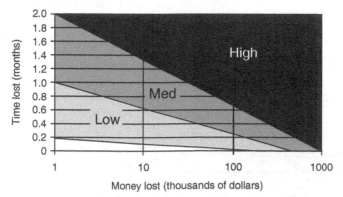

Figure 8.8   Risk profile chart.

For example, if a specific risk has an associated expected delay of 2 months and an expected monetary loss of $150,000, it would be a high-risk event and we would need to develop a new approach to address that part of the project in which the risk might appear.

To use this technique on real projects, we would ask our core team to brainstorm the events that might occur and which would result in major delays or major costs. We then develop estimates of the cost and/or delays that would result if these events did happen. We also estimate the probability of their occurrence by assigning subjective probabilities to each risk event. If these probabilities are developed by the core team, they could be produced using the Delphi technique that was discussed in Chapter 3. If, for example, we have no feeling for whether the event will occur or not, we might assign a probability of 0.5 to that event because its occurrence or lack of occurrence is equally likely. If, on the other hand, we feel almost certain that it will occur, we might assign a probability of 0.9. Then we ask ourselves, "If the event occurs, how much will it cost and by how much time will it delay our project?" A handy format for performing and documenting discrete event analyses is shown in Fig. 8.9.

To complete that form, we would first assign a name to the event and record it as item 1, the risk item title. Then we try to describe the event in an IF ... THEN format. That is "IF the event occurs, THEN what happens?" We record that statement on the form. If there is any additional information required to understand the IF ... THEN statement, we briefly describe that information in the comments section. We next record the money lost and/or the time lost if the event occurs in the Section 3. Risk Evaluation portion of the form and record our subjective estimate of the probability that the event will occur. In the second column, we multiply the estimated cost by the probability that the event will occur and multiply the time that will be lost by the probability that the event will occur to get an "expected" monetary loss and an "expected" time lost.

1. Risk item title: _____

2. Description:
IF _____
_____
_____
THEN _____
_____
_____
Comments: _____
_____
_____

3. Risk evaluation:
3a. *Money* at stake: _____
3b. *Time* at stake: _____
3c. *Probability* of event: _____

3. Risk evaluation (cont):
3c×3a. *Expected* money lost:_____
3c×3b. *Expected* time lost: _____

Risk severity (from risk posture chart)

None	Low	Med	**High**

4. Countermeasures:
Plan 1 summary _____
(Risk =) _____
Plan 2 summary _____
(Risk =) _____

5. Plan chosen _____
Trigger: _____
Trigger owner: _____
Trigger date: _____

Figure 8.9   Risk event analysis form.

We would then consult the risk profile chart shown in Fig. 8.8 to determine if the risk was negligible, low, medium, or high and circle the box on the form corresponding to the location on the profile chart where the expected time lost and the expected money lost values intersect. If the point is in the white area of the chart, we do nothing. If it is in the low-risk area of the chart, we simply track the status of the potential event. If the point falls in the medium risk area, we develop a contingency plan to determine what we will do if the event occurs by selecting a trigger that will determine when that contingency plan should be executed then track its status regularly. If it falls in the high-risk range, our rules say that we should develop a new approach to mitigate the possibility that the event will occur or undertake our countermeasures immediately.

If that is the case, we should develop an alternative plan and analyze the level of risk after those plans are implemented. If they reduce the impact to none or low, then we are finished. All we need to do is to track the risk and determine when, and if, we need to trigger the plan. We then document our plan by specifying, on the form, when the alternative plan is, who is responsible for its implementation, and when its execution should begin.

8.3   SOME THINGS TO REMEMBER

The most important things we have discussed in this chapter are the following:

1. Brainstorm for risky items.
2. Quantify their, usually negative, impacts in terms of schedule and budget.
3. Develop countermeasures or mitigation plans when necessary.
4. Track the status of the risk and take action when necessary.
5. And, finally, implement risk management as a part of your plan for managing the project.

CASE STUDY 8   *Event Analysis*

Purpose

1. Practice discrete event risk management that was discussed in this chapter.

Activity

You are working on a project that requires the use of a special purpose computer for testing the software that you and your team are developing. Unfortunately, the order for the equipment was placed quite late. You are not sure that the computer will arrive in time to start testing on schedule. Your purchasing department has estimated that there is a 70% probability that delivery will be delayed by 2 months, which will delay your team's delivery by a comparable amount. The contract that you have with the customer reduces the customer's cost by $200,000 for each month of delivery delay. So, if the computer is delayed by 2 months, your delivery will be delayed 2 months and it will cost you $400,000 in reduced revenues from your customer.

Using the risk event analysis worksheet (Fig. 8.9) and the risk profile (Fig. 8.8), determine if you need to take any action to address this issue. Complete the first risk event analysis worksheet based on this information and indicate if you should find a countermeasure to reduce the risk.

Your purchasing department has suggested that if you offer the computer vendor a fee of $200,000 for on-time delivery, the probability of a 2-month delay will be reduced to 20%. We will call this "Countermeasure—Plan 1."

Should you seriously consider this option? If you pay the $200,000 and the probability changes as anticipated, do you need to take any further action? Analyze this situation by completing a second risk event analysis worksheet that is shown in Fig. 8.9. If you can think of an additional alternative that would further reduce the risk on this project, complete a third risk analysis worksheet for that alternative.

Outputs

1. You should complete a set of risk analysis sheets to analyze this situation.
2. If you are studying this material in a class, you will be asked to share your findings with other members of the class and to compare your results with those of other students.

REFERENCE

GOLDRATT E. (1997) *Critical Chain*. Great Barrington, MA: North River Press.

Chapter 9

Audits, Reviews, and Assessments

This chapter is about a variety of methods and techniques that can be used by the manager of a development project to provide some assurance to that manager, to their team, and to their organizational management that the project has been appropriately planned and that it is being executed properly. We frequently hear that projects fail because development teams are being overly optimistic about what they can achieve within the planned schedule or budget or that they are under such budget and schedule pressure that they are unable to develop and execute an appropriate plan, or that their customer changes the requirements so frequently that the project is never able to stabilize their execution of the project.

To address these concerns, it is important that the plan that is developed by the core team is reasonable and that teams have a reasonably high probability that they can deliver the features and functionality that is needed by their customer, with an appropriate level of quality, on a schedule that is negotiated with the customer and within the budgetary constraints that may be imposed by either the customer or by the development organization of which the team is a part.

The best way to complete a project successfully is to spend sufficient time up front figuring out what the customer needs, putting together a plan for producing what the customer needs at an appropriate level of quality on a schedule and within a budget with which the customer has agreed. It is very hard to walk away from a project that the core team believes cannot be accomplished within the available time and budget. However, sometimes, that is the best thing to do. After the core team has gone through the sometimes grueling process of developing a thorough project plan, there is no one who knows better than the team and its manager what it will take to produce what is needed by the customer. However, customers and organizational management will sometimes take the position that the teams are requesting too much time and too much budget to execute the plan that they have developed. This is seldom the case. The team leader needs to be able to use the content of the project plan as a basis for negotiating with project funders and sponsors. If that negotiation does not reach a suitable conclusion, the team manager should always

Managing the Development of Software-Intensive Systems, by James McDonald
Copyright © 2010 John Wiley & Sons, Inc.

feel free to say, "This is the best we can do. If you (the customer) can find someone else who can do the work faster or at a lower cost, you should seek them out and perhaps choose them over us."

The techniques discussed in this chapter are intended to provide the project manager with enough assurance to say that to their customers in a polite and logical way. I have personally started approximately 25 different projects during my software/hardware development career. In three of those cases, I was unable to reach agreement with the customer and I told them that they should look elsewhere. All three initially decided to do that, but all three eventually returned and were able to reach an agreement on the plan that we had proposed. This is much better, for the manager, for the team, and for the customer, than starting with an impossible combination of features, schedule, and budget and a year or two later deciding that the project is so hopelessly in trouble that it either needs to be canceled or rescued by appointing a new team leader.

So, let us get started. Figure 9.1 shows the high-level view of the development process that we looked at in Chapter 1. Superimposed on Fig. 9.1 are three ovals that show the various kinds of audits, reviews, and assessments that we will discuss in this chapter.

We will start by discussing project management audits and management reviews, which concentrate on the activities included in the upper part of this figure, but which frequently touch upon some of the underlying business and technical processes. Then we will go on to talk about process audits and assessments that are based upon

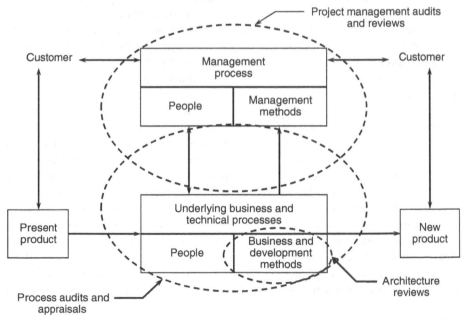

Figure 9.1 Project and process assessments (from Crawford and Fallan (1985), reproduced with permission from IEEE © 1985 IEEE).

the Capability Maturity Model (CMM) of the Software Engineering Institute and the International Standards Organization's (ISO) ISO 9000 standards for product development processes.

9.1 PROJECT MANAGEMENT AUDITS

Anyone who has served in the U.S. military is probably familiar with "the inspector general's visit." That is an annual visit made by a team from the military service's inspector general's office to each military base. During the visit, the team compares the methods being used at the base to the military manuals that describe how a base should be run. When they find inconsistencies between the manuals and what is actually being done, they issue nonconformances, which call out things that must be changed in order to be in compliance with the manual. The story is told that says that during the inspector general's visit, two lies are told. The first lie is told by the leader of the visiting team when he salutes the base's commanding general and says, "We are here to help you." The second lie is told when the commanding general returns the salute and says, "We are glad to have you."

Project management audits are not like the inspector general's visits (McDonald 2002). The purpose of a project management audit is to provide feedback to management on the technical and managerial feasibility of the project, including recommendations for improvement. It includes a review of the business case (or contract), the project plan, requirements, the architectural description, and interviews with project team members by an independent group of experienced development managers. It takes place at the location, or locations, where the work is being performed. It should be requested and arranged by the project manager and their direct line of management using a team of their friends who are experienced in doing similar kinds of work. The best time to conduct a project management is shortly after a detailed project plan has been completed. Sometimes, unfortunately, project management audits need to be used later, in the middle of a project, when the project has gotten out of control. That is a situation we want to avoid because it frequently results in either canceling the project or replacing the management. Using the audit early in the life of a project will help avoid that unfortunate situation. Figure 9.2 shows the optimal timing of a project audit.

It should take place after a baselined business case or contract, a final project plan, a baselined architecture, and at least a portion of the detailed requirements are available for review. Project managers should arrange the audit without waiting for someone to tell them that it should be arranged. They should plan to use the feedback to their advantage and should be open minded and nondefensive about the feedback that they receive.

It is sometimes difficult for the manager to sit through a feedback session without telling the auditors why they are wrong, how they were mistaken about their findings, or why things are as they are. I have found that the best way to combat that kind of reaction is for the manager to view the auditors as a group of consultants. Consultants can do two things for an organization: (1) they can sometimes find

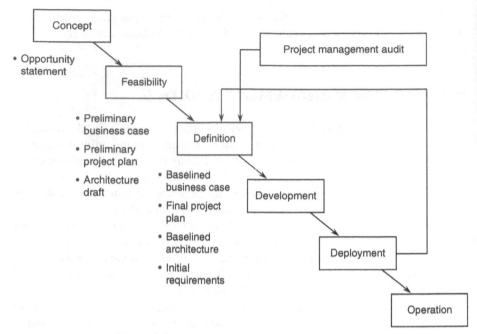

Figure 9.2   Optimal project management audit timing.

information from the project team members that has not flowed freely to the manager, and (2) they can support, or objectively critique, positions that the manager has taken or wants to take with their customers or with their upper management.

Before the audit, the project manager should spend time scoping a project and developing a project plan, as we have discussed in earlier chapters. Then they need to find a willing and able team leader. They need to clarify the scope and objectives of the audit and set dates that are convenient with the leader. By scope, we mean which portions of the project the audit should cover, for example, all of the development tasks, just the design and implementation of the design, only the verification and validation portions of the project or the entire project, including the business relationship with the customer, as well as delivery and continuing support after delivery. By objectives, we mean questions for which we would like the auditors to provide answers, such as "Can you suggest any ways to reduce the cost or the schedule for the project?" or "Do you feel that there are any additional things we need to do to achieve the necessary performance characteristics of the product?"

Then, the project manager needs to assist the assist the audit team leader in recruiting a few additional team members. When the audit has been completed, the project manager should be sure to thank the team members in writing for conducting the audit. And, finally, the manager should arrange to provide the auditor's feedback to the entire project team and to anyone else who might benefit from receiving this information.

The audit team members do not need to be experts in the domain of the project being developed, but they should have had both technical and managerial experience associated with some aspect of the project. At least one team member, preferably the audit team leader, should have had some prior project management audit experience. None of the audit team members should be in a position where they could directly influence team members' performance evaluation. This is not because they would do that but because we want the team members to feel free to talk openly and honestly with the members of the audit team. Team members need to be willing to spend 2–5 days, depending upon the size and complexity of the project, doing the audit. And I like to recommend that the auditors be at an organizational level that is above the level of the project manager. This is not because wisdom comes with organizational level, but because, if the project manager wants to use the results of the audit more broadly than simply as feedback to the project team, it would be helpful if the auditors' names and reputations are well known to the stakeholders to whom the information is being provided. The higher the level of the auditor in the organization, the more likely it will be that the auditor will be known personally, or at least by reputation, to the stakeholders.

Here are some ground rules for the auditors: When giving their feedback, they should provide positive as well as negative feedback. They should be prepared to provide estimates of the probability of project success if the project team does not implement their recommendations and if all of their recommendations are implemented. The auditors should prioritize their concerns when providing feedback and, for projects that need only nominal improvements, raise no more than five or six concerns. I have frequently found that, even though this issue does not arise when the scope and objectives of the audit are being discussed, it almost always gets asked during the audit feedback session. So, auditors should discuss those estimates among themselves and be prepared to provide them when the question is asked. Finally, auditors should be willing to agree to not discuss the results of the audit with anyone other than the requestor and with those whom that person might ask the auditor to share the results.

Table 9.1 outlines the schedule for a typical midsized project audit. This project was scheduled to consume a total of 70 staff years of effort over a 3-year period of time. It required the development of both hardware and software for a telecommunications application. At the time the audit was done, there were approximately 35 people working on the project. It was being done in two different locations with the hardware being developed at one location and the software being developed at the other location, which was about 1600 miles from the other location. I, along with three other managers, was a member of the audit team. One of the other team members was the team leader. This audit was conducted a little later than the optimal time. It occurred about two-thirds of the way through the first release development cycle.

About 3 weeks before the start date, the audit team members received copies of the business case, the project plan, a description of the system's architecture, and the requirements document. During the 3 weeks prior to the audit, we individually

Table 9.1   Schedule for a Typical Midsized Project Management Audit

	Day 1	Day 2	Day 3	Day 4
a.m.	• Travel	• One-on-one interviews with managers and staff on project • Lab environment tour	• Sit in on Project Meeting • Interview with project manager's direct boss • Continue one-on-one interviews	• Feedback meeting with project manager, audit team, and Audit requester
Lunch	• Supervision and audit team members	• Audit team	• Audit team	
p.m.	• Slide presentation by project supervision	• Interview with project manager • Continue one-on-one interviews • Begin formulation of concerns	• Interviews with supervision of supporting functions • Prepare feedback	• Travel
Dinner	• Audit team only	• Dinner with project supervision	• Audit team only • Discuss feedback	

reviewed those documents and made note of our questions and comments about their content in the margins of the documents.

We spent the first half of the first day traveling to one of the locations where the project manager's office was located. We met for lunch with the project manager and with several members of the management team who were involved with the project. During the afternoon, we asked the team to provide a stand-up presentation using only slides that they had developed for other purposes. We asked them to plan using only about half of the available time because we were likely to ask many questions. During that time, they described the project objectives, their plan, their architecture, and the current project status. We did, indeed, ask many questions based on our prepared notes and stretched the total time to occupy the entire afternoon. That evening, the audit team met for dinner and, over dinner, began to outline those areas into which we thought we might want to dig deeper. We produced a list of approximately 10 items about which we agreed that we would ask additional questions as the audit progressed.

The next morning, we began one-on-one interviews in private offices with staff and managers who were working on the project. Each interview lasted 45 minutes to an hour. The interview typically starts with a question about whether the interviewee knows what we are doing and why we were there. Answers usually range from full knowledge of the undertaking and an understanding of the audit objectives to "I don't know. My boss told me that I needed to be here at 8:30 a.m." In that case, the interviewer provides a brief overview of what we were doing and what the objectives of the audit were as well as a few words about their own background and responsibilities. They also ask if it is OK for them to take some notes so they can remember what they have heard and promise that they will not attach any specific names to the feedback they will be providing to management. Then the interviewees were asked to spend some time describing their background, including academic training and work experience, and providing a description of their involvement with this project and what they were currently working on. That introductory discussion usually takes about 20 minutes. The next 20 minutes are reserved for asking the interviewees some specific questions about the project. Some of my favorite questions for this segment of the interview are

What are the primary objectives for the work that you are currently doing?

Who provided the input for the work that you are doing and in what form did you receive it?

To whom will you be delivering the results of your current work and what do you expect to deliver?

When are your results scheduled for delivery?

When will the first release be delivered to the customer?

Then I usually ask any questions that I noted during my pre-audit reading that are related to the work that the interviewee is doing. For each question, the interviewer tries to ask a follow-up question to indicate that the interviewer understands what the interviewee is saying and that the interviewer has some technical expertise in the area.

Next, the interviewees are asked what they foresee as the greatest risks for the project and what they would suggest be done to address those risks. Finally, they are asked if they have any other concerns about the project or their work environment or if there is anything more that the auditors should know. I have always been surprised by the openness and honesty of the answers that I get at this point after spending only about 45 minutes meeting the interviewees and establishing some rapport with them. Responses have ranged from "No, I think I have told you about everything that I can think of" to "I'm having a really difficult time working in my office because I have an obnoxious officemate. Can you do anything to get me moved?"

In the case of this project, the auditors interviewed 23 of the 30 people working on the project.

During that morning, the audit team was given a brief tour of the working environment and the laboratories in which the work was being done. The team members met for lunch and exchanged some of the salient points about what they heard during the one-on-one interviews. In the afternoon, some of the audit team members continued the one-on-one interviews while two of the team members interviewed the project manager. During some free time that afternoon, the audit team started to formulate some of its concerns. In the evening, the audit team went to dinner with the organization's management, primarily socializing and spending virtually no time talking about the project.

On day 3, two members of the project team sat in on the project's biweekly project meeting. That meeting was conducted via a teleconference between the two major work locations. Two other team members interviewed the project manager's direct boss and after that continued their one-on-one interviews. The audit team members met again over lunch and narrowed their concerns down to a relatively short list of topics. In the afternoon, the team interviewed the supervision of several supporting functions such as the data center operations manager, the manager of the organization that prepared computer-aided design/computer-aided manufacturing (CAD/CAM) drawings, the shop that built prototype hardware models, those who provided human resources services, etc. The remainder of the afternoon was spent with the audit team creating a set of PowerPoint slides that would be used during the feedback session on the fourth day. That evening, the team members met again over dinner to discuss how they would present the slides and more precisely what they would say during the feedback session.

On the morning of the fourth day, the team provided feedback to the project manager and the project manager's boss.

During the feedback session, the audit team members described what they had done, summarized a few positive points about the project, described their primary concerns in detail, and, for each concern, described one or more recommendations about how the audit team members would address the issue and summarize the results of the audit.

In the example review being discussed, the positive points were

- enthusiastic people excited about project,
- good staffs who respect their management,
- a well-structured project plan,
- excellent project meetings (with one exception), and
- teams willing to reuse hardware and software.

The primary concerns, in order of importance, were

- lack of formality in monitoring and control,
- absence of baselined performance requirements,
- no provisions for risk mitigation,
- late delivery of interface specifications to other systems, and
- minimal interactions with customer who will be responsible for first field application.

For the first issue, a lack of formality in monitoring and control, we observed that at the project meeting, the project manager simply asked, "Is anyone having a problem with the work that they are doing?" Then, he depended upon meeting participants to speak up if they were experiencing any problems. Instead of that, the team recommended that, because the team was already using inspections to find and stimulate the correction of errors, they establish inspection sign-off as the criterion for milestone completion of requirements, designs, code, and test plans. Second, the team recommended that they should establish test passing as the criterion for completion of unit tests, integration tests, functional tests, and beta tests. Then they should formally compare the inspection and test milestone completions with their planned completions at each meeting. The team made similar recommendations for the other concerns that have been raised.

After the feedback meeting and after the auditors had left, the project manager reviewed the audit findings with the entire team and described to the team what would be done to address the issues that had been raised by the auditors.

9.2 MANAGEMENT REVIEWS

Many organizations and almost all externally contracted development work require regular management reviews at predetermined points in the development life cycle. These reviews consist of a formal examination of the project status by management of the organization doing the work and the customer's management. The official purpose of these reviews is to determine if the project should be continued or if it should be terminated.

The format usually includes completion of a checklist of items before the review that serves as the entry criterion for the review. A typical checklist for a management review that might take place at review point III is shown in Table 9.2. If that checklist is completed and documented successfully, the project is usually reviewed during a formal presentation to upper management of both the customer and the supplier's organizations.

There are usually three to six reviews scheduled during the course of the project. They could take place at the points designated by the roman numerals shown in Fig. 9.3. However, it is more likely that reviews will be scheduled at

Table 9.2   Typical Checklist for Management Review III

• Is business case baselined or contract signed?	• Has the project plan been audited?
• Is project plan consistent with the business case/contract?	• Has an architecture review been conducted?
• Is the architecture baselined?	• Have requirements been shared with customers and approved by them?
• Are requirements available?	• Have development and support personnel inspected the requirements?
• Is the project still aligned with the original business plan?	• Has relevant best current practice usage been evaluated?
• Have market assumptions been verified?	
• Has customer agreed with the cost and the schedule?	• Have all organizational business requirements been met?

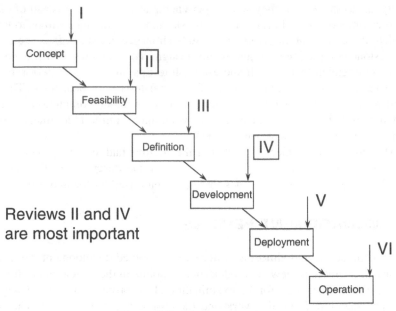

Figure 9.3   Management reviews.

the end of the feasibility and the development phases. These are the most important points at which to schedule management reviews because shortly after review
point II, the project will usually begin to spend larger amounts of money as the
development phase begins. After review point IV, the organization usually makes
a long-term commitment to support the product and therefore commits to the
use of additional funds and resources, possibly for many years into the future.

Some organizations do not require periodically scheduled management reviews
and I have worked in several organizations where they were not required. However,
I have found that as a project manager, even though these reviews usually consume
some project resources, they are worth doing. The value consists in making sure
that upper management is aware of the project, the work being done, and the
major project risks. This knowledge on the part of upper management is important
to the project manager because most projects at some point in time take a turn
with which the project manager needs to seek assistance from his or her upper
management. If the upper management does not have some familiarity with the
project team and the project, it is unlikely that the team will get the necessary
support when the upper management is faced with a request for assistance from
a project with which they are not familiar. Therefore, when it has not been required
of me, I almost always try to schedule management reviews, at least at review
points II and IV so that when I need to ask for assistance, it does not come as a
surprise to my management. This is sometimes the greatest value of management
reviews.

9.3 ISO 9000 AUDITS AND CERTIFICATION

ISO audits are more similar to the inspector general's visit than project management audits are. ISO 9001:2008 is an international standard that has been developed and agreed upon by the ISO. It specifies the requirements for quality management systems (QMSs) and can be applied to the processes used for the development of software-intensive systems and the associated hardware. An organization doing that kind of work that has been independently audited and certified to be in conformance with the standard may advertise that it is "ISO 9001 certified." Use of this standard is particularly important if an organization is developing products that they expect to see in the international market.

To become ISO certified, a development organization has to first prepare a policy and quality manual that describes the upper management's policies and support for the processes used to carry out development work in the organization. Then the manual goes on to describe the processes used for carrying out the work of the organization, the methods used for monitoring those processes, the documentation that is produced by those processes, the system used for filing and retaining those documents, and the methods used for regularly reviewing and improving those processes. ISO certification does not guarantee the quality of the product produced by the organization. However, it does certify that the processes being used are appropriate for the kinds of work being done and that those processes are being followed uniformly throughout the organization. This assurance somewhat relieves the need for functional managers and for the project manager to ensure that every employee is following the defined processes when they are doing their work.

The processes and the quality manual must declare the upper management's support for quality management then define how the development process addresses a series of topics related to quality. It would typically include sections that address the following topics:

- development of the QMS,
- documenting the QMS,
- management responsibilities,
- resource management,
- product realization, and
- measurement, analysis, and improvement.

Because the ISO standard was initially based on QMSs for manufacturing environments, some of the topics may not be relevant to software and hardware development. If that is the case, the quality manual can simply say that the topic is not applicable for this environment. The process descriptions contained in the quality manual usually start with a flowchart similar to the one shown in Fig. 9.4. This is a portion of the flowchart describing the development process for a quality manual that I was involved in preparing. For each block shown in the figure, the document contains a paragraph describing what gets done inside that block, who does the work,

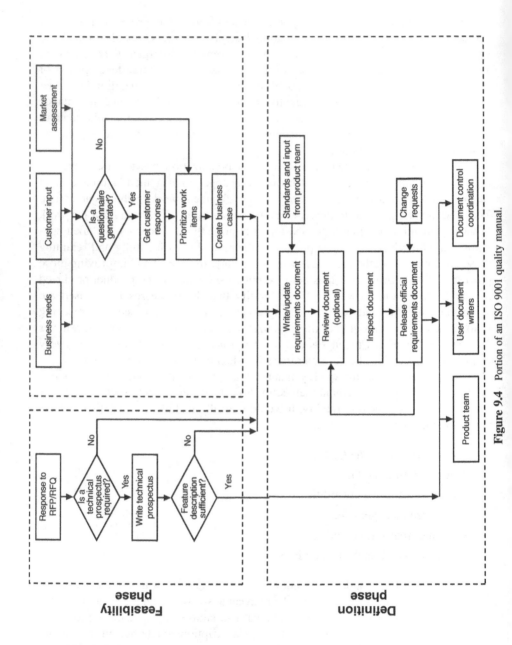

Figure 9.4 Portion of an ISO 9001 quality manual.

164

and what documents get produced. One of the things to keep in mind when developing a process description is that the description should not be overly detailed. There needs to be enough flexibility in the description to allow for differences in how individual employees do their work, but detailed enough so that it is obvious that the process being described is appropriate for the projects being carried out in the organization.

To become certified, the organization needs to employ an external audit agency. The auditors study the policy and quality manual, look at documents that have been produced by the process, and interview a cross section of people employed in the organization being audited. They issue an opinion on whether the process that has been defined is appropriate for the work being done and nonconformances when they find deviations from the process as defined in the manual. In response to nonconformances, the organization then must define procedures to keep those cnonconformances from occurring again and, in some cases, incorporate those procedures into the process.

While pursuing ISO 9001 certification can be expensive, it does provide some advantages. It can be used in support of selling products and applications to customers whose acquisition procedures only allow procurement of products that have been developed by an ISO-certified organization. It also relieves the management of the organization of some of the burden of monitoring and ensuring that the defined processes are being followed.

9.4 CMM ASSESSMENTS

The Capability Maturity Model (CMM) was developed by the Software Engineering Institute at Carnegie Mellon University to model the maturity of the processes used to develop software in the late 1980s. Since that time, it has been expanded to include the development of hardware products with which the software will be integrated and for a variety of other business processes such as the development of services, the development of an organization's human resources, and several others. The latest releases of the model are known as Capability Maturity Model Integration (CMMI). Software and hardware development organizations typically have used the model as a basis for conducting an assessment and for earning a maturity rating that compares their actual level with the model. Their reasons for doing this are usually one or more of the following: (1) to determine how well their development process compares with the best practices specified by the CMMI and to identify areas where improvements can be made, (2) to inform customers how well their process compares with CMMI best practices, and (3) to meet contractual requirements specified by some customers.

Figure 9.5 shows the maturity level of the CMMI and the activities that are required at each level. There are five maturity levels specified by the model. Level 1, called initial, is a level that requires no particular methods but which usually depends on the availability of highly qualified individuals working long hours to produce its products. Levels 2 and 3, which require many of the activities described in this book, are known as the managed and defined levels. Many modern software/

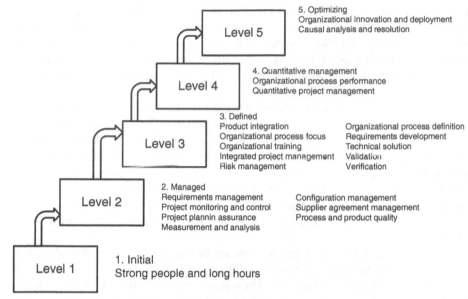

Figure 9.5   The Capability Maturity Model.

hardware development organizations have implemented the key activities specified at these levels. Assessment at levels 4 and 5, the quantitative management and optimizing levels, has been achieved by a relatively small number of development organizations, most notably by organizations that develop embedded aerospace and medical applications, by some organizations that develop software primarily for the defense industry, and by some of the offshore software development organizations.

An evaluation of the value of CMM assessments and ratings typically concludes that it is reasonable to expect that assessment up to level 3 is appropriate for almost all development organizations and product teams employing more than a few people working in small teams. Achieving levels 4 and 5 is usually appropriate only when it is necessary to achieve those levels to assure customers of the organizations' capabilities or when it is necessary to ensure high quality and reliability in the designs produced by the organization.

9.5 ARCHITECTURE REVIEWS

The final type of review that we want to touch upon is the architecture review (see Bass et al. 2006 and Kazman et al. 2000). Like the project management audit, an architecture review is intended to provide the project manager and the project team with additional assurance that they are headed in the right direction, in this case with the technicalities of the architecture specification.

Architecture reviews concentrate on the architectural design of the product or application. It tries to answer the question of whether the proposed architecture will adequately solve the problem being addressed. The review is conducted by a team of technical experts who have previously architected and designed similar systems. It starts by having the project team, usually the person who has primary responsibility for the application's architecture, providing an explicit and brief statement of the problem being addressed. The purpose of the review is to discover weaknesses in the overall design and to recommend improvements. One of these reviews usually requires a few days of the team members' and reviewers' time.

The Software Engineering Institute has developed a formalized process for conducting architecture reviews. It is called the Architecture Tradeoff Analysis Method® (ATAM®). It has also published a summary of the findings from a set of 18 architecture reviews that were conducted using this method. Those evaluations revealed that the most common architectural weaknesses were related to performance, requirements, and unrecognized needs.

9.6 SOME THINGS TO REMEMBER

The most important things we have discussed in this chapter are the following:

1. Use project management audits to pressure yourself, as the project manager, and the core team to produce a sound project plan.
2. Use ISO audits and CMM assessments to insure that you have both business and technical processes that are being used properly.
3. Use management reviews to make go or no-go decisions with management and (sometimes) with customers and to educate your project's "sponsors" and "champions."
4. Use architecture reviews to critique proposed architectures and to stimulate architectural improvements.

CASE STUDY 9 *Responding to Audit Findings*

Purpose

1. Learn how to use objective criticism provided by an audit team.
2. Determine how and when to share audit results with the upper management and with customers.
3. Learn to use the audit results to your advantage.
4. Learn how to avoid misuse of audit results by your team, by your upper management, or by the customer.

Activity

This case is based on the same project as the one described in Case Study 3. You are the project manager. You have had a discussion with your boss and relayed the results of your conversation with the marketing manager to him. His reaction was that you need to find ways to shorten the development interval and to lower the development cost for the project.

He also passed along a comment from the marketing manager's boss indicating that you were getting a reputation for being difficult to deal with. There seemed to be an impression that you were more interested in protecting development jobs than you were in developing products that were needed by your customers at an affordable cost.

To address these issues, you suggested to him that you would arrange for the project and the plan to be audited by a few of your peers. You would ask them to provide recommendations for improvement, to suggest ways that the development interval and total cost could be reduced, and to estimate the probability of successful execution of the plan as it is currently understood by the project team.

You found a few experienced development managers who were willing to do an audit as a favor to you. The team conducted an audit and provided a verbal readout using the attached slides (Figs C9.1–C9.19) to you and to key members of your team in a 2-hour review. You have decided that you would like to keep your major stakeholders aware of the project status by sending them a copy of these visuals with a description of how the project team plans to respond to each recommendation made by the auditors.

You have decided to produce a report to your stakeholders outlining the feedback as well as your planned actions. You will need to pay particular attention to the wording of this report and the influence it might have on the market management organization (remember the problems involved in Case Study 3 and the comments that your boss relayed to you). Could the audit results help the business discussions, or could they hurt?

Output

You should prepare a report addressed to your marketing manager and your boss, with copies to other appropriate stakeholders, describing how you intend to respond to each of the recommendations of the auditors. You should explain why you chose to implement the recommendations associated with each issue or why you chose not to follow the auditors' recommendation. In preparing your response, you should consider the following questions:

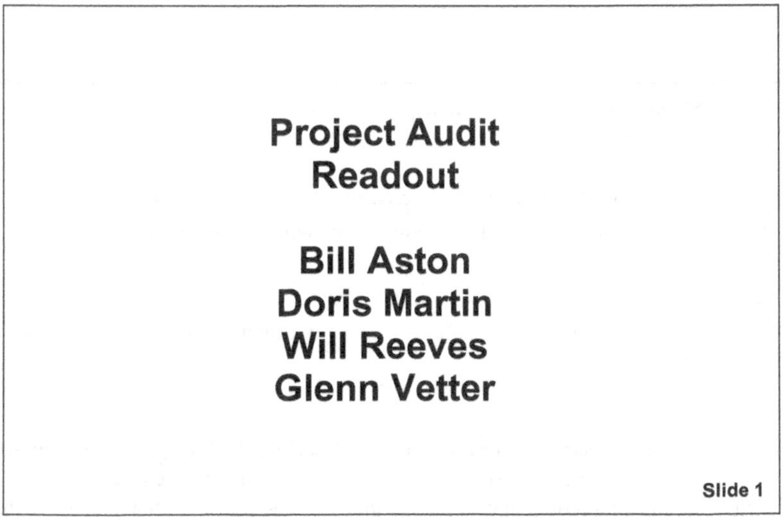

Figure C9.1

Audit Objectives

Conduct a general project review.

Objectively appraise project status and the methods being used to manage it.

Recommend ways to reduce the development interval.

Recommend ways to reduce the total cost.

Estimate the probability of success (delivering the features specified, on the proposed schedule for cost estimated in the project plan).

Slide 2

Figure C9.2

Audit Process

Reviewed:
- HW and SW architecture documents
- Requirements
- Detailed project plan

Conducted three pre-site interviews

Participated in a half-day overview presentation

Interviewed 13 members of the development team

Toured the system and integration test

Attended a project meeting

Summarized our findings and recommendations

Slide 3

Figure C9.3

Project Strengths

The team has developed a very thorough project plan.

The team members are very experienced and have worked well together on other projects.

The hardware and software architectures have been thought through very well.

The functional managers work together on other projects that are under way in the organization.

The requirements are well understood by the team.

The marketing manager and the principal requirements developer have worked closely on the business case and the requirements.

Slide 4

Figure C9.4

**Areas of Concern
(in priority order)**

Competition for development resources

Difficulty in meeting manufacturing cost objectives

Memory and performance budgets

Methods for tracking project status

Cost of testing

Identification of beta customers

Slide 5

Figure C9.5

Concern
Competition for Development Resources

There are five other projects under way in the organization that is doing this project.

Two of those projects are experiencing difficulty in meeting their objectives.

Three of the people working on the project being audited could be of great assistance to the projects that are experiencing difficulty.

They have been asked several times to assist with crises on those projects.

This interference is beginning to have a negative impact on their primary assignment.

Slide 6

Figure C9.6

Recommendation
Competition for Development Resources

The management of the organization should prioritize the importance of the six projects under way in the organization.

The three key people on the current project need to have it as their primary assignment.

A process needs to be put in place that will allow only higher-priority work to interfere with the primary assignments of those three people.

Slide 7

Figure C9.7

Concern
Difficulty of Meeting Manufacturing Cost Objectives

Hardware developers recently learned that it would be very difficult to meet manufacturing cost objectives.

The cost problems were discovered when the manufacturing organization conducted a manufacturing/procurement review of the hardware design.

The primary reason for the problem is the current high cost of the DRAM devices being used and the decision to use the newest microprocessors and digital signal processing devices in the product.

Slide 8

Figure C9.8

Recommendation
Difficulty of Meeting Manufacturing Cost Objective

The hardware design should be carefully reviewed to determine if any of the presently planned memory and processing capability can be eliminated.

Software developers should determine if memory requirements, as currently specified, can be reduced.

The overall physical design and the need for meeting international design standards should be revisited.

More standardization of parts that are used in other currently manufactured products should be considered.

Slide 9

Figure C9.9

Concern
Memory and Performance Budgets

Software developers indicated that there was plenty of memory available.

They also said that the processing capability of the hardware was more than enough for the application.

No memory or processing "budgets" have been allocated to specific functional modules or objects.

Given the hardware cost problem and the lack of software developers' concern for processing and memory usage, it is likely that performance and memory problems may occur in later releases.

Slide 10

Figure C9.10

Recommendation
Memory and Performance Budgets

Appoint an overall system architect (for hardware and software).

Characterize memory and processor utilization based on current early designs of both hardware and software.

Develop "budgets" by function and software subsystems for general purpose processors, digital signal processors, and memory.

Hold software development sub-teams accountable for keeping within their processing and memory budgets and/or for negotiating trade-offs.

Slide 11

Figure C9.11

Concern
Method for Tracking Project Status

The overall project status was not reviewed at the project meeting.

The team members did not know the overall project status.

Our analysis of the raw project plan/status data indicated that 13% of the tasks that should have been completed by now have not been completed (see the following chart).

None of the team members, except the project manager, seemed to be aware of this shortfall.

Slide 12

Figure C9.12

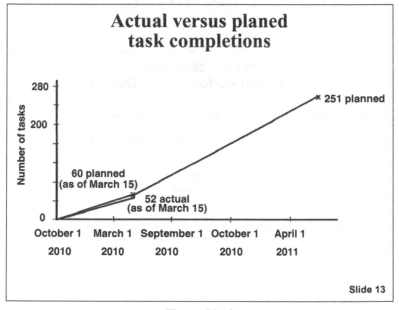

Figure C9.13

Recommendation
Method for Tracking Project Status

At each project meeting, the following should be reviewed:

- Tasks that have been completed since the last project meeting

- Incomplete tasks that should have been completed by now

- Tasks scheduled for completion before the next project meeting

- Open action items due for completion by the current date

These should be recorded in the meeting notes and circulated to the team and all stakeholders.

Slide 14

Figure C9.14

Concern
Cost of Testing

Responsibility for testing is now spread among three managers' groups:

1. One for hardware unit testing

2. One for software unit testing

3. One for integration and system testing

Overall project work is spread among six managers' groups.

Management overhead is contributing to the overall project development cost.

Slide 15

Figure C9.15

Recommendation
Cost of Testing

Merge integration and system testing into the software development manager's group where software unit testing is being done.

This will somewhat reduce the cost of the project because one less manager will be involved.

We understand that management overhead currently accounts for approximately 14% of development project cost.

Slide 16

Figure C9.16

Concern
Identification of Beta Customer

First release is scheduled at the end of this year (9 months from now).

First friendly (beta) customer has not yet been identified

Normal customer planning interval is approximately 12 months.

Slide 17

Figure C9.17

Recommendation
Identification of Beta Customer

Identify at least two potential beta customers.

Work with both of them as if there will be two beta customers.

One will probably drop out.

Then the team might have at least one beta customer by the end of the year.

Slide 18

Figure C9.18

Summary and Conclusions

Have found no silver bullets that would dramatically reduce development interval or cost

The probability of project success is currently about 80%.

That probability could be increased by implementing our prioritized recommendations

We recommend that you share these review results and your action plan with the entire team.

Slide 19

Figure C9.19

1. An audit will almost always produce some recommendations that you do not want to implement. How should you trade off the "pain and suffering" associated with the embarrassment generated by a long list of audit recommendations with the benefits of a project audit?
2. What are some of the benefits of an audit to both the project team and to the members of the audit team?
3. What negative impacts could the exposure of audit results to stakeholders have and how can they be turned into positive results?

4. How can project managers, who do a good job of developing a detailed plan, avoid the impression that they are not "team players" when stakeholders try to negotiate objectives that the project manager knows cannot be met within the constraints being imposed?

REFERENCES

BASS L., R. NORD, W. WOOD, and D. ZUBROW (2006) Risk themes discovered through architecture evaluations. Technical Report CMU/SEI 2006-TR-012, Carnegie Mellon Software Engineering Institute.

CRAWFORD S. G. and M. H. FALLAH (1985) Software development audits—A general procedure. *Proceedings of the 8th International Conference on Software Engineering*, pp. 137–141, IEEE, Piscataway, NJ, August.

KAZMAN R., M. KLEIN, and P. CLEMENTS (2000) ATAM: Method for architecture evaluation. Technical Report CMU/SEI-2000-TR-04, Carnegie Mellon Software Engineering Institute.

McDONALD J. (2003) Software project management audits—Update and experience report. *Journal of Systems and Software* **64** (3), February, 247–255.

Chapter 10

Multi-Projects

The topic we will be discussing in this chapter is multi-projects. Multi-projects cover four different kinds of operations: (1) multiple projects being done in the same organization, (2) single projects being done by more than one organization, (3) single projects being done at two or more geographically separated locations, and (4) programs consisting of two or more projects.

10.1 MULTIPLE PROJECTS IN THE SAME ORGANIZATION

Up to this point in the book, we have been generally assuming that our projects were being done in isolation from all other projects and that the project manager needed to be concerned only about the project that he or she was managing and the resources that were assigned to that project. However, in most industrial organizations that develop software-intensive products, that is not the case. It is quite common for multiple projects to be going on simultaneously in the same organization. It is quite common that organizational managers, functional managers, and sometimes even project managers are responsible for the management of multiple projects, whether the organizations in which they are working is a functional, a project, or a matrix organization as we defined them in Chapter 5.

In organizations where this is the case, we would find that the projects usually use similar technologies. They usually produce similar products and have similar customers. And they frequently use similar technical processes.

Some of the issues that are seen in these organizations are related to budget or personnel constraints, skill mix across projects, relative priority of projects, and accuracy of estimates. Readers who work in organizations can probably add several more issues that they observe in their workplaces.

Let us look at a simplified version of what goes on in an organization with constraints on its total staff size. Figure 10.1 shows the preferred kind of operation that we would like to see in a multi-project environment.

Suppose that in the past, before this chart begins, the entire organization was working on only one project. We will call it project 1. We start at year 0 with the

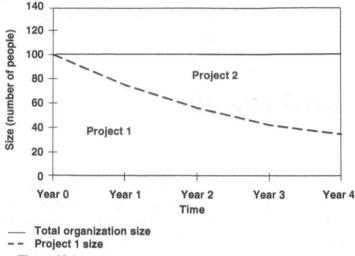

--- **Total organization size**
- - **Project 1 size**

Figure 10.1   Preferred operation when organization size is constrained.

entire organization of 100 people working on one project. We will call it project 1. Because of our definition of a project, that project must eventually come to an end, so we see the number of people working on project 1 declining over the 4-year period shown in the figure. If the organization size remains at 100, we would probably like to have a second project coming along so that, as people complete their work on project 1, they can roll off and start work on project 2. If project 2 has been planned in such a way that it needs the numbers and types of people rolling off project 1 at exactly the time that they become available, everyone will be satisfied. The organization will not have excess resources and the project manager for each project will have exactly the number of people that they need to execute their project when those people are needed.

Even in the case where the organization is not so tightly constrained and it is allowed to grow, we can envision a similar situation. In Fig. 10.2, we show a case where the total number of people in the organization is growing at a modest rate.

In this case, the organization also starts at time zero with 100 people working on project 1, and during the 4-year period shown in the figure, it grows to a total of 120 people. As time moves along in this case, we would also expect that as people finish their work on project 1, they would roll off to project 2. However, we might also expect that at least a few more people would roll off project 1 and move to project 2 than we saw in Fig. 10.1. This is because as the organization hires more people, it would probably start some of them working on project 2 and some of them on project 1. This should free up a few more people to roll over form project 1 to project 2 than we would normally expect.

All of this is very nice. However, the project managers for each of the projects need to be careful of a couple of things. The first is that if the organization grows too rapidly, or if it decreases its size too rapidly, it is likely that the productivity of both teams will start to decline. Why is this true?

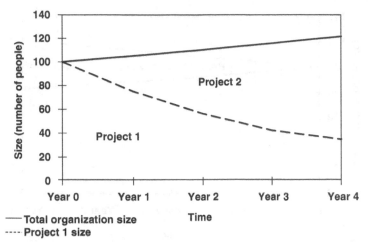

Figure 10.2 Preferred operation when the organization is allowed to grow at a modest rate.

Well, on the growth side, as new people come into the organization, it is likely that, on the average, it is absorbing new people who are not as experienced with either the products that the organization is developing or with the development processes being used by the people who have been there for a while. The new people will initially produce less than the old timers and will use up some of the experienced resources who will have to spend time educating the newcomers. So, the negative impact is greater than just the inexperience of the new people. This double negative impact on the productivity of both the new people and the experienced people can quickly take its toll.

On the reduction side, if the decline needs to be a greater decline than that which normally occurs through attrition, we see similar productivity declines. Why does that happen? In this case, as soon as it becomes known that the organization size needs to be decreased, some of the most productive and sharpest people in the organization start looking for jobs elsewhere and probably do not pay as much attention to their primary responsibilities. Because the very best people start looking early and usually find alternative positions very quickly, the projects are left with people who are not likely to be the most productive employees and who will have to spend even more of their time looking for alternative jobs while their attention to their primary responsibilities decline. (See Fig. 10.3 for an illustration of this.)

That figure shows a relatively narrow productivity envelope. I have managed in organizations that have been growing and in those that have been declining. In the places where I have worked, the normal turnover rate was usually about 5% per year. I found that when the growth or the decline in organizational size went outside plus or minus that range, the project teams and the organization could very quickly see the impact on productivity of the development teams. Of course, there have been other organizations where the normal attrition rate has been considerably higher than 5%. In those cases, I would expect that the productivity envelope would be somewhat wider than the one shown in Fig. 10.3 because their historical productivity

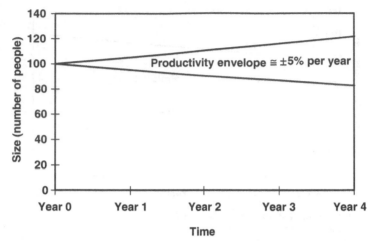

Figure 10.3 Organizational growth or decline.

would likely be lower than it would have been in an organization with a smaller attrition rate.

So, our preferred kind of operation is to keep the organization size close to flat, with perhaps a slight increase or decrease in size, preferably not more than a few percent per year in either growth or size reduction. In that case, people can roll off the old projects as they finish their work on the old ones and can start up the new ones at a reasonable pace without a significant negative impact on productivity. However, doing that requires centralized management and control of staffing among the projects. The higher management of the organization needs to manage the staffing, roll off from old projects, and ramp up on new projects. Project managers cannot be expected to accomplish this independently within their organizations because they will always plan ramp-up and roll-off of staff from their projects independently of other projects.

Table 10.1 shows a simple example of what needs to be done at the organizational level to manage this multi-project organization When I was the manager of an organization at Bell Laboratories and had responsibility for seven or eight different development projects and about 90 people, I created data like the information shown in this figure three or four times each year. Listed in the first column is the name of each person in the organization, the function that they perform, and the projects they are currently working on. For the small portion of the data shown in the example, we have Anderson, who is a systems engineer working on project 1; Banks, who is a software developer, working on projects 2 and 3; and Albright, who is a system tester, working on projects 1 and 2. Then, in my real organization, there would be similar data for 87 other people in the organization. Across the top of the first row is a calendar with each column corresponding to 1 month, and across each row next to a project name and under the person's name, we have listed the percentage of time that each person is expected to be working on each project during each

Table 10.1 Spreadsheet Showing Resource Availabilities

Month	Jan	Feb	Mar	Apr	May	Jun	Jul	Aug	Sept	Oct	Nov	Dec	Year
Name													
Anderson, Systems Engineer													
P1	1.00	1.00	1.00	0.60	0.60	0.20	0.20	0.00	0.00	0.00	0.00	0.00	0.38
Busy	1.00	1.00	1.00	0.60	0.60	0.20	0.20	0.00	0.00	0.00	0.00	0.00	0.38
Available	0.00	0.00	0.00	0.40	0.40	0.80	0.80	1.00	1.00	1.00	1.00	1.00	0.62
Banks, Software Developer													
P2	0.20	0.20	0.20	0.20	0.20	0.20	0.20	0.20	0.20	0.20	0.20	0.20	0.20
P3	0.80	0.80	0.80	0.80	0.50	0.30	0.30	0.30	0.30	0.30	0.30	0.30	0.48
Busy	1.00	1.00	1.00	1.00	0.70	0.50	0.50	0.50	0.50	0.50	0.50	0.50	0.68
Available	0.00	0.00	0.00	0.00	0.30	0.50	0.50	0.50	0.50	0.50	0.50	0.50	0.32
Albright, System Tester													
P1	0.60	0.60	0.60	0.60	0.50	0.50	0.30	0.30	0.20	0.20	0.20	0.20	0.40
P2	0.40	0.40	0.40	0.40	0.50	0.50	0.50	0.50	0.50	0.50	0.50	0.50	0.47
Busy	1.00	1.00	1.00	1.00	1.00	1.00	0.80	0.80	0.70	0.70	0.70	0.70	0.87
Available	0.00	0.00	0.00	0.00	0.00	0.00	0.20	0.20	0.30	0.30	0.30	030	0.13
Date for others in the organization													
⋮	⋮	⋮	⋮	⋮	⋮	⋮	⋮	⋮	⋮	⋮	⋮	⋮	⋮
Available for new projects	0.00	0.00	0.00	0.40	0.70	1.30	1.30	1.70	1.80	1.80	1.80	1.80	1.04
Systems Engineer	0.00	0.00	0.00	0.40	0.40	0.80	0.80	1.00	1.00	1.00	1.00	1.00	0.61
Software Developer	0.00	0.00	0.00	0.00	0.30	0.50	0.50	0.50	0.50	0.50	0.50	0.50	0.31
System Tester	0.00	0.00	0.00	0.00	0.00	0.00	0.20	0.20	0.30	0.30	0.30	0.30	0.09

month. For example, the first person is Anderson. Anderson is a systems engineer and he is working full-time on project 1. Therefore, he is busy 100% of the time and remains that way through March. In April, he starts to become available for about 40% of his time and by year end is available full-time to work on a new project. Averaging across the year shown in the figure, Anderson will spend 38% of his time on project 1 and will be available for new work for 62% of her time during the year.

The next person is Banks, a software developer who is working on two projects at the beginning of the year. He starts the year fully occupied and, by year end, it is expected that he will be available 50% of his time.

At the bottom of the spreadsheet is a summary that shows how much of each type of resource is expected to be available each month throughout the year to work on new projects. For the small sample shown, it is expected that during the year, slightly over 1 staff year (1.04) of total resource will be available with about 0.61 staff year of a systems engineer's time, 0.31 staff year of a software developer's time, and 0.09 staff year of a system tester's time becoming available on the schedule shown.

I developed my data by wandering around among both the functional managers and the project managers in the organization with a large spreadsheet in my hands. I asked them for their best estimates of what each person was doing and when they expected them to become free of their current responsibilities. I usually got pretty good agreement on the numbers, but occasionally, they did not agree. In that case, I would need to get the managers and the individual members of the staff together to come up with consistent estimates. This procedure was a bit clumsy, but it worked well. The purpose in doing this kind of an analysis is to determine the capacity of an organization to start a new project. A project manager and his or her core team, left to their own devices, would probably develop a plan for the next new project that gets the work started as soon as possible and would plan to ramp up the project's staff to optimize the operation of that project. The inevitable result would be that there would not be enough staff available to get started as planned and the project would be in trouble from the start. New projects should be planned with a knowledge not only of what needs to be done for that project but also with the knowledge of what resources will be available to work on that project, and when. In the simple example discussed above, if there were no other resources in the organization. The new project could not start until April when a systems engineer becomes available on a part-time basis. A small amount of software development work could be undertaken in May when a part-time software developer becomes available. Test planning might start in August when a tester becomes available for 20% of his or her time.

The point of all of this is that the resources in an organization involved in multiple projects need to be managed and controlled by the organizational manager. Functional managers and project managers within the organization cannot and should not be expected to do this part of their jobs. If this is not being done in the organization where you work and if the available staff is constrained, you need to start your lobbying campaign to get it started.

A second problem that frequently appears in multi-project organizations, and it can be seen in our example above, is that the projects are under pressure to get started as soon as possible. This results in making use of people who are rolling off other projects in the organization. It is unusual for a person who has been working on a project, perhaps for several months or even years, to completely roll off on a specific day and immediately to be available 100% of his or her time to start on the next project. It is much more common to see situations like the one that we have just discussed in which people gradually roll off their old work and become available for the new work over a period of several weeks or several months. This leads to a person trying to share his or her time across projects and, probably more frequently, across tasks on the same project. Some task and project sharing is almost inevitable. But let us look at a situation in which, while it may be inevitable, it is not desirable.

Figure 10.4 shows the potential impact of assigning three tasks, perhaps all on one project but possibly on different projects, to the same person. If the objective is to complete the tasks as early as possible, the first row shows the order in which they might be completed if each was being done by different people. However, if they are all assigned to the same person and that person works on them as shown in the second row of the figure, we see that tasks 1 and 2 are delayed and task 3 is completed no earlier than it would have otherwise been completed. There has been no gain as a result of multitasking, and there has actually been a penalty.

While it would be desirable to avoid such multitasking completely, it is frequently not possible. So, the second best alternative is to ensure that the project manager lets the person who is being multitasked know the priorities for each task to which they have been assigned and the due date for each. This is particularly important if any of the tasks are on a project's critical path. An even more difficult situation is when the three tasks are parts of different projects. In that case, the project managers for each project need to negotiate with each other to determine the relative priorities of each task (and perhaps each project). This is sometimes difficult because if I am the project manager for one project, it is likely that the priority for my project is almost always higher than the priority of other projects. In that case, it may be necessary for a manager who has responsibility for all projects to make the call on which of the tasks should receive the undivided attention of the person doing the work and which tasks can wait for the completion of higher-priority tasks.

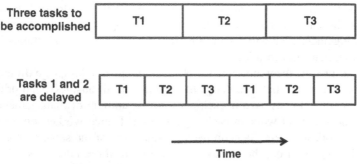

Figure 10.4   Potential impact of multitasking.

In an organization that I managed several years ago, we decided that we should prioritize the projects under way in the organization a few times each year. I and the functional/project managers who reported to me met one day and we prioritized all of the projects under way in the organization. The criterion that we used for prioritization was a combination of the time to the customer delivery date (the closer the time, the higher the priority) and the financial impact of a missed delivery date (the higher the cost, the higher the priority). After some discussion, we were able to reach an agreement on a prioritized list. Our purpose in doing this was partially to handle the multitasking issue that we have just discussed and to determine, without the necessity for a long meeting and many discussions, from which projects we should we pull resources when it became necessary to address an issue on another higher-priority project. This worked very well over a period of several years. However, when we started doing it, we made a mistake by announcing to the entire organization what the priorities for each project were. As you might expect, the people working on the lower-priority projects were very disappointed to hear that their project had been given a low priority and it took some effort to recover from our error. We did continue to reprioritize about every 3 months and to use the priorities to assign and reassign people to tasks. However, we never announced the priorities to the organization again.

10.2   MULTI-ORGANIZATION AND MULTILOCATION PROJECTS

Now let us look at multi-organization and multi-location projects. These are projects being executed in more than one part of a parent organization and/or at more than one geographic location, which might be only a few hundred yards or many miles apart. In this case, you will usually see similar technical work being done in both organizations and at both locations. That means that we see similar experts, or at least people who feel as though they are experts, in both organizations and both locations. This is not an ideal way to work from the point of view of productivity, but it is usually done to share the workload or to balance staff shortages and surpluses. Sometimes, it is done to grow the size of the staff outside the "productivity envelope" that we talked about earlier in this lecture. Sometimes, it is done to add local content from nondomestic locations so that customers in those locations will be encouraged to buy the products being developed. When we make these arrangements, we will usually find that there are different cultures in each of the organizations and locations.

By culture, we mean not only the obvious things like language differences and time zone differences but also things like the technical, business, and project management methodologies used in each place or the amount of management involvement in the technical work in each organization. I once worked on a project for which the work was being done in two different parts of the same company. In one part of the organization, the management at two to three levels above the people doing the work was frequently involved in some of the technical details. In the other part of the organization, no one above the direct functional or project manager had any idea of how the work was being done, what its status was, or why it was being done the way it was. Needless to say, these two parts of the same organization had difficulties working together.

When work is being done on the same project in two or more parts of the same organization, we frequently hear comments like the following about the organization on the other side of the boundaries:

- They have different priorities in the other location/organization.
- They make decisions unilaterally without consulting us.
- Some of the people there are not very technically competent.
- People who are assigned full-time appear to be unavailable for large portions of the time.
- Our managements do not get along.
- Management on other side of boundary is very loose.
- They do not seem to follow business and technical processes on other side of the boundary.

In one case, I was the leader of a development organization that was designing an application that would be installed in and would work as part of a product that was being designed at a location about 40 miles from my location. That project got started because the leader of the other organization and I had been friends for several years and we both realized the value of developing an integrated solution. We were able to convince our joint managements that we should work together to develop this product. We both developed excellent project plans and decided that we should conduct a project management plan as described in Chapter 9. One of the findings of the audit team was that the management of the two parts of the development team did not get along with each other. This came as a surprise to my friend and me because in our opinions, we got along very well. However, to follow up on the finding, we decided to dig more deeply to find the cause of that perception. What we found was that both I and my friend had made what we thought were joking comments about each other, our styles of management, and the status of the work in each of the organizations. We usually made these comments when the other person was not present. While we thought we were joking, we found that members of our teams took these comments quite seriously and concluded that we did not get along with each other. So, for the next several months, we had to appear together frequently, put our arms around each other's shoulders, and be very careful of what we said when the other person was not present. Eventually, the perception of interpersonal problems disappeared.

To manage some of these perceptions, there are many things the project manager can do. They include

- getting the two parts of the team to meet, face to face, at beginning of a project (perhaps for development of some parts of the project plan);

- getting at least some members to meet face to face regularly (perhaps quarterly) to socialize;
- getting individuals to work with each other face to face frequently;
- using audio, or preferably video, for weekly or biweekly project meetings;
- requiring team members to use e-mail and voice mail only to leave messages or to send formal documents and not to use these methods for conversation; e-mail and voice mail messages are frequently misunderstood;
- encouraging the use of live telephone calls (not e-mail or voice mail) for substantive discussions;
- never disagreeing, criticizing, or arguing via e-mail;
- using similar project management methodologies and having similar people doing the project management work on both sides of the boundary;
- setting up a joint change request review board and automatically transferring and displaying change requests across the boundary;
- appointing one (and only one) project manager who is recognized and agreed upon by people on both sides of the boundary; this person will need to travel frequently between locations;
- setting up similar and consistent cost and staff tracking structures in both parts of the organization; and
- creating name/address and responsibility lists for cross-organization/location distribution.

Notice that the first few items on this list require that people on both sides of the boundaries must get to know each other at the start of the project. This is frequently an expensive part of the operation, but if the project manager is ever faced with this kind of project, he or she should never give in to the management who might claim that budget pressure do not allow team members to travel extensively or to spend some time working in the other location or organization. Without those up-front expenditures, the project will surely fail or the cost will be incurred later when everyone realizes that team members need to get to know each other.

Those in the middle third of the list have to do with methods that should be used for communications, not only across the boundaries but also within the whole project. Project managers should pay particular attention to those having to do with the use of e-mail. The misuse of e-mail within these kinds of projects can be particularly harmful. I was once an auditor for a project management audit on a project that was being done at three different locations, Chicago, Phoenix, and New Jersey, by teams that had never previously worked with each other. During some e-mail conversations among the primary architects in New Jersey and Phoenix, the architect in New Jersey, who was also a functional technical manager, responded to a suggestion that was made by his counterpart in Phoenix about an architectural issue by saying something like, "That's a really dumb idea. Whoever suggested it doesn't know anything about designing systems like ours." That was not very polite, but, in addition, within an hour after the message was sent, the message appeared on bulletin boards at the Phoenix location. Everyone there knew the person who had made the suggestion who was one of the most experienced and respected members of the Phoenix team. At the time we conducted the audit, which was several months after this incident occurred, several people in Phoenix mentioned it as an example of how difficult it was to work with the people in New Jersey, even though the original perpetrator had profusely apologized to everyone for his indiscretion and had traveled to Phoenix several times to help alleviate the opinions there that he was extremely difficult to work with.

The last third of the items on the list say that project managers need to do all the same things that they would normally do if the project were located entirely within one organization and at one location.

10.3 MULTI-PROJECT PROGRAMS

That finally brings us to multi-project programs in which the results depend upon bringing together several projects to produce a common unified result. Programs like these are sometimes created to subdivide very large projects into more manageable subprojects, but, in my experience I have seen them created to obtain a variety of expertise available only in widely disbursed organizations. In this case, we usually see different technical expertise within each subproject. It is sometimes done to integrate the products that were independently developed by separate organizations, which might still be undergoing continuing development. They sometimes involve products and organizations outside the parent organization, which we will discuss in Chapter 11.

Figure 10.5 illustrates the structure of a multi-project program. At the top we have a block illustrating the program then several, somewhat independent, projects. The objective of the program is to produce a unique product or service within a predetermined interval of time and a budget that needs the outputs from all of the subprojects to achieve the program's overall objectives.

First, a program manager should be appointed at an appropriate organizational level that allows them to exercise appropriate authority over all of the subprojects.

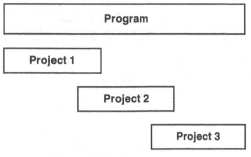

Figure 10.5   Program structure.

As an example, the Boeing 787 Dreamliner program manager is Scott Fancher, a vice president of the Boeing Corporation and general manager of the program. That program is extremely large and is made up of several internal Boeing projects and many external supplier projects from around the world.

The program manager should have personal management experience on projects that are similar to some of the program's subprojects. Mr. Fancher had been vice president and general manager of Boeing's Missile Defense Systems division where some of the airplane's subsystems are being designed and developed.

The program manager needs a staff with expertise in each subproject area in which the program manager does not have personal expertise.

This typically results in a structure that looks like the one shown in Fig. 10.6 with a technically competent staff at the program management level. They are typically responsible for managing the development of the program's requirements, including user interfaces, technical oversight of the subprojects, and management of the projects being executed by external vendors. Our U.S. government's National Science Foundation (NSF) manages several programs under which projects are done at hundreds of universities and some industrial organizations across the United States. The NSF program management staffs typically consist of 5–10 people who are either permanent NSF employees with research experience or university people on 1- or 2-year temporary assignments at the NSF.

The program managers and their staff need to ensure that there is a clearly designated project manager, not just a contact person, for each subproject. At least one program staff member should participate in each subproject meeting, or at least participate with the management of the subproject in regularly scheduled joint governance meetings. Both the subproject and the program personnel should participate with the customer in developing requirements to ensure that the subproject members clearly know why they are striving to meet the requirements imposed on them. The program manager must require the subprojects to develop project plans that are audited by managers with experience in the area of the subproject work. Because there are more opportunities for delays in programs than there are in individual

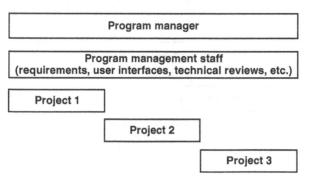

Figure 10.6   Program management office and staff.

projects, more contingency time and effort need to be included in the program plan than in individual project plans. For example, the Boeing 787 Dreamliner project mentioned above was delayed by approximately 2 years because of the inability of some of its subproject suppliers to meet the requirements for new technology, high-quality products.

Subproject interface specification documents must be produced early and inspected by two or more subprojects and the program management staff and approved by all. In a program environment, the management of the individual sub-projects is similar to the management of isolated projects. However, the program manager and the program management staff need to recognize that the subprojects may have objectives in addition to those required for the program, and those sub-project managers may sometimes be under pressure to prioritize those other objec-tives above those of the program. That is one of the reasons that managers with high levels of authority should be the program managers so that they can exert appropriate pressure when such discrepancies are recognized.

The program staff must have detailed visibility into each subproject, much deeper than high-level milestones. The program manager must assure the availability of sufficient funding of each subproject and sufficient staff within each subproject's organization. And multi-project programs require special attention to the specifica-tion of interfaces, integration test planning, and integration test execution so that mismatches can be detected as early as possible.

Program managers need to build a strong but small program management staff. They need to hold regularly scheduled program meetings with each of the subproject managers participating. They need to hold program reviews at checkpoints with a high-level and broad management participation. And, finally, if the program manag-ers are new to program management, they need to get external expert program and project management consulting help.

We could continue to go on with guidelines for managing multi-project pro-grams because that effort is very difficult and is well beyond the content of this book. But the reader should be able to recognize when program management is called for and when they need to get appropriate help in doing it.

10.4 SOME THINGS TO REMEMBER

The most important things that we have discussed in this chapter are the following:

1. Be sure to provide appropriate organizational resources and technical man-agement in multi-project organizations.
2. Monitor and control resources at the organizational level.
3. Follow the guidelines contained in this chapter when managing multi-organization/location projects, even when budgets are tight.
4. Get lots of help for multi-project program management.

CASE STUDY 10

Purpose

1. Identify potential causes of poor communications.
2. Outline some things that can be done to address these issues before they become serious problems.

Background

The Operational Services Software Development (OSSD) organization has been working for 4 years on the development of the third generation of the Network Management System, which is used in your customer's telecommunications network. They are in the middle of the development cycle for Release 3. All of the development to date has been done at their location in New Jersey. Releases 1 and 2 both had significant problems during development and after introduction into the field. Release 3 has been going very well. Most of the project team members believe that the reason that they are in good shape now is that they are following an appropriate, well-defined development process and that they have an outstanding manager who is providing project management leadership to the team.

Release 3 was kicked off with a series of team meetings in which the entire team of about 30 people participated in outlining what needed to be done and how those tasks were interrelated. They subsequently formed several smaller teams that spent a few weeks putting together plans for each of the sets of features that would be included in Release 3. These results were then assembled by the project manager and the sub-team leaders into an overall project plan. Because their development process was ISO (International Standards Organization) certified, they did not have to devote significant effort to defining the development process in the project plan, but they did do a very thorough job of writing a project plan that contained all of the other recommended information.

Because of the team's poor experiences with Releases 1 and 2, and because the effort and cost associated with Release 3 were significantly smaller than those of the earlier releases, the team had little difficulty getting approval for the budget and staffing that they requested. Project meetings were being held biweekly, and the project manager was providing very useful status information to the team, to higher management, and to the customer.

About 6 months ago, a new opportunity had come along. The International Systems subsidiary of your customer's organization approached the OSSD organization, indicating that it now had a need similar to their parent's domestic needs and was willing to pay several million dollars for a system that was very similar to the Network Management System. Their version would require some minor interface changes to operate with the telecommunications facilities used internationally. Because the OSSD organization was just getting into development of Release 3, we indicated that we were not able to take on the job in time to meet the international subsidiary's needs.

We did work out an arrangement, though, to give all of the system software to another development organization, which was part of our own corporation, so that they could modify it for international use. We offered a nominal level of consulting help and expected to receive a portion of the revenues when the sale was completed. That part of our company was located in Germany and they began the work there.

The independent jobs have progressed reasonably well in both locations. Now a second challenge has appeared. The domestic customer's major service competitors in the United States recently announced that they would shortly be providing new services that could easily be matched (or bettered) by the domestic customer if several of the features that have been on the Network Management System's "wish list" for several years were implemented quickly. The first increment of these additions would be needed about 4 months after Release 3 goes to the field. Once again, the OSSD organization was faced with a shortage of experienced talent. It was still in the middle of Release 3 development and was being strained by the consulting that it was being asked to do by the development team in Germany.

The upper managements of both organizations discussed this dilemma and came up with a resolution that they felt would be workable. As a result of some unrelated decisions that had been made by the organization in Germany, there were several people coming available at the European location where the modifications were currently being made on the Network Management System for use by the international customer. The people there were all very experienced software developers. In addition, a group of software developers were coming available at the OSSD's location in Colorado who could assist with the next generic. If the work could be shared among those locations, and if the OSSD organization could afford to pay the standard cost per year for each of the developers, then the work could be accomplished on a schedule that would meet both the domestic customer's and the international customer's needs. This would also help stabilize our company's work force and avoid major dislocations of very experienced employees at both locations.

A decision has been made to proceed with the development of features to be called R4 under this organizational arrangement.

You have been assigned the job of project manager for the OSSD organization's R4 project. You have frequently heard that projects spanning more than one location were difficult to manage. This one will span three geographic locations and two business units of your company.

Start by identifying, in the form of a list, some of the more obvious communications problems that could be encountered in an arrangement like the one outlined above. Instead of simply describing possible symptoms, try to make some guesses at what the underlying causes of the communications problems might be. We want to address these root causes, even before their symptoms appear. Indicate on a second list the actions that you, as the project manager, need to take now to address these root causes.

Output

You should prepare a summary of the problems and planned actions that address the following issues:

1. How does the project change when you move from the hierarchical project management structure that we assumed earlier in this book to a more distributed structure as outlined in this exercise?
2. What is different about the role of the project manager as an individual under each of these structures?
3. What needs to be different about the project management process with the different structures?
4. What do you think that the impact of geography, culture, and history might be in a situation like this one?

Chapter 11

Managing Outsourced Development Work

Traditionally, software-intensive applications were developed by relatively small teams of people who all worked for the same first-level manager and who worked at a common location. The manager frequently performed some of the functions that we now ascribe to a person whom we call the project manager. That person sometimes managed both hardware and software development if the applications were relatively small and they depended upon the people within their groups to integrate the various parts of the ultimate product. This resembled the project structure that we discussed in Chapter 5. We started our discussions in this book with a tacit assumption that this was still the case. In reality, this situation is far from normal today. Over the years, development teams became larger and most industrial organizations were faced with economic pressures to increase the span of control of their first-level managers. As the teams became too large for one manager to handle entire projects, team managers started to specialize in various specialties required for realization of the final product. This led to organizational structures that looked similar to what we called the functional structure in Chapter 5, with the functional specialties being things like systems engineering, hardware development, software development, and system testing. As projects and the organizations became more complicated, the concept of project management was introduced to provide resources that would assist in managing and coordinating projects that spanned multiple functional groups. The first-line functional managers gradually came to depend on what we call today "team leads." These are individual technical contributors, usually within the various functional groups, who the functional manager depends upon to work with the project manager and the members of the functional group who are assigned to a specific project. These changes tended to produce organizational structures that looked similar to the matrix organization that we discussed in Chapter 5. That is probably the most common structure that we see in the industry today.

Figure 11.1 traces the evolution of these structures from the relatively small colocated project teams in the upper left, which depended heavily on the

Managing the Development of Software-Intensive Systems, by James McDonald
Copyright © 2010 John Wiley & Sons, Inc.

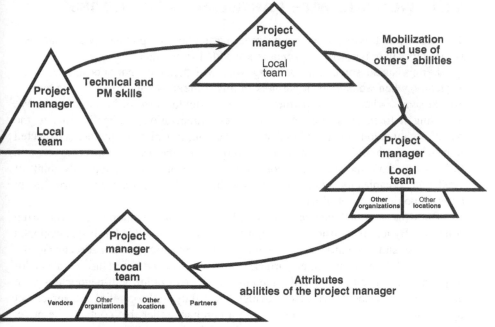

Figure 11.1   Old versus new project management.

technical and project management skills of first-level managers, to the expansion of the spans of control of those managers and their dependence upon project managers and team leads within their groups. This forced those first-level managers to develop the ability to mobilize and use others' abilities, not only for technical contributions but also for management of the resources within their management groups.

The next step that occurred was the addition of resources from other organizations, initially within the parent organization, and from other geographic locations to supplement the resources available within the original management groups. This forced the successful project managers to become more adept at managing resources at other geographic locations and in other organizations that may, or may not, report directly to them. This resulted in many cases drawing in both partners and vendors to the projects of the parent organization to produce a combination of resources shown in the lower left portion of Fig. 11.1 including not only people who reported directly to the project manager but also people in vendor organizations, in other organizations within the parent organization, people at other locations, and partners whom the parent organization depends upon for either services or products. In this configuration, the operation becomes crucially dependent upon the project manager's personal attributes and abilities, particularly their interpersonal and general management skills and, to a lesser degree, their technical capabilities.

11.1   WORKING WITH PARTNERS AND VENDORS

The one step in this evolution that becomes particularly perplexing for the managers is the step where partners and vendors are added to the mix.

Let us spend some time defining what we mean by partners and vendors. Typically, when we talk about partners in this context, we are not using the term in a legal sense, where a legal partnership is a particular form of business entity. We are using it to mean a relationship between organizations, either internal to the parent organization or external to that organization, in which the partner is expected to provide some of the investment in the project and the partner expects to share in the rewards from the successful completion of the project. We typically think of vendors as organizations that promise a specified delivery for a specific price on an agreed-upon date or set of dates.

Both partners and vendors can supply off-the-shelf solutions or customized solutions. By an off-the-shelf solution, we mean something that has been developed in the past and something that is being sold to other customers. Procuring off-the-shelf solutions from either partners or vendors is the safest use of a vendor or partner arrangement. Typically, the customer organization will negotiate a price and a delivery schedule with the provider. Then they will formalize the agreement by signing either a contract or by issuing a purchase order that contains the price, the specifications, and the schedule for deliveries.

Another alternative is the procurement of new or customized solutions. In this case, the product being purchased is sometimes currently under development and the development work is being paid for by the partner or the vendor with the intent of selling the product to the customer and to other customers as well. An alternative use of partners and vendors is to have them develop a product especially for you and you are paying for the development work. Both of these arrangements increase the risk on your project as compared to the use of an off-the-shelf product. There might be good business reasons for accepting that increased risk, perhaps because of limited internal resources, cost advantages, or market positioning. However, one of the things we need to remember is that no matter how tightly the contracts for this kind of work are written, they cannot reduce the risk of negative schedule or performance impacts to your project. The agreements with partners, if they are well written, can protect the parent organization from major financial losses, but they usually do little to protect the specific project from negative impacts.

Figure 11.2 illustrates the relative risks with the use of partners and vendors for off-the-shelf solutions and custom designs.

The upper left corner, corresponding to procuring off-the-shelf solutions from vendors, is the minimal risk situation because the partner already has the product available and stands to lose profitability if they do not deliver as promised. This might correspond to an arrangement that a software development team might make with a provider of commercial computer hardware and its operating system software on which the software development team's software will run. In this case, there is little risk that the commercial hardware will not be available as planned and will perform as it has for the partner's other customers. They might make a deal with

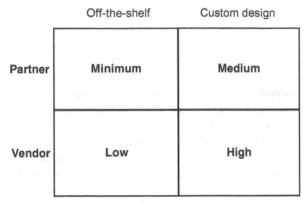

Figure 11.2   Relative risks of various arrangements.

the software development organization that if more than a specified quantity of the commercial hardware is purchased by end customers of the software development team, they will give deep discounts to the end customers when they buy the hardware for the purpose of running the newly developed software. In my experience, discounts in this situation can typically be 35% for even modest numbers of purchases and can be considerably higher for large purchase quantities. Sometimes, the hardware partner may be willing to provide a limited amount of hardware at no cost to the software development team if they develop the software specifically for the partner's hardware and software environment. The advantage to the software development organization is that its customers see a lower total cost of implementing its solution and the hardware supplier sells additional volume.

The next riskier arrangement is purchasing off-the-shelf solutions from a vendor. This would include the use of commercial off-the-shelf (COTS) software that is integrated into the software product being developed by our team. In this situation, the risk is somewhat higher than the situation described above because, unless the development team does an extensive evaluation of the COTS software under conditions that rigorously simulate the ultimate operating environment of the final product, it is possible that the integrated COTS product may not perform well enough to meet the end customers' need for reliability and high throughput. In this case, many software development organizations that have experienced this problem have found that it is difficult, if not impossible, to get the COTS vendor to address the problem because the software development business and its customers make up only a small portion of the total business for the COTS product, and most of the COTS customers are not experiencing the same problems with its use. In addition, the functionality of the COTS product may not precisely match the needs of the end customers, and it is usually very difficult, if not impossible, to get the COTS vendor to modify the product to meet our needs.

The next category of relationship has our partners providing custom designs to be incorporated into our projects. If you search the World Wide Web looking for "software partnerships," you will get thousands of hits. They are usually companies who are not looking to be partners but are rather companies who have entered into a partnership with another firm to make use of one of that partner's products in developing custom solutions for our use. You usually cannot find many suppliers who are willing to enter into a partnership relationship with another development team if both are developing new products that must be integrated to make them successful. Occasionally, you might be able to find a supplier who is developing a new product and who is willing to treat you as a beta partner for the first, or nearly first, application of their product.

I was involved with one such relationship several years ago in which my company was developing software and hardware to upgrade and modernize a line of telecommunications switching products. Traditionally, systems like this had been built using entirely custom-designed hardware to implement both the necessary switching function and the control and interface functions that were necessary for the operation of a switch. The argument for doing it this way was that the speed and reliability that was required for the control functions were so stringent that they could be achieved only by computers that were customized for that application with redundant processors, redundant nonvolatile memory, and operating system functionality that also performed continual monitoring of all redundant hardware. However, at the time this work was being done, several commercial computer suppliers were developing new, highly reliable, high-capacity, and high-performance computers. So, our development team decided to partner with one of those suppliers to use the commercial hardware and its new operating system to control the switch. Shortly after the development work began, in fact, it was while detailed requirements were being developed, our team recognized that they needed some very specific capabilities to be provided by the commercial computer system. When they began serious negotiations with the "partner," they found that, not only was the computer development already delayed but that the vendor was also treating our team like a beta customer. By this time, the vendor had also acquired several other beta customers and in their view, some of the other beta customers' markets were likely to be much larger, and less demanding, than ours. The estimate that they provided for the cost of modifying their product to meet the necessary needs was extremely high, and it quickly became clear that they were not willing to treat this relationship as a two-way partnership.

Successful partnerships are more frequently successfully arranged within a parent corporation in which pressure can be applied to both partners to successfully meet their obligations and in which accountability can be demanded of both partners.

The highest-risk situation is the development of customized designs by vendors. Despite its relatively high risk, this arrangement has, during the past few years, become a very common arrangement. It is used widely by various parts of the U.S. government, including the military, for acquiring software, hardware, and combined software/hardware development services. There have been notable failures observed in this kind of environment, particularly when it was clear at the beginning of the project that the vendor would need to use new and untested technologies, or use technologies in ways that they had not been previously used (McGroddy and Lin

2004; Dixon 2008; Feickert 2009). On the other hand, this arrangement has become quite common and, in some cases, very successful for the development of business software that uses well-established technologies. It is now most frequently used for the international outsourcing of software development work where the ultimate solution might cost considerably less than if it were developed domestically using in-house software development teams. We will talk more about this later when we discuss international outsourcing.

11.2 MANAGING PARTNER AND VENDOR RELATIONSHIPS

So, what are we to do if we need to get involved in one of these arrangements and we are still responsible for delivering our results with appropriate levels of quality, on time, and within budget?

One possibility is that our partner or vendor is an internal partner or vendor, meaning that it is organizationally located within another portion of our parent organization. If we work in a corporation, that means that the other organization is located in another part of the same corporation. If we work for a government entity, it would mean that the partner or vendor is an organization in another entity of the same government. In this case, we should always start with a written "contract" with the partner or vendor. We have put the word "contract" in quotation marks here because it cannot usually be a legally binding contract. An agreement made between two parts of a corporation or two parts of a government is similar to an agreement that we make with ourselves. It can put pressure on us to comply with the terms of the agreement, but it is not binding in the legal sense in that there are no legal remedies under available to either party if one of the parties does not deliver. In these cases, the validity of the agreement is only as good as the reputation of the person who signs the agreement. If that person leaves the organization for which they signed the agreement, the agreement no longer has any validity. On the other hand, if the agreement is between two corporations or a government entity and a corporation, and if it was signed by individuals who have the authority to make commitments on behalf of those organizations, it is valid even if the individual who made the agreement is no longer employed there.

Despite the fact that internal agreements within a corporation have no legal standing, they can frequently be used very effectively to insure that both parts of the organization have a clear understanding of what needs to be done. Therefore, the agreement should contain a clear and complete statement of the technical work that both parts of the organization agree to do. The receiving part of the organization should be sure that the affected members of both teams have opportunities to socialize and get to know each other. They should make sure that technical specifications describing any necessary interfaces and the methods that will be used for integrating and testing the joint application are completed as early as possible. The receiving organization should insist that their partner manage their portion of the project properly. To help do that, the receiving organization might want to suggest that that the joint plan be subjected to a project management audit. We might try to negotiate open access to their project meetings, or even better, schedule joint project meetings. Finally, for all projects involving partners, it is advantageous to set up a joint steering committee that meets regularly to monitor the status of the joint project.

If we are planning to work with an external partner on a custom design, one of the first things we should do is to negotiate a solid contract. We should feel free to call on our internal legal and procurement people to assist with these negotiations because, while sometimes it appears to us that the involvement of those parts of our own organization may slow down the negotiations, people who work full-time in those positions are usually better than we are at negotiating and they can frequently add things to the agreement that provide us with additional protection. However, when we ask them to get involved, we cannot turn over the entire responsibility to them. We need to insist that the agreement contains very clear and complete technical scope or work statements. Any interfaces that need to be met by the hardware or software being developed by the partner must be clearly and completely specified in the agreement, or at least in an addendum that is made a part of the agreement. The agreement should specify that there will be frequent face-to-face interactions between technical members of our team and members of the partner's team and should be specific enough to determine how frequently these interactions should occur and who will be involved in the interactions. One of the first things that the agreement should call for is the development of a joint integration and system testing plan early in the project development. And, finally, our team should develop a fall-back contingency plan describing what we will do if the partner does not deliver its portion of the project according to the terms of the agreement. This contingency plan is necessary because in most partnering situations, nondelivery by the partner will put our project into the high-risk portion of the risk profile that we discussed in Chapter 8.

That brings us, finally, to the riskiest arrangement of needing to manage external vendors who are providing custom designs for incorporation into our project. In this case, the first thing we need to do is to arrange for the development of a solid contract between our parent organization and the vendor. Of course, that implies that we should draw our procurement people and our legal people into the development of the contract. In this case, our organization might want to consider a two-phase project in which the first phase consists of the development of detailed specifications and the second phase includes the development and deployment of the product. To go to the extreme, some organizations actually contract with two or more organizations for the first phase of a two-phase contract then use the specifications produced by the first phase to help identify which vendor should be chosen for the second phase. Two-phase contracts, unfortunately, can stretch the total development and deployment time significantly. However, it sometimes reduces the overall project risk particularly when new technologies are being incorporated into the project.

In the case of a two-phase contract, it is quite easy to make the specifications a part of the contract for phase 2. However, if possible, it is sometimes a good idea to make the specifications, whenever they are produced, an addendum to the contract. This makes it relatively simple to determine when a change that becomes necessary during the course of the project calls for a renegotiation of the specifications and, perhaps, a change in the cost of the work. The process for handling change requests and the decision to change costs based on those requests should also be included in the contract agreement.

In any case, the receiving organization should require that the vendor has a project management process in place that is at least as good as that of the receiving organization and that it has enough visibility into the vendor's organization to determine if this is the case. The receiving organization should assign a member of the project team to work with the vendor for as much time as it takes to insure that the receiving organization knows the status of the work being done by the vendor. If the receiving organization does not have technical expertise in the work that is being done by the vendor, it should acquire one or more experts who are capable of evaluating the vendor's plans and the status of its work. They should also require the vendor to allow members of the receiving organization to participate in the vendor's project meetings.

It will usually not be easy to get the vendor to agree to these last few requirements. Therefore, it is important that these needs are identified when the contract with the vendor is being negotiated and that they get incorporated into the contract. This also makes incorporation of these conditions into the contract the responsibility of the legal and procurement people who are usually more capable of negotiating difficult inclusions than are members of the project team.

In the last few pages, we have referred several times to procurement and legal people. The procurement people in some organizations have, within the last several years and in some organizations, become known as vendor managers. These people, along with attorneys in the legal organization, usually have expertise in the contracting process and in the types of contracts that are most appropriate for each situation. By the contracting process, we mean the pre-award phase, which typically includes development of requirements, cost estimating, invitations for bidding and issuing of requests for proposals and requests for quotes, the award phase, which includes cost analysis, risk analysis, negotiating and contracting, and the post-award phase, which includes contract execution and contract change management.

They also have expertise in the types of contracts, shown diagrammatically in Fig. 11.3. These range from those preferred by the vendor such as those contracts pay the vendor based on their costs plus a percentage of costs (CPPC contracts)

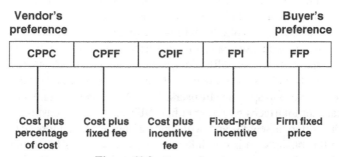

Figure 11.3   Types of contracts.

to those preferred by the buyer such as firm fixed price (FFP) contracts. Because of their detailed knowledge of the issues related to the contracting process and the types and content of appropriate contracts, it is important not to exclude them from the preparation of an agreement and to get them involved early.

11.3 MANAGING INTERNATIONALLY OUTSOURCED DEVELOPMENT WORK

During the past several years, one of the most commonly seen kinds of outsourcing has been the outsourcing of software development work to offshore vendors in India, Eastern Europe, Southeast Asia, and several other offshore locations. The earliest vendors of software development services were located in India and some of the Indian companies that entered this business early, such as Wipro, Infosys, and Tata Consultancy Services, have grown to become powerhouses in the provision of these services. Most organizations that have outsourced their work have done it to take advantage of the relatively low labor rates in these areas. On the other hand, some have been exported portions of their software development work upon the insistence of their upper managements or by venture capitalists who have taken an ownership position in the firm without clearly specified objectives for taking that step. Organizations that have made use of offshore software development services have related a variety of experiences and widely differing levels of success. Some have reported extreme difficulties in getting the offshore vendors to understand user requirements. Others have expressed disappointment with the capabilities of the people who have been assigned to develop the software by the offshore vendors and what sometimes appears to be rapid turnover of personnel. Yet others report what appear to be highly successful uses of these services.

Because of these widely varying results, we want to spend some time describing in this section the things that can be done by the outsourcing organization to help ensure that the internationally outsourced work is successfully completed.

The first, and most important, factors to consider when an organization is considering outsourcing is what work should be outsourced and which vendors should be considered for doing that work.

While a casual search for outsourcing success stories can produce positive results for applications in virtually all software domains, the most successful outsourcing experiences are usually those associated with the development of software that involves business applications making use of a back-end database built on commercially available database management systems such as Oracle, SQL Server, or DB2. These applications typically require the development of business logic software that interacts with users and with the back-end database and produces standardized reports or reports as specified by users. They also usually require the development of graphical user interfaces based on either. NET or based on customized Java software. With a diligent search, and with the assistance of vendors who are heavily involved in this business, it is possible to find success stories for virtually any business domain in which the reader might be interested. However, the further one gets from traditional business applications like those described here, the more difficult it becomes to find solid success stories. As one moves from traditional business applications to business applications that involve numerous automated interfaces, particularly those with rigid time and performance constraints and with volatile data, to control applications that are embedded within the hardware on which they run and which have high reliability and safety requirements, to scientific software applications, it becomes more difficult to find international outsourcing success stories.

Therefore, if one becomes responsible for managing an internationally outsourced software development project, he or she probably has the best probability of success if the project involves the development of traditional business software as described above. If the project requires the simultaneous development of both hardware as do some examples in the earlier chapters of this book, the project is probably not a good candidate for international outsourcing because of the need to keep the software developers and the hardware developers tightly integrated and in close communication on a day-to-day basis.

Now, suppose you, or your organization, has selected a software project, or area of work, that is a likely candidate for outsourcing. Which international outsourcing vendors should be considered? There are hundreds, or perhaps even thousands, of vendors to choose from. While labor rates and cost is one set of things to consider, it is probably more important to find an international outsourcing vendor that has experience in the industry and business domain in which your project operates. Some of the large vendors mentioned above have expertise in a wide variety of industries and business applications. These include, among others, the industries shown in Table 11.1.

When faced with making a vendor choice, it is important for the organization considering outsourcing some of its software development work to understand the capabilities and reputation of the supplier in delivering similar applications. Experience in an industry and successful delivery of results to other customers, based on recommendations from those customers, are one of the best ways to prescreen potential vendors.

Another way to evaluate the capabilities of a potential supplier is to examine the results of its most recent Capability Maturity Model (CMM) assessment. Most of the large offshore software vendors have sought and achieved a level 5 CMM assessment. They have also typically set up internal process audit operations to

Table 11.1 Typical International Outsourcing Vendor Specialties

- Aerospace and defense
- Banking, financial services, and insurance
- Energy and utilities
- Health care
- Life sciences
- Retail
- Telecommunications
- Travel and transportation

insure that the outsourced software development projects undertaken by their organizations are properly using the processes upon which their assessments were based. When we get involved with a new offshore software vendor, their possession of a level 5 CMM assessment and an audit process to ensure that the development process is being followed should be a basic requirement. This is a good start. However, we must remember that the use of an appropriate process does not guarantee a successful project completion.

An outsourcing organization should not rely solely on one offshore vendor. However, most outsourcers would not want to bear the cost of working with more than a total of two or three vendors. Work that is outsourced for a single project should not be placed with more than one outsourcing vendor.

Most successful relationships with offshore software suppliers have started slowly. These relationships typically start by employing a small staff from the potential vendor's organization to work side by side with the onshore development team, initially taking on responsibilities for continuing maintenance of a legacy system. As their experience with the application and the organization grows, they gradually take on more responsibilities for designing and adding functionality to the existing system, still working onshore with the customer's staff. When they have developed sufficient expertise, it is time to consider moving responsibility for continuing maintenance work to their offshore location, but, at least initially, keeping responsibility for the specification, design, and development of new capabilities onshore. When the offshore vendor employees have developed sufficient capability with the application and the customer organization, then it is, finally, time to move significant portions of the development work to the offshore location. In the typical successful transition to an offshore vendor, approximately 75–80% of the total project staff will ultimately be located offshore. The 20–25% who remain at the customer's onshore location is usually a mix of both customer and vendor employees, perhaps one-half being customer employees and one-half being vendor employees. The customer, in most cases, retains responsibility for developing high-level requirements, overall application architecture, and project management.

Even with a very successful transition, it is very important that the customers continues to provide at least a reasonable amount of effort by their own employees to insure that the relationship with business customers continues to be healthy and that the project is well managed, both within the customer's organization and within the vendor's organization. Let us take a look at what the customer's project manager needs to do, and what they need to avoid doing, during the transition and in the longer-term steady-state operation of the project to help ensure project success. This will usually require 10–20% of the total project effort, considerably more than the normal 5–10% typically required for project management of in-house projects.

It is common for project managers who have been very good at managing software development projects that are done completely within the customer's environment to experience great amounts of difficulty with outsourced work. Let us make some assumptions about how the outsourced work is organized then discuss some common problems that occur in such an outsourcing environment.

Within the customer's organization, the work that is outsourced is usually the primary responsibility of the chief information officer (CIO) organization or of some comparable part of the organization that usually manages the development of new software. The users of the software usually reside in some other part of the organization and have primary responsibility not for software development or computer operations but rather for a portion of the business that has profit and loss responsibility, or for operational support of a part of the business that has that overall profit and loss responsibility. We will call these users, who have been traditionally the internal customers of the CIO organization, the "business customers." We will call the CIO organization or other organization with primary software delivery responsibility in this structure the "outsourcing vendor's customer," or the "customer's project manager." The vendor will also typically have a person who is the designated project manager residing in the vendor's organization. See an example of this arrangement in Fig. 11.4.

Some of the common problems and the solutions that have been reported when using this structure are the following:

1. The customer's project manager does not have a good relationship with the business customers. It is important that someone in the outsourcing customer's development organization is responsible for managing the relationship with the business customer. This means that the customer's project manager needs, at a minimum, to understand the business needs of the business customer. That project manager needs to manage the development of requirements for the work that is being outsourced. They need to know which of the business customers can provide detailed requirements or, if the business customers cannot provide detailed written requirements, which

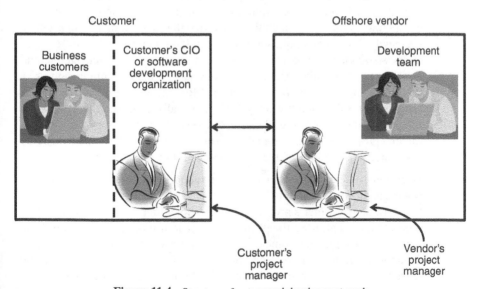

Figure 11.4 Structure of outsourced development work.

people in the business organization should be consulted when the requirements are being written.

2. The customer's project manager does not adequately control requirements change. The project manager needs to put the requirements under change control. This means that as soon as the first version of the requirements is written, they should be baselined. After that point in time, the requirements should not be modified unless the changes go through a formal change process that would entail an analysis of the impact of the change, a determination of whether development work on the modified requirements has begun, and an economic analysis of the impact of the change on the cost of work being done by the outsourcing vendor. Of course, the outsourcing vendor would like the requirements to remain as stable as possible, particularly after development of software to provide the features impacted has begun. We frequently hear from outsourcing vendors that one of the most negative impacts on their work is rapidly changing requirements. So, one of the major contributions that the customer's project manager can make is to stabilize the requirements as much as possible while still being responsive to the customer's business needs.

3. The customer's project manager sometimes tries to micromanage the outsourcing vendor. When work has been outsourced to an external vendor, the customer's project manager needs to carefully manage the intensity with which he or she attempts to manage the vendor while at the same time remaining deeply enough to understand the status of the work and to be able to provide assistance from the customer's organization when such help is appropriate. They do need to continue managing in detail the portions of the work for which the customer is responsible. This might include development of requirements, control of requirements changes, installation and staging of computing facilities on which the software will run, training of end users on the newly developed application, and installation and interconnectivity of the new software in its operating environment. The project manager should not become overly involved in day-to-day scheduling and monitoring tasks that are being executed by the vendor. Monitoring status, particularly of critical path tasks, on a biweekly basis, is usually enough. However, when major deviations from the plan are observed, it is necessary for the customer's project manager to find the reasons for the deviations and to provide assistance when help from the customer would be appropriate.

4. Occasionally, the business customer or support people in the outsourcing organization resist attempts to internationally outsource work. When this happens, the customer's project managers, sometimes with assistance from their management, have the primary responsibility for working with those who are resisting to overcome obstacles being put in the way of success. It is difficult to say what needs to be done in these circumstances because the reasons for the resistance can be so varied. Sometimes, the outsourcing has been initiated on the assistance of upper management or, in some cases, by

venture capitalists who have taken ownership positions in the outsourcing organization. Sometimes, the objectives of outsourcing are not clear particularly when there appears to be no overall economic justification for the undertaking. And, sometimes, it is simply a feeling on the part of the people whose work is being outsourced that "we can do a much better job here." The project manager and his or her direct management sometimes can have very little influence in reducing the level of resistance under these circumstances. The project manager and his or her management, of course, always have the option of leaving their positions, but, if that is not feasible, the best they can do is to provide strong support in making the outsourced project successful.

5. Vendors sometimes report that customer project managers hide from them changes that are likely to occur in the future. As all of us who are involved in developing software know, it is helpful when we can at least make guesses about what parts of the application are likely to need change in the future. These changes might come about for operational reasons, for example, changes in the way the business is operating, changes in legal requirements, for example, financial reporting regulations, or various kinds of regulatory requirements, such as those that occur frequently in the medical, telecommunications, utility, and transportation industries. Predicting these changes in advance is very difficult. However, responding to them retroactively when they occur is usually even more difficult. So, it behooves the project manager to keep abreast of likely changes and to keep the offshore vendor informed of where and when changes like these might occur.

6. Occasionally, outsourcing vendors experience both financial and legal problems. One of the most important decisions that need to be made after a decision has been made to outsource some work is to which vendor, or vendors, the work should be outsourced and how much work should be outsourced. Most participants in the international outsourcing industry agree that the work that has been outsourced should not be spread among a large number of vendors. However, they also agree that not all of the outsourced work should be placed with the same vendor. While the amount of work to outsource and the choice of vendor(s) will probably not be a primary responsibility of the customer's project manager, that person should participate to the extent possible in vendor evaluation. Some of the considerations that should be considered in the selection of international vendors are their financial stability, their reputation for delivering results of appropriate quality on time, their costs (not only per person costs but also overall estimated project costs), their abilities to match their cultures with the culture of the outsourcing customer's company, and, probably most important for the customer's project manager, their experience in doing similar technical work for others. The customer should not depend on the claims of quality, delivery, and experience provided by the vendor. They need to talk with some of the vendor's customers to examine their experience and the reliability of the vendor's services.

7. There will frequently be cultural differences between employees of the customer organization and employees of the vendor organization. It will usually fall to the customer's project manager to both understand these differences and to manage them. It is sometimes helpful if the customer's project manager has a personal cultural background that is similar to the backgrounds of the vendors' employees. If this is not the case, the project manager should attempt to learn about these differences by visiting the vendor's location, discussing these differences, engaging in some formal learning about the culture of the vendor's environment, and, sometimes, organizing and running a cultural workshop in which some of the vendor's employees participate along with the customer's employees.

8. Customers sometimes try to manage outsourced work with virtually no resources being assigned to do that work. Managing outsourced work cannot be a part-time job. The customer's project manager must be assigned full-time to the project management position and should rarely be expected to manage more than one or two outsourced projects. Managing this kind of work, if it is located in Asia or eastern Europe, will frequently require that the project manager be involved in teleconferences late at night, so they cannot be expected to be in their offices for the entire day then to participate in these late evening calls. Both vendors and customers who have made use of those vendors continually emphasize the importance of having the customer's project manager continually involved with both the business customer and with the offshore vendor. The project manager usually needs to have at least one formal meeting each week at which project status, action items, and current risks are assessed and acted upon. The project manager should document those meetings very shortly after they occur and route that documentation to both the vendor's management and to key personnel in the customer's organization.

9. At a minimum, the person doing the project management job in the vendor's organization should lead a weekly project meeting. Beyond the project manager's involvement in weekly project meetings, he or she should set up a governance structure involving the management of both the customer's organization and the vendor's organization. This would include the weekly project meetings, perhaps a monthly meeting among the project manager's direct manager and the corresponding person or persons in the vendor organization, and a quarterly meeting among one of the project manager's upper management and upper management from the vendor's organization. The project manager, his or her immediate manager, and the upper management representative should visit the vendor's offshore location at the time the project is starting up and at least once a year, or more frequently, after the project gets going. The purpose of these visits is so that the managements of each organization can get to know each other, to keep them involved in some of the details of the project work, and to get them comfortable enough with each other so that they feel free to talk openly and honestly when problems arise.

10. Frequently, projects experience risk events that are completely outside the scope of the technical work associated with software development. The customer's project manager needs to manage these risks in the customer's organization. This activity is similar to the risk management activities that we discussed in Chapter 8. However, in this case, it will focus primarily on risks that might develop within the customer's organization. It would involve brainstorming for those risks, estimating the impact of those events if they occur, and developing mitigation and contingency plans when they are sufficiently great to require that.

11. Sometimes, the software being developed offshore will need to interface with other applications or systems in the customer's environment. Frequently, those interfaces will be old, and possibly undocumented, or they will be developed and maintained by another software provider who may or may not be part of the customer's organization. Sometimes, they will be provided by a second vendor who competes with the current vendor for business. In all of these circumstances, it is helpful if the customer's project manager is able, from both management and technical perspectives, to assist the vendor in obtaining and/or negotiating those interface specifications. In one case in which I was involved several years ago, the interfacing vendor simply would not provide the interface specifications. As the project manager, I had to make arrangements to have the interface links monitored and the data flowing over them interpreted so that the interface specification could be inferred from the protocols and from data flowing over the links. That is a very difficult job and requires access to highly specialized communications and network analysts.

12. Finally, while it is not an absolute requirement, it is helpful if the customer's project manager has both business expertise in the part of the business that is being addressed by the software that is being developed and technical expertise in the methods and techniques that are being used to implement the application.

With that long list of things that the customer's project manager needs to do, we will bring this discussion of managing projects that are outsourced to offshore vendors to a close.

11.4 SOME THINGS TO REMEMBER

The most important things that we have discussed in this chapter are the following:

1. The changing software development environment has resulted in the use of teams that do not report directly to the manager who has overall responsibility for the project.

2. The use of partners, both internal and external, as well as vendors has become increasingly common.

3. Acquiring off-the-shelf software from partners and vendors involves relatively low risk if the off-the-shelf software requires little or no modification. However, the acquisition of custom-designed software from partners and vendors can become quite risky.

4. Managing the acquisition of custom-designed software from partners and vendors consumes significant resources, and the acquiring organization needs to dedicate resources to this endeavor.

5. If an organization decides to acquire custom software from domestic partners and vendors, they should follow the guidelines that have been outlined in this chapter.

6. International outsourcing has become quite common in recent years. That kind of acquisition can reduce costs, but it almost always increases risk. To address those risks, the acquiring organization must dedicate significant management resources to the management of offshore software development.

7. Managers assigned to the management of internationally outsourced projects should follow the guidelines that have been described in this chapter.

CASE STUDY 11

Purpose

1. Begin to learn some of the complexities of program management in a typical development work environment.

2. Make some basic decisions regarding program management that need to be made at the beginning of every new, large program.

3. Develop a preliminary plan for managing a new program.

Background

You have been requested to lead a group of six employees who will provide the New Product Introduction Program Management function for a major new corporate program that will offer, develop, and deliver a new system to a major customer. It is expected that the customer will be the only customer for this specific product. Providing the product requires development of a proposal, and ultimately a contract, under which this work will be done. The primary responsibility for the sale and contracting is with your company's marketing/sales organization. However, during the negotiations, they will require the participation of systems engineers and developers, both hardware and software, who are members of the new product development organization. To develop overall project costs, they will also require inputs from your manufacturing and procurement organizations as well as from those organizations that will be responsible for deployment and continuing support after the product is generally available for wide deployment.

This will be a large undertaking.

It is expected that the total cost of development will be approximately $300 million and will be spread over 5–6 years. At the peak, we expect approximately 500 developers working on the project with about 60 of them responsible for hardware development, 300 responsible for software development, and the other 140 responsible for systems engineering, testing, customer documentation development, initial field deployment, and a variety of support functions. The development organization is being assembled from well-established development groups at two different geographic locations (and two different organizations). The current organizations will be supplemented by approximately 200 new hires—about 100 from the market and 100 from campus.

About one-half of the hardware will be developed internally and will be manufactured by our company. The other half will be procured from commercial vendors and integrated with the hardware and software that will be developed internally.

Because the hardware being procured from external vendors is currently under development by those vendors, and because we will be one of the first customers for that hardware, the development organization must be involved in early management of those vendors. As the vendors' products mature and our deployment program ramps up, we expect vendor management responsibilities to transition to our procurement organization. The internally developed and manufactured hardware (custom devices, bare boards, circuit packs, equipment units, and cable) will be manufactured using manufacturing processes that are already in place at our large manufacturing locations. At each of these locations, several hundred people will be involved in the manufacturing processes.

Field deployment will be done by our customer service organization, which provides service, local engineering, and installation services. It is expected that the developed product will be deployed at approximately 150 locations throughout the world. For each deployment location, it is anticipated that one customer service person, two engineers, and three installers will be required, each for approximately 26 weeks. Therefore, each location will require approximately 3 staff years of effort in this area plus the management loading normally associated with field activities. Because the engineering and deployment organizations are not currently staffed to handle a job of this magnitude, they, like the development organization, are probably going to have to do this job with approximately 60% of their currently employed people, 30% experienced hires, and 20% new employees.

Each of the functional areas, for example, the customer business unit, development, and manufacturing, has agreed to participate in the development of a program plan. Your organization has agreed to staff a program management organization and to develop a program plan. At the current time, however, only the development organization has done any significant planning work. They have developed a work breakdown structure for the work that they expect to do during the first 2 years. They have identified approximately 3850 tasks, determined the predecessor/successor relationship among those tasks, and assigned resources for those tasks that are currently staffed. They have entered the data describing this work breakdown structure into a project scheduling tool and have agreed to share the contents of that tools file with you and your people. The manufacturing organization has just begun to think about its work breakdown structure but has not developed any details. They expect that they will staff the management of this project with three experienced project engineers from the manufacturing organization. The deployment organization has not yet staffed its project management organization and has not given any indication of how many people or who would be involved in that activity.

Activity

First, draw a high-level diagram showing all of the functional organizations that you would expect to be involved in a program of this kind. Also show the major handoffs between each pair of organizations indicating the kinds of information that would normally be passed among the organizations.

Next, decide what the purpose and objectives of your six-person program management group will be, for example,

1. Will you try to manage the program in the broadest sense by being responsible for its entire scope, schedule, cost, and quality?

2. Will you be responsible for facilitating the development of project plans for each of the subprojects and the integration of those plans to form a coherent program plan?

3. Will you be primarily responsible for identifying and monitoring the planned task completions within each subproject (or functional organization) and for escalating those that are seriously delayed?

4. Will you be primarily responsible for interfacing with the external customer, providing them status on our work and insuring that they receive the information that they need on the schedule that they are expecting?

5. Will you provide project/program consulting services to the subprojects and execute the mechanics of Microsoft Project data entry, scheduling, resource allocation, etc., for them?

6. Will you provide some other set of capabilities or a combination of some of the items outlined above?

Remember that you have limited resources (six people at various individual contributor levels and yourself at the manager level). Whatever objectives you choose will have to be achieved with those resources, or with additional resources that you might be able to obtain if you can make a good case for their benefits versus their costs.

If you are doing this case study with a group of other people, you should discuss these issues as a group and decide what your objectives for the program management function should be. Then you should develop a set of guidelines, or rules, for how you will operate in order to achieve your objectives.

For example, you will need to decide which tasks you will include in the program-wide work breakdown structure. How many of these tasks should there be for a program of this magnitude? How will you obtain descriptions of these tasks? Will you need to know the resources required to execute each task, and what will you do with that information? Which tasks from each of the subprojects will be directly included? How will you use summary task information from the subproject? How will you determine the critical path for each project and the overall program?

You will also have to decide what should be included in the written version of your program plan and who should be responsible for writing the various sections of the plan. What methods will you use to facilitate the development of the plan? Will this plan be updated as the program progresses, or will it be used only to get the program started?

What kind of program meeting structure will you use; that is, who will participate? How often will they be held? What will be on the agenda? What information and in what form will need to be collected from the subprojects before the meetings and in what form will participants provide their input?

Finally, what additional means of formal communications will be used? How will e-mail, teleconferences, paper reports, and other means of communications be used routinely in this program and what will they be used for?

What other decisions will need to be made by your program management group before getting started with this undertaking?

Output

You should prepare a summary of your analysis and decisions. In that report, you should include a very brief overview of the program as described in the Background section of this exercise. You should then describe the results of your analysis concerning the organizations that will be involved, your program management objectives, and the guidelines or rules that you have developed to manage your group's involvement in the management of the program.

REFERENCES

DIXON L. E. (2008) Air traffic control modernization: FAA faces challenges in managing ongoing projects, sustaining existing facilities and introducing new capabilities. FAA Report Number AV-2008-049, Federal Aviation Administration, April 14, 2008, Washington, DC.

FEICKERT A. (2009) *The Army's Future Combat System (FCS): Background and Issues for Congress,* Congressional Research Service, No. 7-5700, March 13, 2009, Washington DC.

MCGRODDY J. C. and H. S. LIN (eds.) (2004) *A Review of the FBI's Trilogy Information Technology Modernization Program,* National Research Council, Computer Science and Telecommunications Board, National Academies Press, Washington, DC.

Chapter 12

Is a Heavyweight
Process Required?

The techniques that we have discussed in this book are quite extensive. They cover virtually all of the project management methods that would be required for the largest, most complex undertakings, even those requiring extremely high quality and reliability, whether they are done by colocated or disbursed teams or whether they are done in-house or outsourced.

Starting in the mid-1980s, several organizations began to develop what have come to be known as life cycle development processes and frameworks. These include models like the Software Engineering Institute's (SEI) Capability Maturity Model Integration (CMMI) and the International Standards Organization (ISO) Standard 15504, both of which are intended to evaluate an organization's development capabilities and to serve as a basis for process improvement. Generally, these models require that the organization make a commitment to a series of process objectives, put in place a set of well-specified activities or processes to achieve those objectives, and measure their success, or lack of success, in achieving the objectives.

Figure 12.1 shows a portion of the description of the SEI's Capability Maturity Model, which we reviewed briefly in Chapter 9. The ISO 15504 standard describes a similar multilevel structure. Each of these models includes a description of each key process area, a statement of the commitment that must be made by the organization, and the evidence that must be provided to show that the process is being implemented effectively. Paper copies of the models are several hundred pages long.

In parallel with the development of the SEI and ISO maturity and process improvement models, several organizations like the U.S. Department of Defense, the Institute of Electrical and Electronics Engineers (IEEE) Computer Society, the Electronic Industries Association (EIA), the American National Standards Institute (ANSI), and the ISO developed a set of standards that define software life cycle processes. These have included, among others, MIL-STD-1679, DOD-STD-2167, MIL-STD-7935, MIL-STD-498, EIA-640, ANSI J-016, IEEE 1498, and IEEE/ISO 12207. These standards define a comprehensive set of processes that cover the entire

Managing the Development of Software-Intensive Systems, by James McDonald
Copyright © 2010 John Wiley & Sons, Inc.

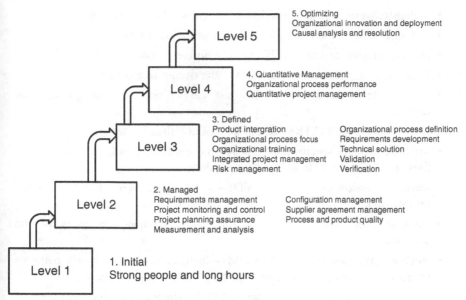

Figure 12.1 Capability Maturity Model.

life cycle of a software system, from concept to retirement. They describe the processes, activities, and tasks that are typically involved in the development of large, mission-critical software-intensive systems. They also define the documentation that should be produced when these processes are used. For example, a key component of the 12207 Standard is the description of 22 data items, which are documents that should be produced by the process. They are

- software development plan (SDP)—a plan for performing the software development;
- software test plan (STP)—a plan for conducting qualification testing;
- software installation plan (SIP)—a plan for installing the software at user sites;
- software transition plan (STrP)—a plan for transitioning to the support agency;
- operational concept description (OCD)—the operational concept for the system;
- system/subsystem specification (SSS)—the requirements to be met by the system;
- software requirements specification (SRS)—the requirements to be met by a computer software configuration item (CSCI);
- interface requirements specification (IRS)—the requirements for one or more interfaces;

- system/subsystem design description (SSDD)—the design of the system;
- software design description (SDD)—the design of a CSCI;
- interface design description (IDD)—the design of one or more interfaces;
- database design description (DBDD)—the design of a database;
- software test description (STD)—test cases/procedures for qualification testing;
- software test report (STR)—test results of qualification testing;
- software product specification (SPS)—the executable software, the source files, and information to be used for support;
- software version description (SVD)—a list of delivered file and related information;
- software user manual (SUM)—instructions for hands-on users of the software;
- software input/output manual (SIOM)—instructions for users of a batch or interactive software system that is installed in a computer center;
- software center operator manual (SCOM)—instructions for operators of a batch or interactive software system that is installed in a computer center;
- computer operation manual (COM)—instructions for operating a computer;
- computer programming manual (CPM)—instructions for programming a computer; and
- firmware support manual (FSM)—instructions for programming firmware devices.

The standards produced by these efforts are available from IEEE and ISO. The documents are many hundreds of pages in length, and, with all of their appendices and supplementary information, they run to several thousand pages.

Primarily because of the volume of these standards documents and the documentation requirements that they imply, they have, sometimes, derisively been called "heavyweight" processes. Alternative names for them are "plan-based" or "disciplined" processes. The management methods that we have described in this book, when applied properly, meet virtually all of the content of the standards that have to do with managing the development of software-based systems.

Well before the development of the modern life cycle processes and models described above were created, engineers, primarily those associated with work being done for the government, began to use a method called iterative and incremental development (IID). IID was based upon work done by Walter Shewhart at Bell Laboratories in the 1930s. Shewhart proposed a series of short Plan-Do-Study-Act (PDSA) cycles for quality improvement, which, during the 1940s, was promoted by W. Edwards Demming. During subsequent years, many successful development projects, some involving only hardware, but others involving both hardware and software, were completed under government contract. These included the development of the X-15 jet aircraft in the 1950s, National Aeronautics and Space Administration's

(NASA) Project Mercury in the 1960s, the Command and Control System for the first U.S. Trident Submarine in the 1970s, and the Navy's Underwater Sound Surveillance systems in the 1980s and 1990s. IID proved to be particularly useful for large system development projects which were making use of unproven technologies for which the requirements were dynamically changing. While these system developments were under way and while proponents were promoting the use of IID, the U.S. military clearly headed toward the development of life cycle development standards which clearly did not depend upon IID concepts, but which concentrated on models and methods that were based on the waterfall method that we discussed briefly in Chapter 1.

Since the mid-1990s, a somewhat quiet (although sometimes not so quiet) revolution in opposition to the use of methods based on the waterfall model, or plan-based methods, has developed. This movement has been called the "agile revolution." Agilistas object to what appear to them to be the overly burdensome requirements of heavyweight methods. They see the life cycle models requiring that the development team be able to foresee far into the future to develop complete system requirements, even when those requirements are likely to change during the development process. They see the development of detailed architecture and design documents as being overly confining, limiting the development team's creativity and flexibility. They believe that the interval between project initiation and delivery to the customer becomes unduly long and results in the loss of business value for the customer.

To address these concerns, the proponents of lighter-weight methods have developed and promoted a number of methods. They have names like Scrum, Adaptive Software Development, Lean Development, Crystal, and e-Xtreme Programming. These agile methods are most appropriate for small products and product teams. They generally rely on knowledge that is resident in the heads of team members rather than on written documentation. They are not well suited for use on safety-critical systems. They are excellent for use in highly dynamic environments in which requirements or the environment changes rapidly. They require the availability and involvement of a critical mass of scarce resources such as domain and architecture experts. And they frequently appear to be chaotic, which is acceptable if team members, their management, and their customers are comfortable with that kind of operation.

In reality, well-run projects based on the project management methods we have described in this book look more like IID projects than they look like either waterfall-based projects or agile projects. They use the best of IID, agile, and, yes, even the heavyweight methods.

12.1 SCALING BACK

Let us discuss how, when we use the methods described in this book, we need to tailor them to be most appropriate for the project we are managing.

Table 12.1 Lists the techniques that we have discussed in this text.

Table 12.1   Techniques Described in Earlier Chapters

Major Topic	Specific Method	Sub-Method	Page	Yes or No
Planning	What are we going to do?		21	
	How are we going to do it?		21	
	Who is going to do it?		21	
	When will it be done?		21	
	How much will it cost?		21	
Estimating	Top–down estimating models		62	
	Top–down experienced-based estimating		61	
	Network diagrams and Gantt charts		72	
	Delphi method		73	
Verification and validation	Inspections	Requirements	83	
	Inspections	Designs	83	
	Inspections	Code and schematics	83	
	Inspections	Test cases	83	
	Testing	Black box (functional)	91	
	Testing	White box (unit)	92	
Organizing	Organization structures		102	
	Project kickoff and maintenance		106	
	Conflict resolution		109	
Monitoring	Project meetings		114	
	Quantitative status monitoring		116	
	Written status reports		122	
Control	Project control		126	
	Artifact control		129	
Risk management	Simulation		144	
	Discrete event analysis		148	
Audits, reviews, and assessments			153	
	Project management audits		155	
	Management reviews		161	
	ISO certification		163	
	CMMI assessment		165	
	Architecture reviews		166	
Multi-projects	Multiple projects in the same organization		179	
	Multi-organization and multilocation projects		186	
	Multi-project programs		189	
Managing outsourced development work	Working with vendors		196	
	Working with partners		196	
	Managing internationally outsourced work		202	
Backing off from heavyweight processes			214	
Retrospectives			232	

The methods displayed in this table provide a virtually complete listing of all the things that can and, in some cases, should be done to properly manage a large, complex, mission-critical software/hardware project that resides in an organization with multiple project responsibilities and which makes use of the services of partners and vendors who may be geographically, or even internationally, dispersed. The table can actually be used as a checklist by someone who becomes responsible for managing such a project by inserting a "yes," indicating that the technique is or will be used for this specific project, or a "no," indicating that this method will not be used. The choice is obviously that of the manager and the management team responsible for the conduct of any specific project. However, we should expect to see the word "yes" on a large number of the rows in this table if the project is one with the characteristics outlined here.

On the opposite end of the spectrum, the management of a project that involves only the development of software, which is being done by a relatively small, colocated, in-house team of developers, does not have any particularly stringent safety or reliability requirements, and which will not depend upon goods or services being provided by any external partners or vendors, would probably feel that the long list of topics included in Table 12.1 was major "overkill." They and their organization would probably not want to incur the cost and bureaucracy associated with overlaying these methods on their project. So, if they were to complete the "yes" or "no" column of Table 12.1, we would expect to see the word "no" on a large number of the rows in this table. This result would be close (although not precisely) to what we would expect to see from a project that decided that they should be an "agile" project.

The extremes are easy. We should expect to see mostly "yes" on one extreme and mostly "no" on the other extreme. However, unfortunately, most real projects are not at one end or the other of this distribution of projects. On the size scale, I have been personally involved with projects that involve a very small number of people (two to four) to projects involving over a thousand people. It was obvious for these projects how much and what kinds of management were necessary. However, in the organizations in which I have worked and those with which I have been associated, the average project staff size was typically 15–20 people, and the distribution of project sizes was grouped pretty tightly around that average. A very subject estimate of projects in most organizations, based on my personal experience, is that about 90% of projects have staff sizes from about 12 to 30 members. The size, complexity, and variety of projects that are near the average staff size make the decision about which techniques to use and which not to use a very difficult one.

Let us assume that we start with a large, complex, high-risk project and that we have placed a "yes" in all of the rows in the right column of Table 12.1. What we want to do is turn some of the "yes" entries to "no" entries by changing the characteristics of the project and the environment in which it is being executed. We will start with some of the easier ones, then get into those that are more difficult.

A few of the "yes" entries can be assumed away. If the development team has the freedom and chooses not to work with external vendors or partners and not to place any of their work with international outsourcers, then the three techniques listed under Managing outsourced development work can be changed from "yes" to "no." These are Managing internationally outsourced work, Working with partners, and Working with vendors.

The same idea can also be similarly applied to the techniques listed under Multi-projects. However, decisions on these topics will probably need to be made by both the development team and their upper managements. If the project can be kept small enough (based on my own experience, less than about 600 tasks with an average duration of 4–6 weeks per task), then the overall undertaking can probably be managed by one person without the need for the management of a multi-project program. If that is the case, then the Multi-project programs row can be changed from a "yes" to a "no." Of course, most of the time, the development team will not have complete control over the amount of work that needs to be done. It is likely to be determined by the nature of the project. The decision to place the work in one organization or in multiple organizations or the choice to colocate the development team or to have it reside at multiple locations is frequently made by either the upper management of the organization that is doing the work based on its local business conditions or, sometimes, by broader business considerations across the parent corporation. Based narrowly on the needs of the project and its management, it is almost always better to organize the work into one organization and to colocate team members within a short distance of each other. That will eliminate the need to manage multi-organization and multilocation projects and to reduce the management overhead associated with such complicated arrangements. If this can be done, then the "yes" on the Multi-organization and multilocation projects can be changed to "no." There are almost always multiple projects under way in a development organization. However, sometimes, a small team, working on a high-priority project, can get agreement from its management to operate as if it were a completely separate entity that will be semipermanently staffed and budgeted independently of other parts of the organization. If that is the case, they can make good estimates of the resources that will be available to the team for the foreseeable future. Therefore, they would not need to be concerned with the issues discussed when we described Multiple projects in the same organization. In this case, the "yes" on the Multiple projects in the same organization could be changed from "yes" to "no"—or at least to a maybe!

We have now disposed of the topics that were easy to dispose of, that is, those that would not be necessary because we have made decisions that would preclude the need for them. That still leaves numerous items on our list of topics. Let us now start from the other end of the spectrum and examine our list as if we were going to apply it to the simplest, smallest, and least critical projects.

The first item on our list is planning. That includes some determination of what we are going to do, how we are going to do it, who is going to do it, when it will be done, and how much it will cost. We have implied in our discussion of planning that the planning process would result in the publication of a substantial document that would answer those questions in considerable detail. If you worked through the exercise at the end of Chapter 2 completely with a simulated core team, you should have produced a document that was at least 50 pages in length. Very small teams would not want to do that. They might simply document in a page or two what they plan to do, generally describe how they plan to do it, the names of the team members who will be involved, how long they plan to work on the project, and perhaps not feel compelled to even estimate a cost. If the team doing this project has a management, and perhaps a customer, that is willing to proceed under those conditions, that may be all the formal documented planning that is necessary.

My first software development project was similar to that. I was a new summer intern who knew nothing of budgets, schedules, or costs. My boss asked me to do some research to determine if a computer program could calculate the transmission characteristics of the copper cables that were used at that time primarily for transmission of voice frequency communications. I did that, wrote a short report on my findings, and developed a prototype of a program that provided the requested functionality under a simple set of environmental conditions. It was called the Universal Cable Circuit Application Program (UNICCAP). When I returned as a full-time employee a year later, I was assigned to a systems engineering job which had responsibility for examining the economic feasibility of the development of a new line of electronic products that might help reduce the cost of telecommunications service providers' distribution plant. And, oh, by the way, if I wanted to continue expanding the prototype program that I had worked on the previous year, I should feel free to spend about 30% of my time doing that. I did, and over the next 2–3 years, I expanded the prototype to handle many more conditions and many more types of cables. I also expanded the frequency spectrum for which the calculations could be done well beyond the traditional voice spectrum and added a user interface that made the product more user friendly.

That version was enough to stimulate the interest of a few people in the engineering organization of the AT&T Co. who thought that if it were made to look a little "prettier," some of the engineers who designed special service circuits and trunks throughout the United States might make use of it. So, funds to support three people were allocated and the people were directed to develop a production version of the prototype. The only plan for this project was a short memorandum that I wrote specifying what the production version should do (similar to a requirements document) and a 1-year commitment to fund three people to do the development work. At the end of a year, they had made enough progress to get a funding commitment for a second year. They completed their work about three quarters of the way through the year and made the product available for use. Little use was made of it until several years later when it was integrated into a system called Trunk Investment Record Keeping System (TIRKS), which was used by all telecommunications circuit designers in the former Bell System. Over the years, the TIRKS team, using the original structure and software of the UNICCAP application, greatly enhanced the capabilities of the product by adding the ability to analyze the effects of incorporating a variety of active devices into circuit designs. To my knowledge, that same application is still being used for its original purpose, more than 45 years after it was developed. This project had only a very loose plan and a customer who was close and understanding and who was willing to take the risk that this three- or four-person project might produce nothing useful. That does not happen often, but when it does, it can be very beneficial and exciting.

So, while some planning is important, and for larger complex mission-critical projects, it is extremely important that the planning effort for small projects can be kept to a minimum.

The same is true of estimating, and estimating is really a part of planning. Developing high-quality estimates for a large, complex project can take a considerable amount of time and effort. If the work is being done under contract for external customers, those customers deserve to know what they will be getting, when they will be getting it, and how much it will cost. In order to provide this information for all but the simplest and smallest projects will require real work. If, on the other hand, the customers are close enough, and understanding enough, they might be willing to settle for delivery of whatever three people can produce in 12–18 months. In that case, almost no estimating is necessary and a brief project plan could say that.

Next, we come to verification and validation, which, for most projects includes inspections and testing. Most projects, other than those that are very small or very unimportant, will produce some kind of requirements, even if those requirements are only in the form of an informal proposal saying what the objectives of the work will be. All projects that are software based, of course, produce codes, some of which are well commented and easily understood, and some of which are completely uncommented and obscurely written. Virtually all large projects develop test cases that are archived for future use. These can be unit test cases, which are sometimes only developed and captured by the person who developed the code, integration test cases, which assist in initially putting the pieces together, and functional test cases, which are intended to search for defects that will negatively impact the operation of the system when it is being used in practice. We talked about inspecting all of these artifacts when we discussed inspections in Chapter 4. We also discussed inspecting designs. If I were to rank order the importance of inspecting each of these types of artifacts, I would put designs (of both software and hardware components) at the top of the list. The reason for this is that they are closest to the beginning of the development process, and defects in the requirements or the designs can have large negative impacts if they are found late in the development life cycle. I would rank test case inspections second and codes third. The reasons for this relative ordering are that, while test cases come near the end of the process and if they have defects, they can appear as surprises late in the game; it is usually relatively easy to fix them quickly while testing is under way. Code inspections were the subject of the earliest inspection efforts in the 1970s, and many researchers have shown that code inspections are economically viable when that is the only inspection activity being done. However, the major problems discovered during code inspections are usually faults that were introduced during the requirements or design stages of a project, so why not get them then?

We next discussed testing. Many of the agile or lightweight methods that are being promoted heavily emphasize the importance testing, that is, unit testing, functional testing, and even stress testing. Several agile methods advocate a design-to-test strategy, which encourages developers to first develop the tests they plan to use then to design the product so that it will pass those tests. That is a very reasonable approach for unit testing. However, for functional testing, I have some reservations because, ideally, even for small relatively simple systems, we would like to have someone other than the developer preparing the test cases and executing them. This would argue for using the functional testing methods discussed in Chapter 4, even for small, simple systems developed by small teams.

The next topic that we discussed was organizing, in Chapter 5. Certainly, for very small teams, the topics that we discussed under Organizational Structures will not be relevant. For very small teams attempting to follow an agile paradigm, their formal organizational reporting relationships should have minimal impact on the management and operation of the team. On the other hand, if the small team members report formally to several different managers, it will be important for those managers to agree that the team members are available for the current project full-time and are likely to remain available to the team for the duration of the project. If the members of a small team are selected carefully, if they have previously worked together, and have worked together well, the activities that we have discussed associated with project start-up and continuing management are unlikely to be relevant to the small team. However, even if the team is small and its members know each other well, conflicts among its members might occasionally arise. In a small informal team, it will fall to the team members to recognize symptoms of conflict and to resolve those conflicts among the team members by seeking assistance from someone from outside the team.

All projects must monitor their status, even if the project is being done by a small team, the members of which are colocated, perhaps in the same room. What can vary considerably is the formality with which monitoring is done. For a team of four, whose desks are in the same room, there may be no need for formal monitoring beyond the normal everyday conversations that frequently take place in these environments. This is particularly true if the team members are continually integrating their work results with the work of other team members on a frequent basis. On the other hand, once the team size gets beyond the relatively small numbers of people who can be informally gathered by rolling their chairs together, some form of regularly scheduled project meeting is required to insure that all team members are getting exposed to all of the information they need. For teams of 5–10 people, this could be as simple as a daily or weekly stand-up gathering in one of the team's office spaces. When the team size gets into the 16- to 18-member range, which is about the size of an average project, then more formal project meetings, scheduled on a weekly, biweekly, or monthly basis become important. At this size, there should be a plan available containing specific tasks with expected completion dates so that team members can report and demonstrate in an objective way what has, or has not, been accomplished. With meetings that are expected to have more than about 15 attendees, we should expect that one or more people will be missing due to vacation, other commitments, or emergencies. This is when it becomes important to produce written summaries, or status reports, indicating what was discussed at the project meetings.

Project control is related to the actions taken by the team manager and the team in response to deviations from a plan. If it has been determined that there should be no fixed plan because the team is small enough, the requirements are flexible enough, and the criticality of the project is low enough so that the team does not produce a plan containing a detailed schedule, then there is no need for a formal project control process. Small, informal teams may have to occasionally change direction, which is similar to the exercise of project control. But in those circumstances, team members are usually not thinking much about where we are, how we go there, and where we want to go. So, these situations usually do not require any formalized project control process. However, once again, when a project reaches a size and complexity such that the development of a detailed project plan is appropriate, the project also needs some way to compare the project status with the plan and to determine how to respond to deviations. This usually becomes appropriate when the team size reaches the range of 8–10 people.

Artifact control is almost always important. No matter how small the project is, someone needs to know well and tightly control the configuration of work products, whether they are requirements, design, schematic diagrams, code, or test cases. Think about working as an individual writing a document. If the document is subject to change, either based on comments from others, changing external circumstances, or just because of the way the author wants to express himself, there are likely to be multiple copies of the document produced and, perhaps, saved in different places with different names. Unless the author either has a method for keeping track of versions of the document or rigidly keeps a good current copy that cannot be easily changed, there will be some confusion in the process about what changes have been made to the document and which version of the document is the current one. Likewise, when requirements, designs, code, etc., are changing over time, the team needs to have a method for controlling the artifacts either very simply by having one good current copy or with a more elaborate version tracking method. So, artifact control appears to be something that virtually all projects need.

In Chapter 8, we discussed risk management. We covered simulation and discrete event analysis. The simulation method that we discussed is probably not necessary or applicable to very small projects. We should consider using that method only when project team sizes get into the range of 20–25. Discrete event analysis is something that could be done on even the smallest projects. It can be done using the quantitative methods we discussed in Chapter 8 or much more informally by brainstorming major project risks, classifying them by importance to the project, and developing mitigation or contingency plans. The important thing here is not only to identify the risks but also to be ready to reduce their negative impact proactively or to determine what we will do if the event occurs. So, simulation is probably not appropriate for use on small informal projects, but discrete event analysis is probably always worth considering, even if done in a qualitative way.

Project management audits, reviews, and assessments are a collection of techniques closely related to project monitoring and control. Of these, my favorite, and in my experience the most useful, are project management audits. They can frequently provide the team with useful feedback. However, they can also be quite disruptive to the project and, sometimes, to the relationship with the project's stakeholders. I would recommend that anyone who is managing a project involving more than 20 employees, particularly when the team is a multidisciplinary team, consider doing a project audit. Management reviews are always important. They keep the team's management and, perhaps, its customers up to date on the status of the project and prepare them for times when the team might want to call upon them for assistance. For small, informal projects, they do not have to be impressive presentations with checklists and slides. They can sometimes simply involve inviting management and customers to participate in a team gathering at which the project status is summarized. They are very important and should never be eliminated completely.

A decision to seek a CMMI assessment or an ISO 9000 certification is more of a business decision than it is a development management decision. While it is true that using CMMI as a basis for development process improvement or using ISO 9000 certification primarily as a basis for publicly announcing that the organization has reached a specific CMMI level or has been ISO certified, can assist development managers in improving and stabilizing their development processes. These methods are usually not applied on an individual basis but are usually applied at an organization or an organizational physical location basis. They require the availability of process documentation and documented evidence that the process is being followed. If those things do not exist, then the project probably does not need to be concerned with them. This does not preclude, however, the existence of small, informal or agile projects within an organization, which is subject to CMMI assessment or ISO certification as long as the process documentation prepared at the organizational level includes an option for using these methods and the conditions under which a decision will be made to choose that option.

Architecture reviews represent an area that truly presents the team or the manager of the development team with a decision that should be made on a technical basis. If the team is working in a domain that it knows well and if it is planning to use a well-known architecture that it has previously used, it should probably decide that an architecture review is unnecessary. This might be the case when a team is developing an interactive web application for the retail industry for which it has previously developed several versions; the team is using the same back-end database that it has previously used and the same presentation layer that it has used before. However, even if the application is very small and the team is faced with some unusual situations that it has not previously faced, or if the application is particularly complex, the team should probably opt to have an external architecture review. If the project is medium to large, if it involves the need for real-time responses, if there are possible safety issues involved, or if the work is being done in a domain that the team has not previously addressed, then an architecture review is almost always in order.

Table 12.2 is a rearranged listing of the topics, or activities, shown in Table 12.1. It has been rearranged based in the intervening discussion about the importance of each topic or activity and the frequency that we should probably see each topic being addressed by real projects. Those items in the first section of this list are those that should almost always take place in some form, even on very small, noncritical projects. For large, complex projects, all of the things in the upper portion of this table should always be done in a formal way, as we have described them on the

Table 12.2   Techniques Described in Earlier Chapters Arranged in Relative Order of Importance

Major Topic	Specific Method	Sub-Method	Page	Yes or No
Activities that are almost always required				
Planning	What are we going to do?		21	
	How are we going to do it?		21	
	Who is going to do it?		21	
	When will it be done?		21	
	How much will it cost?		21	
Verification and validation	Testing	Black box (functional)	91	
Monitoring	Project Meetings		114	
Control	Artifact control		129	
Audits, reviews, and assessments	Management reviews		161	
Verification and validation	Inspections	Requirements	83	
Estimating	Top–down experience-based estimating		61	
Activities for case-by-case decision				
Backing off from heavyweight processes			214	
Verification and validation	Inspections	Designs	83	
	Testing	White box	82	
	Inspections	Test cases	83	
Monitoring	Quantitative status monitoring		116	
	Written status reports		122	
Control	Project control		126	
Audits, reviews, and assessments	Architecture reviews		166	
Estimating	Top–down estimating models		62	
	Network diagrams and Gantt charts		72	
Audits, reviews, and assessments	Project management audits		155	
Estimating	Delphi method		73	
Verification and validation	Inspections	Code and schematics	83	
	Inspections	Test cases	83	
Organizing	Project kickoff and maintenance		106	
	Conflict resolution		109	
Retrospectives			232	

Table 12.2 Continued

Major Topic	Specific Method	Sub-Method	Page	Yes or No
Risk management	Discrete event analysis		148	
Organizing	Organization structures		102	
Audits, reviews, and	CMMI assessment		165	
assessments	ISO 9000 certification		163	
Risk management	Simulation		144	
Activities that may not be necessary				
Multi-projects	Multiple projects in same organization		179	
	Multi-organization and multilocation		186	
	Multi-project programs		189	
Managing outsourced	Working with vendors		196	
development work	Working with partners		196	
	Managing internationally outsourced work		202	

pages shown. Those in the middle section of the chart need to be seriously considered for implementation by teams of 4 to 5 people up to teams of approximately 20 people. For projects employing 20 or more people, all of the things listed should almost always be done, and done quite formally. The third section of the table includes those items that should or should not be done based on the organizational circumstances in which the project is being executed.

If we were to use this chart as a checklist for a real project, we should see Y's on all of the rows in the upper section of the table. For projects being done by teams of 5–20 people, we would expect to see Y's on some of the rows in the second portion of the tale and N's on some rows. For teams of 20 or more members, we should see Y's on all of the rows in the middle section of the table. Finally, in the last section, we should see some mixture of Y's and N's, sometimes seeing all Y's and sometimes all Y's depending upon the circumstances and the nature of the project.

This analysis and discussion has used primarily project team size as the determinant of which methods and techniques should be used. An alternative, somewhat more complex approach to the appropriate trade-offs between the use of disciplined (heavyweight) and agile (lightweight) methods of project management has been proposed by Barry Boehm and Richard Turner (2004). They used five determinants, one of which is team size, to determine the appropriate balance between using a plan-driven approach and an agile approach. The other factors used in their method are the criticality of the project (loss due to impact of defects), dynamism (rate of requirements change), technical capability of the staff, and the culture in which the project is in operation (the degree to which chaos vs. order is preferred and tolerated). For those wishing to learn more about this aspect of making decisions regarding appropriate management methods, their book is well worthwhile.

12.2 SOME THINGS TO REMEMBER

1. We have described virtually all of the management techniques required to manage the largest, most complex, safety-critical software and hardware projects.

2. The life cycle development standards developed by the U.S. Department of Defense, the IEEE, and ISO call for the use of all of these methods, and these methods can be used to satisfy the requirements of those standards.

3. There are some circumstances when it is not necessary to rigorously meet all of those formal standards, and a faction within the development community has been promoting the use of agile methods that consider the methods described in the standards and the methods described in this book to be heavyweight methods.

4. For projects and environments in which not all of the methods described here do not have to be rigorously applied, the project team or its manager can decide which methods should be used and to what extent.

5. The methods that should always be used are the following:
   a. Planning—what, how, who, when, how much?
   b. Black box (functional testing)
   c. Monitoring via project meetings
   d. Artifact control
   e. Management reviews
   f. Requirements inspections
   g. Top–down experience-based estimation

6. Those methods that are sometimes not required because of the specific environment in which the project is being executed are
   a. management of multiple projects in the same organization,
   b. management of multi-organization and multilocation projects,
   c. multi-project programs,
   d. working with vendors, and
   e. managing internationally outsourced work.

7. Activities that need to be chosen on a case-by-case basis, and which need to be given most thought by the team and by the team manager, are
   a. design inspections,
   b. white box testing,
   c. test case inspections,
   d. quantitative project status monitoring,
   e. written project status reports,
   f. project control,
   g. architecture reviews,

    h. top–down estimating models,
    i. network diagrams and Gantt charts,
    j. project management audits,
    k. the Delphi method,
    l. code inspections,
    m. project kickoff and maintenance,
    n. conflict resolution,
    o. discrete event analysis,
    p. organization structures,
    q. CMMI assessments,
    r. ISO 9000 certification, and
    s. simulation for risk management.

CASE STUDY 12   *Conducting a Project Management Audit*

Purpose

1. Learn how to organize and conduct a project management audit.
2. Practice gathering appropriate information about the status of a project.
3. Practice the steps involved in developing useful audit results.

Activity

This is an optional exercise to be done only by readers who are using this text in a classroom environment in which other groups of students have spent the past several weeks developing a project plan for the CCPS project presented in Case Study 2. During the past several weeks, those groups have been developing a project plan for a project that requires the development of a significant amount of software and, possibly, some hardware. You have been asked by the project manager's boss (Mark Money) to do a friendly audit of that project.

One of those other groups should share a paper copy of the plan that was prepared by that group with your group and you should provide a paper copy of your completed plan with one of those groups. Your group will now become the audit team for the group who provided their plan to you. You should start by having each member of your group read the paper copy of the other group's project plan and make notes on any questions that they have about its content. Each of the members of your audit team should select one member of the group whose project you will be auditing. Try to find a private quiet spot where you can interview the selected member of the other group in a one-on-one interview. These interviews should last for about 45 minutes to 1 hour.

During the interview, you should do the following:

1. Provide some background on the purpose of the audit and put the interviewees at ease (purpose should be to identify major project risks, uncover any weaknesses in the plan, and make recommendations for improvement). Assure them that your conversation is confidential and that you will not associate their name with any information that they provide to you.
2. Determine what the role of the interviewees has been in the project to date, particularly their role in preparing the project plan.

3. Try to understand whether the planning work has appropriately addressed issues with which many projects traditionally have had implementation difficulties. (These are specification of the business and technical processes that will be used, estimation of total staff effort and cost, development of a work breakdown structure to an appropriate level of detail with observable end points for each task, performance requirements and their relationship to the system architecture, plans for appropriate audits and reviews, inspection planning and time for inspections, test plans and facilities, communication mechanisms, and team building.)

4. Ask the interviewee any questions contained in the interviewer's notes based on reading the plan.

Here are some hints about other questions to ask:

- Has a feature/release matrix been developed?
- Has the work breakdown structure gone down to the level of individual tasks of durations that do not exceed 6 weeks?
- Are the tasks the work that one individual can do in that period of time?
- Have specific, observable, task end points been specified for each task?
- Have cumulative milestone charts been developed?
- Have milestone lists (containing 50–150 milestones) that will be used in project meetings been developed?
- Has adequate attention been paid to estimating total effort as well as individual task duration?
- Has an appropriate plan for developing detailed architecture and requirements been included?
- Has an inspection program been defined?
- Has a systematic test program been specified?
- Have the major risks been analyzed, and have appropriate contingency plans been put in place?
- Have management reviews and status reporting mechanisms been specified?
- Has an adequate staffing plan, with appropriate assumptions about availability of staff, been included?
- Does the plan contain planned staffing and cost profiles?
- Ask the interviewee what they think the greatest risks are and what they would recommend be done to address these risks.

After completing the interviews, your audit team should reconvene. You should organize your concerns into a small number of major categories. You should prepare a list of strengths and a list of areas of concerns (with backup data to support your concerns). For each area of concern, you should develop one or more recommendations for improvement.

Before your next class, your group should prepare the audit report (10–15 slides that follow the structure outlined in Chapter 9 would be appropriate) that you will present to the project team, its management, and its customers. During your next class, each team should make a presentation describing their project plan. That presentation will be followed by the audit team's presentation. Based on the team's project plan presentation and the audit team's findings, the management will make a decision to proceed or to cancel the project.

The outcome is obviously important to the team, to its customer, and to the corporation, so please do the best job you can do in the limited time that is available.

Outputs

Choose one of your group members to be the audit team leader. Identify that person to your instructor and to the team that you are auditing. That person will coordinate arrangements for the interviews with the project team and will lead the audit readout presentation. Prepare a set of slides that will be used as the basis for your audit team's presentation. Those slides should cover

- purposes and scope of the audit,
- what you did,
- project strengths,
- prioritized areas of concern,
- recommendations for each area of concern, and
- overall summary.

Give a presentation that outlines your findings. The audit team leader should make the presentation, with other team members contributing as appropriate.

REFERENCE

Boehm B. and R. Turner (2004) *Balancing Agility and Discipline.* Boston: Pearson Education, Inc.

Chapter 13

Retrospectives

The topic for this short chapter is project retrospectives.

Anyone who has been involved in total quality management or process improvement activities know that the quality improvement process requires that you plan what you are going to do, do the things specified in your plan, check on how well it worked, and, finally, make improvements for the next cycle. That well-known cycle is illustrated in Fig. 13.1.

A famous Spanish philosopher, poet, and novelist educated in America, named George Santayana, wrote in 1905, "Those who cannot remember the past are condemned to repeat it" (Santayana 1905). Mr. Santayana probably knew very little about the development of software-intensive systems.

However, he could have been talking about many development organizations that develop software-intensive products. Many have no institutional method for remembering the past and learning from their experiences. In these organizations, most knowledge is passed on as folklore and the process improvement loop is sometimes left open. The use of retrospectives is one way to address this issue for the kinds of projects we have been discussing. Retrospectives are sometimes called post-release evaluations, postmortems, and, perhaps, several other names. During a retrospective, teams try to look back to see what they did well, to identify what could have been done better, and to develop plans for improvement.

To initiate a retrospective, which corresponds to the "check" step of the quality improvement cycle shown in Fig. 13.1, the development manager finds appropriate space for a meeting and insures that the space is properly prepared for an initial meeting. He or she selects and notifies appropriate people from the project, possibly, a representative from the customer's organization and at least one manager, other than the project manager from the development organization. The retrospective starts with a brainstorming session during which team members provide facts. They try to identify things that went well and things that could have been done better. Then they set priorities among the things that could have been done better.

Then a less structured strategy session is arranged during which a subset of the attendees from the retrospective session meets to develop improvement plans. Those plans are documented and distributed to the members of the project team, the

Managing the Development of Software-Intensive Systems, by James McDonald
Copyright © 2010 John Wiley & Sons, Inc.

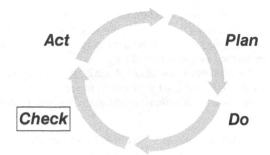

Figure 13.1   The quality improvement cycle.

customer team, and the management. Finally, based on the priorities, improvement actions are taken.

To make the improvements happen, the highest-priority changes need to be incorporated into the plan for the next project or project development cycle. Those that have been chosen for implementation should be assigned to someone for action and tracking. If this is not done, they will probably not be implemented. Implementation problems frequently occur when the team selects too many items to address or does not assign an owner to each. So the guidelines are to select a small number of improvements to be made and to assign someone to be responsible for each.

In summary, what we want to do is review the past, learn from that review, and change the way we do selected things in the future.

13.1   SOME THINGS TO REMEMBER

1. After the completion of each release or each project, arrange a retrospective.
2. Ask the team to identify things that went well and things that could have been done better.
3. Among the things that could have been better, prioritize their importance.
4. Choose the highest-priority improvements for implementation.
5. Assign implementation responsibilities, include changes in the next plan, and track the impact of the improvements.

CASE STUDY 13   *Conducting a Retrospective*

It would be preferable if this exercise were done by a group of four or five readers of this book. If you are in a class for which the book is being used as a text, this case requests you to assemble privately to identify what you believe to be the major pluses and minuses of the text (and perhaps of the course), prioritize the minuses, then recommend a very small number of changes (two or three at the most) that could be made to improve the book and the course.

I would like to see your lists of pluses and minuses, your prioritization of the minuses, and your recommended improvements. Please send your results to me at jamesmc@monmouth. edu, and I assure you that your inputs will be used to improve the structure and content of the book if and when another edition is published.

If you have read this book as an individual, please do the same exercise as an individual, concentrating only on the book, and send your results to me.

The following step-by-step directions might assist groups in completing this case efficiently:

- Break up into workgroups of four or five members (2 minutes).
- Pick up a marker or chalk (20 seconds).
- Brainstorm the pluses/minuses for this course/textbook (18 minutes).
- Create a list of pluses and minuses and record the list in a form that can be shared with your instructor and the author.
- Pick one minus (4 minutes).
- Brainstorm two to three actions that your instructor and the author could take to improve that aspect of the text/course (4 minutes).
- Provide verbal feedback to your instructor on the one minus that you have chosen and the actions that could be taken to improve it and send that information to the author by e-mail (2–6 minutes).

The author will thank you for your input.

REFERENCE

Santayana G. (1905) *Reason in Common Sense*, p. 284. New York: Charles Scribner's Sons.

Index

Managing the Development of Software-Intensive Systems, by James McDonald
Copyright © 2010 John Wiley & Sons, Inc.

Printed in the USA
K028832SCI072916   01S29053000000001316